PRACTICAL SHOOTING TRAINING

BEN STOEGER & JOEL PARK

This is a book that covers aspects of training for pistol shooting, which is inherently a dangerous sport. Never try anything represented in this book without full knowledge and acceptance of the risk associated with that activity. Always follow the rules of gun safety, including but not limited to:

Always treat a firearm as if it is loaded.

Always keep the firearm pointed in a safe direction.

Always keep your finger off the trigger until ready to shoot.

Always keep your firearm unloaded until it is ready for use.

Always be sure of your target and what is beyond it.

An accident that takes place is the responsibility of the shooter. This book covers exercises in live-fire and dry-fire settings – never have ammunition anywhere near your dry-fire area and always be sure that your gun is unloaded when performing drills in dry-fire.

The reader of this book acknowledges and accepts all risk associated with their live-fire and dry-fire activities and hereby accepts all the risk associated with any shooting and related activities.

CONTENTS

Acknowledgements

Many people helped and supported the creation of this book. There are too many to name them all, but we would like to mention a few who without their help this book would not be what it is.

Thank you to:

The group of proofreaders for the ideas, corrections, and additional content they suggested. Special mention to Andreas Yankopolus and Jon Anderson.

Hwansik Kim for his countless contributions to shooting and training through very innovative drills and his analytical mind.

Jamie Watts for the invaluable help with proofing, editing, formatting and logic checking this book as it went through various phases.

Kenny Nguyen for the training and support for building the corrective diagrams and graphics.

Jenny Cook for her expertise and experience in turning this book into a final product and getting our ideas implemented.

Ben: Tim Meyers hassles me about deadlines and keeps me on task. Countless others helped me in some way. There are too many to mention.

Joel: My parents for always being supportive and an important part of my life. Many people have influenced my shooting and training over the years. There are too many to name and I am incredibly grateful for all of them.

FOREWORD

I was at a local indoor range around 2003 and I saw a USPSA style stage from a match in one of the bays. It looked way more fun than just standing in a lane shooting like I was used to, and I wanted to try it. My dad bought a 9mm handgun for me to use and I started competing. After a few months of attending the weekly indoor matches, my friends told me about a local outdoor sanctioned USPSA match. After shooting one outdoor match, I was hooked on practical shooting.

I trained for several years doing the same thing over and over. I would go to the range every Saturday, set up a few targets, shoot a few random drills I had made up that day, then clean up and go home. I did not see the need to own a timer. As far as I knew at the time, I was shooting at the speed my sights allowed, so there was no need to measure what that speed was. I thought with all my time at the range, I was improving my skill, but looking back, I was staying at the same skill level and learning to be consistent. I was already one of the top guys at my club and did not know what to do to improve my skill. My work schedule started to cut into my availability to attend matches. The time I spent practicing and participating became less and less.

In 2014, I got the bug to start practicing and decided to shoot USPSA again. Knowing I wanted to improve my skills, I searched YouTube looking for any videos I could find of the top shooters. I would emulate the videos I found to the best of my ability. I did not quite understand the technical detail of what I was doing at the time, but I could tell I was getting faster without having misses, and that was exciting enough to keep me motivated. As I was searching YouTube, I stumbled across Ben Stoeger's YouTube channel, which led me to his training material, and podcast. Ben explained his shooting technique in a simple and easy to understand method. I was sold by his message that with sustained practice a regular guy could become very good.

I first met Ben in 2015 when I organized a class for him at my local range. The class had a lot of valuable information, but the two main things I took away from the class were how I should be practicing and how to evaluate my performance. Prior to taking his class, those concepts had never been extremely clear to me. With a plan and some direction, I was energized and extremely motivated to start shooting more frequently. I started training every day and noticed I was improving rapidly.

In 2016, I made Master class and was "all in" for practical shooting. I spent a large portion of my free time training, shooting matches, and learning as much as I could. I made Grand Master class the following year and my motivation to improve continued. I had several friends I regularly trained with, but I started receiving more and more requests from friends who wanted to practice with me. In order to not sacrifice my personal training, I started organizing group training sessions for my friends that I lead in a class format.

After a few years of leading training sessions for my friends, I decided that I was ready to start teaching classes. My goal was to teach others the lessons I learned the hard way, and show them in the simplest and most easy to understand format. By this time, I had developed a personal friendship with Ben through taking several of his classes. I adopted a teaching style similar to Ben and I was very excited to share everything I had learned with my current and future students. Teaching has taught me a lot about my own shooting, explaining things in different ways, to learning the most effective way to work on skills and how to deal with pressure.

Teaching classes for several years, it is safe to say most people have difficulty assessing the results they get. It is not uncommon to have an entire class show the same marksmanship issue to varying degrees. Often, the students have vastly different ideas for diagnosing what is occurring. Within that same class, there will be a wide range of skill levels and experience. I noticed the same fundamental issues were happening student after student, class after class. As I gained experience in teaching, I started to know what the target was going to look like before the student even fired a shot on that drill. That knowledge resulted in giving specific corrections for issues that are likely going to happen as I presented the class demos.

The expectations for each student changes based on their skill level. I became a lot more demanding of a student on the verge of making Master class than I was of a student that was about to make B class. With the change in expectations, came different levels of corrections based on where the person is in their shooting. Lightbulb moments occurred more and more frequently when the students were given the appropriate correction for the level they were at. Seeing the excitement in the eyes of the students as I was able to individually give direction and more specific corrections for each student assured me, I was on the right path during my classes. Training and teaching are not a one size fits all.

Choosing the appropriate correction to give each person based on their skill level and experience can be a difficult task. This book breaks down skill and experience into levels, and gives the correction based on where you are in your shooting progression. Concepts are introduced and built upon as your skill improves and the corrective diagrams show what your targets are likely to look like as you train.

This book is a collection of the lessons Ben and I have learned over our years of training, teaching, thinking about and talking about shooting. It has been organized to give you the absolutely best training material we can provide in an easy-to-understand format.

It is common to look at dryfire and live fire as separate things. Some training happens with ammo; some training happens without ammo. I would like to suggest that it is all *Practical Shooting Training*.

-Joel Park

BUILDING A TRAINING PLAN

One of the most common questions students ask is about a training plan. People always want to be handed a list of tasks they can complete and at the end of the plan they get the desired outcome. Shooting does not work like that. Everyone is different.

Life circumstances, age, previous experience and various other factors all influence how quickly and easily people can pick up skills. This is especially true when it comes to something as counterintuitive as practical shooting can be. The skills you need are difficult to acquire and seemingly in contradiction all the time. You are supposed to aim, but not supposed to stare at the front sight for the whole stage. You need to shoot fast, but always aimed. When you aim, you feel slow. When you feel fast, you are probably out of control. The mix of safety rules and marksmanship rules under time pressure, plus adrenaline makes things difficult to figure out.

Learning how to solve all these issues can be challenging. It is only natural to want the plan handed to you. However, how you need to train depends entirely on YOU. Not the "audience" you. I mean specifically to the individual, the "YOU" that is reading the book. What do you understand? What are you good at?

You need to train the "what" part of the whole equation, which is wrapped up with the "how." Until you understand technique and training, you will not be able to utilize the stuff you need to improve. This problem of not understanding the root of some technique issues is tough to solve. There are so few people that understand shooting technique AND have the ability to articulate their knowledge in a way everyone can understand. I can probably name less than 10 shooters who possess that ability. Yes, shooters can win huge championships and still not understand this stuff.

Even after all of my years of training and teaching, I still do not have a solution to this problem. What I can tell you is this book has the answers you are looking for. They may not be the clearest and may not be explained in a way that clicks with you right away, but I promise they are here. Joel and I have organized this book the best way we knew how. Read through the front section of this book and then move to the drill level that is appropriate for you and start training. As you train, more things will start to click. Reading the first section a second time will allow you to develop new ideas as you gain understanding on a different skill level. Keep working at it. It will come. You can see where this is going. It is in here, but unfortunately, the responsibility falls on you.

I was 18 years old when I started on this path. I liked the idea of handguns. I started learning more about them by reading all the gun magazines and books I could. This was back in the age of print magazines and I had every copy of every magazine I could find. I then started going to the range and shooting to try the things I had been reading about.

The magazines told me, the ultimate test of a handgun was how tight of a group it could shoot from a bench at 25 yards, every gun was tested in that way. After the testing, the author would write some stuff about how the gun looked or how they liked the controls. I started trying to shoot groups like they did in magazines, but it was not good. Guns that could shoot a 2-inch group out of a machine rest couldn't shoot an 8-inch group in my hands. I figured out early on that the guns were not the problem, I was.

I was determined to correct the problem. I bought a book about shooting Bullseye. That is the "sport" where you get 10 minutes to shoot 10 shots. I needed to learn to shoot a handgun somewhat straight. I read the book. It taught me about trigger control, and I put what I learned into action.

Soon, I could shoot a good group with almost any handgun I picked up. That wasn't the only thing I learned though. I decided the magazines I read were wrong; how tight of a group a gun could shoot was NOT the ultimate test of the gun. The inherent accuracy of a pistol wasn't that important. Observed reality informed me very few people are capable of shooting a good group with any gun, let alone an especially accurate gun. The real test was not the gun, but the shooter. A good shooter could shoot any gun well and most any gun was way more accurate than it needed to be.

By the time I discovered practical shooting I was 21 years old. As soon as I saw footage of a match, I knew it was for me. A sport where you can run around with a pistol, shoot stuff fast and get a score based on accuracy and speed? Sign me up!

I immediately got a holster, a timer and started training. I read everything out there about practical shooting I could find. I went to the most popular internet forums. I read every book. I bought and watched every video. I soaked up as much information as I could. I did all this in the space of 60 days before my first match. I was a total fiend for the stuff. I liked all that I was learning, and I loved putting it into practice on the range.

As I learned all these things and started competing, I built myself a training plan. I came up with ideas about what I needed to learn and ingrain. I developed my own opinions about technique and started to train and implement these ideas. I did not want to follow someone else's training plan. I continued to hone my technique and update my training plan as I did.

Through my continued training I realized I was wrong a lot. Over the course of every 5-year period I changed my technique, ideas and even my course curriculum. About 80% of all these things changed. This rate of change has started to slow as I have reached my mid-30s. That is how many years of time and study have gone on to even get me close to the answers we all are looking for.

What you need to do now is develop your ideas. Figure out how it works and build yourself a training plan to fit your needs. The plan should fit your lifestyle and your goals. The plan will be demanding in some ways, but I am sure you are up to it.

You want to build a training plan like you would build a house. To build a good house you start with a good foundation. You want a house to be sturdy and functional for your needs. It should work for your lifestyle and last you a lifetime.

The foundation of the house is built with your goals and your motivation. Once the foundation is laid, it is very difficult to alter. Without motivation your house would never get built. If you are not motivated, no one else can give you motivation. You need to find the motivation inside yourself and be truly motivated to be willing to put in the work to accomplish your goal. You cannot be coerced, intimidated, or even threatened to find motivation. Nobody can make you have a desire to shoot at a certain level. That desire comes from inside you. The desire can grow a little faster and burn a little brighter, if you are encouraged by other people. However, nobody can plant the seed of the desire in you. You either have that or you don't.

Everyone has to set goals based on what they desire and want to achieve. For me, that goal was a USPSA National Championship. That goal made sense given my age, lifestyle, and talents, but that goal does not make sense for most people.

Here are a few goals that might be interesting for you along with a realistic assessment of the efforts involved:

Competently compete in USPSA/IDPA (Mastery of Level 1 in this text)

In my experience, to be ready to competently compete at your first match, you will need to spend 40-120 hours doing dryfire (primarily) and live fire (perhaps 500 rounds) of training. You will need to be able to manipulate your pistol, clear malfunctions, load and unload, etc. After learning the manual of arms and being able to shoot a good group, your only worry is safety. Expect to do hours of training just being safety conscious as you move around on stages.

Shoot at a B class level (Level 2)

If you already shoot USPSA, making B class is not complicated. To shoot at a B class level you will need to adopt some kind of regular practice schedule. This means scheduling regular dry training for some period with a focus of speeding up your draws and reloads so you can classify higher.

Shoot at an M class level (Level 3)

Getting to M class requires the same as B class, but also adding in shooting enough live rounds in your training to get comfortable doing fast Bill drills and Blake drills. If you are safe, you can draw and load fast, and you can spray bullets in the center of the targets quickly, at close and mid-range, you can make M class.

Shoot at a GM (Level 3)

In most cases, making a Grand Master is a lot more difficult than Master class. To move from M class to GM, you need to understand the scoring system. You should practice specifically for classifiers. Your skills need to be highly refined, along with a bit of luck to make the move from M to GM. If the right classifier comes along at the right time and you hook up on, then you make it.

Win a Sectional/State match (Level 3)

Plan on being M or GM classification if you want to win sectionals. Not every GM will win sectionals, but every big winner in the country is at least M class. In addition to being M class, you need to be trained well enough that you are consistent. You need to be able to go through the stages at a whole match and not make mistakes that will take you out of contention. For most people this means you have a regular practice schedule consisting of live and dry fire that you maintain over time.

Win an Area match (Level 4)

Winning an Area match is hard. Winning these matches requires M or GM level and training regularly so you are consistent. Even with all of your practice and training you hope that none of the national hotshots show up and take the title. Winning an Area match is not easy to do and it definitely requires some luck and a lot of skill.

Win USPSA Nationals (Level 4 training + total dedication + a bit of luck)

I can tell you from experience, winning a USPSA Nationals, especially in a heavily contested division, is one of the hardest things I have ever done in my life. To compete at Nationals, you have to be ALL IN. You have to train all the time. You have to shoot all the time. Basically, your life revolves around shooting. There is no other way. Winning a National Championship means you need to be an Area match winner type of competitor. Winning the Area match gets you a ticket onto the super squad. From there, you need to shoot a consistent Nationals match (20 or so stages) and then you are in contention for the win. If you get yourself into contention enough times, statistically you should win one.

Looking back at your foundation and your goals, you need to be realistic and honest with yourself. Think about what you want to get out of shooting. Think about what you are willing to put in over time. Pick a goal that works for you. This is your mental foundation; the thing you are working for.

Going back to the analogy that building shooting skills is similar to building a house consider this: the walls and ceiling of your house are built through training. Training is composed of drills; this is the most fundamental part. Each drill is a brick or a 2x4. We combine these drills together into training sessions. As we combine these things, the walls and ceilings are shaped by our training. This book contains plenty of bricks and 2x4's. This book is designed to help you build your house from the foundation up. As you read through this book, do not forget how all of these pieces fit together.

The rest of the house are the remaining aspects of shooting. You likely need to learn to load ammo, clean guns, fix guns, zero dots, etc. There are so many ancillary things. It's like the electricity and appliances in your home. All of them need to be understood because they all serve a function for you. The number of tasks and technical information you may end up absorbing is mind boggling.

None of this comes for free. You will battle frustration. You will spend lots of hard-earned cash looking for some edge over the competition. No doubt you will experiment with equipment. There will be varying costs based on what you choose, but the greatest price you are going to pay is in the form of your time. Your opportunity cost. The reason that practical shooting has built up its own subculture is because this thing does not lend itself to casual participation. It is not easy to be half in.

With the preamble out of the way, it's time for you to start the fabrication of your own custom home. Everyone needs to build their own home and build it in a way that works for them. The foundation comes from within. If you have the competitive flame, this book will help fan it. That fire can forge a foundation made of steel. From there, the sky's the limit.

Having a match or an achievement that is your true goal can help get you into the swing of preparing yourself for an upcoming season. You can train in cycles driven by endless learning and gathering of new knowledge. You can have FUN shooting and learning. Say no to the parts of shooting that you don't want to do. If you don't want to reload because you hate reloading, don't. Say NO when it suits you.

Have fun and we will see you on the range.

HOW TO USE THIS BOOK

Practical Shooting Training is the most detailed and specific training manual for practical shooting that has ever been produced. This book is the culmination of years of steady training, instruction, teaching, and writing. As our understanding of how to "git gud" at practical shooting has grown over the years, the concepts described inside of this book have evolved and taken on a life of their own.

Invariably the first question I get will be from people that have followed my work over the past years. "What is different about this book?" This is a fair question, so let me answer.

Practical Shooting Training is a "layered" approach to training. Instead of dumping out all the information you need for your training and then having you sift through hundreds of pages of drills and training information we have decided to structure this book in a new way.

There are 4 levels of training. Among these different levels, every reader should be able to find where they fit in and get to work from that point. Think of each level as a self-contained training book. Each level has a different mix of drills, goals and standards. The same exercises evolve and change over time as your shooting grows and changes. Each level of training is segregated in the book so it will be easy to work within that level.

If you have never fired a round at a match before, you start out at level 1. If you are chasing your 4th National title, you go to level 4. The structure allows this book to work for a wide audience and will give you plenty of room to grow as you work through the book. The design of this book also allows us to discuss topics when they start to matter. For example, things that do not make any difference to someone finishing in the middle of the pack at a club level match will be particularly important to more advanced shooters. The nuances of activated target strategies or mastery of hit factor scoring do not matter when you are starting out. Similarly, high level shooters do not spend that much time working on slow fire group shooting. As you progress in ability your focus is going to change. This book is set up exactly for that type of evolution.

Broad Concepts

The meat of this text is the 4 largely self-contained training levels. However, please do not neglect to understand the broad concepts that are the foundations of each level of training. There are certain things that everyone, at every level, needs to understand and those ideas are laid out in the front of this book before we even get to any drills or training.

The ideas I am referencing here are the big picture ideas that should guide your training. I will make a small list of these concepts to provide some examples.

- Your grip largely determines your shooting accuracy.
- You should do two or three drills in a practice session.
- You should dry fire regularly.

- Live fire training informs your dry training and tells you what to work on next during dryfire.
- Use training to look for an assessable pattern of mistakes.
- Pay attention to the right cues
- Shoot the same target order every time during a set of runs on a transition drill for easier assessment.

The above list provides a few examples of some statements that someone who has a good understanding of what we are trying to accomplish through training might say. It is not an exhaustive list but does give you a sense of the sort of things you want to understand to be able to effectively train.

Don't worry if there are items on the above list of statements that seem like foreign language. The front section of the book is here to give that common framework and understanding of many of these concepts. Make sure you pay careful attention to the sections about how to train before you jump straight to the level you deem correct for yourself.

Choosing the Correct Level

Many people will have some sort of confusion or uncertainty when it comes to what training level they should go to and operate in. This is a foreseeable issue when you are asking people to essentially train themselves.

The best advice to give is to take a close look at the following description of the training levels. Be honest with yourself in terms of where you think you truly fit in. It is important that you train at the intended level so you can master concepts and improve quickly. Jumping to level 4 as a new shooter will not serve you well.

Many people have mastered a set of concepts and skills to move beyond where they are. The next step is to move out of their comfort zone. They need to fail, and fail frequently, to learn what they need to do to get better. Naturally, people do not like failure. They do not like beating their head against a figurative wall to marginally improve at their hobby, but that is what needs to happen in order to grow.

Other people may have a bit of talent and speed and think they have already mastered concepts they have not even begun to deconstruct and figure out. There are lots of A class shooters in practical shooting with natural speed and basically nothing else. There is nothing wrong with that. If that is you, it is important to understand how to shoot not just fast, but consistently, if you wish to improve. Instead of going fast and hoping for the best, you train yourself into a machine that makes very minimal mistakes.

No matter what your circumstances and skillset are, it is extremely important that you are relentlessly honest with yourself. Do not allow yourself to sit back and be complacent without working to be better.

The Levels

This book has 4 training levels. As you grow and improve, more concepts get layered in and the time *Standards* tighten up. Concepts that are ignored in level 1 are emphasized in level 4. Concepts that are emphasized in level 1 are taken for granted in level 3.

Some of these choices are, in many ways, arbitrary. The borders between levels are a little bit fuzzy. Any of these normal sorts of criticisms when you lay out a training system are expected and, in many ways, healthy. The bottom line is, we wanted to divide things up into a reasonable number of levels and we arrived at the cleanest way we could see to do that.

Level 1 - Complete a club match without a penalty.

Level 1 is designed to make you competent, safe, accurate, and able to shoot under pressure. It contains no time *Standards* and does not have any advanced shooting concepts like different aiming schemes on different targets. It is designed to take you from no practical experience doing competitive shooting and get you through a club match without shooting any misses or no-shoots.

Level 2 - Get to B class.

Level 2 introduces basic time *Standards* for many exercises and it also introduces the concept of different aiming schemes based on different targets. If you understand USPSA safety rules and how to shoot your gun accurately (even if a little bit too slowly), the next goal is to make USPSA B class or a similar skill level.

Level 3 - Get to Master/Grand Master.

Level 3 has advanced concepts like dynamic movement, predictive shooting, multiple aiming schemes, and GM time limits for basic exercises. Once you are competent, accurate and you have some measure of speed, the next challenge is to become one of the best shooters in your club and achieve a high rank inside your shooting sport. Making GM was my first goal when I started shooting USPSA. Setting a goal like making GM will force you to learn a in order to achieve that goal. It will come with practice and dedication.

Level 4 - Achieve competitive excellence.

Level 4 emphasizes consistency of performance and building a deep understanding on how to blend different techniques together to marginally improve scores. If you are basically training every day and have already ranked up inside your shooting sport, you are likely looking to train at Level 4. This level is appropriate to those that are chasing important titles at big matches. It is for the top shooters that are not afraid of challenges. If you can accomplish (after a bit of practice) pretty much any skill with a handgun that you see on Instagram and want to do very well at big matches, this level is for you.

The Drills

The bulk of this text is a series of training drills. Please pay careful attention to these directions so you can get the most out of it. Just as it is important to understand how the training levels work, you will also need to understand how the drills are supposed to work.

There is a lot of variety to the drills in this book. Some of them are small and simple. They have a strict time limit and an easy to assess performance standard. Other drills are complex, open ended and difficult to do a performance assessment on. You will need to engage your brain to understand what exactly you are trying to accomplish for each drill and how that fits into your larger plan for shooting.

Many of the drills are open ended in terms of their physical construction. It will be up to you to build out the shooting positions and targets. Try to build the drill in such a way that it reflects what you are seeing in matches.

It is common that people will build things to be "harder" because they want to feel comfortable at matches. Making the targets much tougher and more punishing than matches is not a bad idea to get you used to difficult scenarios, but you do need to be careful. You should bear in mind that much of your training is getting used to being relaxed and comfortable on challenges that many people consider easier. It isn't enough that you can smash targets perfectly at 25 yards, you need to be able to shoot at warp speed at the 5-yard line without tensing up or inducing errors. You need to work the whole spectrum of potential scenarios so your training should reflect this.

Start positions/conditions and other procedural issues

Many of the drills in the book are left open ended in terms of the start position or some other procedural issue with the drill. This is intentional. Feel free to practice any start position you want to and work that into the drill you are training on. Try to mix it up in your training the same as it would be mixed up in a match. Hands up, hands down, back to the targets are all good options for training (to name a few). Mixing it up from "hands relaxed at sides" is always good.

The standard tests are drills that are strict with a par time are the ones you want to pay careful attention to the start condition. You want to make sure that you measure yourself accurately against the standard, so you have a realistic idea of where you stack up and what you should focus your efforts on next.

Par times

Time goals are referred to as par times. These times should not be considered a pass/fail sort of test, but instead they should give you a good idea of where your times should fall in general on a particular exercise.

For example, if the par time for the drill is 5 seconds, shooting the drill in 5.2, 4.8, 5.1, 4.7, 5.4 and so on means you are pretty much in the range you are meant to be in. Shooting the drill once under 5 seconds does not mean you "pass." Shooting it over 5 seconds once does not mean you fail. Instead, the par time is giving you an idea where your time should be falling. A "bad" rep where you bobble a bit on the reload coming in just over the par time means you are generally where you need to be.

The par times are a guide. They exist to give you a push in the right direction. They should not serve as a hard limit. Use them for the information they provide you, but do not let them take over your life or dominate your training.

Equipment Considerations

There are some equipment considerations that should be addressed, especially as it relates to the par times. This book is designed to be picked up and used by people in different divisions and shooting both in USPSA matches in the U.S., and IPSC matches outside the U.S. The equipment rules vary, and the popular gear varies as well. Some people will be using iron sights and some will be using optics. Some people will be using "race" triggers and others will be using near factory Glocks.

In the same way as the construction and start positions are open ended, you should use your head when it comes to equipment as well. Some things in this book will get a LOT harder depending on the gear you have. This may require you to adjust your expectations or standards. The book is targeted at a wide audience. If there is some time standard or some drill that does not seem to work for you the way your gear is set up, make a reasonable adjustment to the construction or the par time. There is no reason to get hung up on minutia.

Physical Limitations

Many users of this book have one or more physical conditions that may hamper their development in shooting. This book is written from the point of view of an able-bodied adult and is pointed towards the same audience. Just like when it comes to issues of equipment, you should be reasonable when it comes to physical issues. If you are not yet old enough to legally drive a car, you likely have not physically developed to the same extent you will in adulthood. You may have some injury that impacts your results in certain areas. Be smart and adapt this material to suit your own purposes.

Use your head

The primary message for this section is to be smart and use your head. The concepts that are contained in the drills are going to work for you if you are smart and adapt the challenge to your range, equipment, and skillset.

LAYERS

"Why did you give them such different advice? They were both doing a lot of the same things wrong."

This is one of the best questions I have ever gotten from someone. It was such a fundamental question. It cut to the core of training philosophy.

The question was asked by Joel Park in a class he organized for me to teach several years ago. Joel is someone that has become a good friend since taking the class. I suspected he was using this class as an opportunity to shadow my teaching. He was not interested in shooting with the class, but wanted to watch me work, and was asking a lot of "why" questions.

Joel saw me running a class on a target transition drill. He had watched me explain to one guy that he was driving the gun past the target he was trying to transition to. This was causing him to drop points. He needed to relax his shoulders and pinpoint an exact spot to transition the gun where he wanted it to go.

Another attendee was making the same mistake. He would slam the gun onto the next target with very little finesse. He was also dropping a ton of points. I talked to him about the way he was gripping the gun inconsistently and explained if he changed his focus to nailing a good grip while he was drawing, he would get much better results.

Joel did not understand. I explained to him that the first guy was over transitioning the gun and needed to fix it. The other guy was making terrible problems for himself when he was not paying attention to his grip. He was not in a place to correct the transition issue and it is more of a minor issue in the scheme of things. If he fixes nothing else in the class, at least gripping the gun properly would help him in the long run.

The example is quite technical, but it does cut to the core of the concept of layers. This book aims to describe in detail how to strip back the layers of your technique and improve them one piece at a time. It will show you what is most important to pay attention to during specific stages in your development.

One piece at a time

Most things you do during your day are subconscious processes that you direct consciously. When you drive somewhere you do not think through every step of the drive; you just drive. Your conscious desire to go to a particular location is all you need to get started. All the small things you do are the result of your training to drive. The way you signal to turn or brake as you come to a stop are not things you consciously need to direct. These things seem to happen.

Your shooting is no different. As you start out you need to think through each step. Your gun feels strange and foreign in your hands. As you grip the gun you need to think about each piece. Over a period of time, you become trained and do not need to think about every detail. You can shoot a stage to your ability and your conscious mind does not need to control each action.

Why is this important?

Learning to do a thing requires conscious thought as you move through each step in a process. You need to think your way through each thing. For example, loading your pistol before you holster it.

The steps to loading your pistol might be:

- Insert a magazine in the pistol.
- Ensure the magazine is seated properly.
- Cycle the slide to chamber a round.
- Confirm the pistol has a round in the chamber.
- Confirm the pistol is in battery with the slide fully closed.
- Apply the safety.
- Holster the pistol.

It is a well-known fact that your conscious mind can be in one spot at a time. For example, you can be consciously focused on where your vision is directed, or you can direct your conscious mind on how your finger feels. You can move your attention around from moment to moment, but still only think about one thing at a time.

Each step in the process is associated with a physical technique that you need to learn. As you consciously think through each step and perform the associated action, you start to internalize this process. You get faster at it as well. Eventually, you get to a place where you consciously decide to load your pistol and you can subconsciously perform each step without any conscious thought. As a matter of fact, you might be carrying on a conversation with someone while you do these steps and it will not pose a problem. You are working subconsciously at this point.

This is the product of muscle memory achieved through repetition and training. This does not mean it is good or bad; it is the way it works. You internalize the process and then you can repeat it without needing to think through it.

Reality of Training

Throughout your training you have already learned lots of processes for shooting. If you are reading this, you can likely perform all sorts of actions without needing to think your way through the process. I would describe this as being "trained." Once it happens without conscious direction, it is a trained response.

It can also be true that some of your training has been wrong. You may not hold the pistol as well as you could. You may have some hitch in your movement technique that is inefficient. You may focus on your sight as you transition from one target to another. Most of these things you are doing wrong and may not even be aware of.

The nature of competitive shooters is that they are forever training to improve. That means they need to carefully examine each subconscious process that they have trained and then start making changes. To change, they direct your conscious mind to that part of the process they are doing and work to change the habit that they have. After enough time and repetition, that small piece will morph into something new.

For example, if they want to grip harder with your support hand while you are shooting, reading that information in a book will be of little help. They need to actually perform training repetitions and consciously direct that force into their hand exactly the way they want it. After a few thousand repetitions, they will see your grip in the place they want it to be without needing to think about it. This frees the conscious mind to work on the next piece of technique that needs to be modified.

The Path

This text is centered around the path that most competitive shooters are going to take to improve.

First, you learn basic mechanics and safety. This means learning how to load your pistol and work with a holster safely. It means moving around with the pistol in your hand and keeping the muzzle in a safe direction. It also means basic marksmanship and trigger control. A good test for this would be getting through USPSA matches safely and competently. This does not mean you are fast, safe and competent.

After you get that baseline down, you start to go faster. You are comfortable drawing your pistol from the holster and feel safe doing it, so now it is time to go faster. If you are always shooting with a traditional "perfect" sight picture, you can start learning how to compromise that sight picture to go faster. You can refine your grip and stance to maximize recoil control and shoot the gun accurately nearly as fast as you can pull the trigger.

To level up like this it means you need to start paying attention to things that did not matter before. For example, when you are starting out, you focus on the muzzle direction while you move to stay safe. When that becomes an unconscious habit, you can switch your attention to running faster. Each little piece of your technique like this will need to be pulled apart and re-examined.

As you near the top of the heap of the competitive shooting game, you will need to identify subconscious habits that manifest themselves in competition to undermine you. For example, clamping down your firing hand when the targets are extremely close is a common example. Associating tension with speed is a common issue that people create for themselves. Undoing that association takes dedicated time and attention.

The Layers

This book is designed to help you untangle these concepts by operating in the correct layer for you based on your ability level. Different people need different feedback at different times. The drills in this book are designed so you can work on the things you need to, when you need to, to improve. The idea behind this is that lower-level shooters do not waste time trying to master techniques that will provide marginal benefit and that higher-level shooters work towards a deeper understanding and more refined ability as they improve.

TRAINING PHILOSOPHY

Training is teaching. In the case of this book, training is about you teaching yourself. This book is here to help you. Think of it as a guide to help you help yourself.

There are some strengths and weaknesses to training yourself. One strength is you know yourself better than anyone else. One weakness is you are almost certain to suffer from the same cognitive biases that we all suffer from occasionally. You will likely not want to see factual information that makes you uncomfortable. You will make excuses for yourself. You will fall into habit and routine.

The first thing to understand about training is that if you are doing it right, it is not always comfortable. You are working on getting better at shooting and you will likely find plenty of excuses for yourself to keep doing exactly what you are doing. This is normal and natural.

The point I am making is, you are training yourself. This means you are battling yourself in many respects. The battle you need to fight is the one you are avoiding. Many personalities think they need to force themselves to work on uncomfortable or difficult skills. Many people think the battle they need to fight is to force themselves to train in the first place. I think the battle you need to fight with yourself is the one you are avoiding even thinking about. Maybe you do not understand things you take for granted and you will not even allow yourself to ask yourself the question for real.

In order to train yourself you must battle with your own thoughts and ideas. You need to understand how you think and how you can make yourself think better. You need to understand your habits and predispositions, both positive and negative, then work to be better. If you are not willing to do this there will be a ceiling to your performance.

You are a machine

Very few people are going to come to this book without having trained themselves to shoot. I have no doubt there will be a few people that open this that are truly blank canvases to begin with, but the large majority will have already experienced their own training ideas.

You know how to view a stage, make a stage plan, load your gun safely, shoot the stage and assess the stage performance. You know how to do it. You can do it. You have done it. You will do it again.

Think about all the things you learned to get out and shoot a match. You learned how to hold your pistol, how to handle it safely, how to load it, how to use the sights, etc. There is an uncountable number of things that you had to know to participate in a match.

Nobody on earth is in conscious command of all these things simultaneously. You cannot consciously control all aspects of your shooting as you work through something as complicated as a stage of fire at a match. Most of your actions will be your trained responses to certain things. You see a sight picture you like on a target? You pull the trigger without even thinking about it. Out of ammunition? You will grab for a magazine off your belt without needing to wonder where the magazine is.

You are already trained. You are already a machine. You are not a machine in the T-800 crush your enemies' sense, but you are a machine in the way you have inputs come in through your senses and automatically have an output. You get done shooting in one firing position and you push yourself to the next firing position. The way you move your feet and how you move will fade to the subconscious, but there is a pattern to it. If you look closely, you will see that in the same circumstances you perform the same action. The outputs that you give are you subconsciously processing the inputs that come in.

Doing what comes naturally

It is important to point out one of the most important things driving the way your shooting machine operates. Your desire to get better, combined with effort over time, will cause your body to naturally solve some problems. You truly learn by doing.

Most of the things you do when it comes to shooting were not things you chose to do consciously. You may have received instruction on how to hold your gun, or change magazines, but it is quite often the case that even though someone told you explicitly how to do those things you ended up in a similar, but not quite the same place.

An easier way to explain this concept might be to have you think about how you learned to grip your pistol properly. You read some words or listened to a guy giving instruction. It is highly unlikely, almost impossible, that you took every part of what you were instructed to do and implemented it exactly as instructed. There may have been some ambiguous words in the instruction or simply parts you did not understand. More likely there are parts you thought you did as you were instructed, but you did not.

Over time, as your conscious attention moves to other components of your shooting, the way you grip your pistol takes on a life of its own. You may have an idea in your conscious mind that is similar to some instruction you got at one point, but if we take a close look at your shooting under match pressure, we will see that you do not grip the pistol the way you were instructed. If I asked you directly, you would likely self-report that you grip your pistol the way you were instructed. If you were giving an outline of your technique, the surface would probably closely match what you were instructed, but have a few little word changes that may or may not be important.

Take this perverse sort of game of telephone when it comes to learning complicated skills and you can see that your machine is built by ideas you heard here and there, practice you did, matches you shot, etc. Your shooting is a patchwork of ideas picked up from all over the place and in many cases subconsciously invented on your own. You quite naturally solved the shooting problem to some degree. A big part of your continued training is to understand what you have done, so you can redo it better.

Run the machine and then make changes

The training philosophy that guides this text is that *you are a machine* and we need to see you run. You should run at different speeds and under different circumstances to see how you work. Once you build a good understanding of how you work, you can start to tweak yourself in important ways to make you run better.

You must understand, almost nobody comes to a book like this as a blank slate. You have already built some sort of shooting machine in one way or another. You have probably copied some techniques and can probably repeat some talking points about wrist locking or other shooting technique. What we mean to do now is get under the hood of your shooting machine and tweak it a little bit by conscious effort over time to change your habits in a productive way.

Say a newer shooter is working through a stage. Every time they get to a shot they think will be difficult they aim the gun very precisely. A common example for this would be a piece of steel they need to knockdown for score. This shooter aims hard and then misses. They frequently tend to miss left and low. Throughout the whole match and this pattern is a continual issue.

Isolate the issues

Once you see a pattern, then the path to improvement will be clear. You need to make a little tweak here and there and you will get a markedly better result. Remember our example shooter? The shooter is missing a lot low and left when they are engaging specific targets. It is likely that once they get the sight picture the way they want it they are snatching the trigger or pressing their gun down in anticipation of coming recoil. They have associated tough shots with lots of aiming, but have also associated it with smashing the trigger back and getting an errant shot.

The solution for this will be lots of training on precise shots with the focus on holding the firing hand still. In this text I will refer to a training focus as a "cue." As you train, you are going to be able to put your focus on one thing at a time. The correct focal point for our example shooter is to focus on hand pressure so they do not move the gun while firing at a target.

Over time, our example shooter should be able to rewire their machine. When they judge a shot as difficult, instead of staring at the sights longer and aiming more, they instead smoothly press the trigger back and get a hit on the target.

Understand how to build a better machine

The above example is one microcosm of the process I am proposing you undertake while utilizing this book.

Step 1. Run the machine. This means that you do what you do. Go to a match and shoot the match. Shoot assessment drills. Do not try to manipulate the outcome beyond simply doing your best. In order to get a good idea of what is going on you need to let the machine run.

Step 2. Pay attention. When you are assessing your shooting, you should carefully look for patterns like the example I gave earlier in the section. As your shooting improves, the patterns you are looking for will be more obscured and difficult to spot. They will be hidden under layers of technique. If you can find these patterns, they will show you the way to improvement.

Step 3. Train yourself to be better, this is the tricky step. You need to consciously train until your subconscious response is the thing you are consciously training yourself to do. This means dozens, hundreds, or thousands of repetitions on a single item. The item can be the way you grip your pistol. It can be where exactly on a target your eye goes to when you acquire it. It could be even more subtle than that.

You get better by doing step 1-3 over time. You assess, tweak, train the tweaks, and assess again. This is a process that never stops and never has to. As you learn and grow over time, your shooting will grow, as long as you continue to pay attention.

Build your shooting into an unstoppable machine

What I propose you do is to consciously take control of the way you are trained.

This text provides you the tools to test your machine under a wide variety of circumstances. As your level of skill and understanding increases, the way you test your skills will change. The cues you will utilize to get yourself to do a specific thing you are trying to do will get more detailed. Over time, if you apply the test, assess, change model to your shooting you can make yourself into an unstoppable shooting machine as you systematically change the process that you are executing without even thinking about it.

WHY YOU SUCK

You are not as good as you would like to be. That is a fact that holds true of about everyone. It certainly holds true if you are reading this.

This book is not intended to be a detailed description of shooting technique. This is a training guide. However, these two concepts are intertwined in some ways, so it is important to spend some time to understand technique.

If training is the fuel to get you where you want to go, then technique is the car. Even if you load up a slow car with the best fuel, you cannot get around as quickly as the better car.

Training is what makes you better. Most shooters are quicker to put $500 into a new optic than they are to put $500 into training ammunition or a class. Even though the shooting community intellectually accepts that training is what is needed to get exceptionally good, they do not usually act on that information.

It bears repeating, training is what makes you better.

Shooting vs Training

There is a difference between shooting and training. Shooting is just that... shooting.

Shooting in the context of competition preparation means going to the range and doing what you know how to do. This could be shooting drills or mini stages that you are comfortable with. When you are shooting, you just note the scores that you are producing.

Have you ever gone to the range and shot a drill or some test and noted the score, then shot it again trying to get a higher score? As you repeat this process, your focus will shift from the technique you are employing to the result you are trying to produce.

You can improve by going and shooting. Many high-level shooters got there with motivation and a lot of shooting. Their desire to shoot high scores is what made them so good. They kept focused on driving up the hit factors when they shot at their practice range. Guys like this generally focus little on process or technique. They want the result and they will not quit until they get it.

Training, however, is where you take command of specific aspects of your technique and mold them into what you want. Training is where instead of focusing on the score you shoot, you focus on the process by which you produce the score. Instead of focusing on the hit factor, focus on specific pieces of technique. Doing this, you can instill the techniques you choose to and turn those pieces into habits.

Most people do not function this way. They go shoot and focus on getting good results until they get to a point where the results are not improving. They hit this invisible wall and even though they might be shooting a lot, they are not getting better. They cannot go faster; they cannot move up. This happens in B class and sometimes it happens as a GM. For most people, this will happen eventually.

Shooting Produces Habits

The reason people hit a plateau in their performance, even when they shoot a lot is, they have limitations built into their style they cannot see. For example, you have it in your head that before you fire a shot you want to see a "clear front sight." This idea in your head was okay to get you to B class, but it imposes inherent speed restrictions on your shooting.

If you pay attention at a match you will see some mid-level shooters have this issue as well. If you watch closely, you will see that they always want to see a clear front sight on every target irrespective of the distance. If you were watching them and could not see the targets you would think everything was 25 yards away.

The fact is, every time you shoot you are teaching yourself habits. The way you understand shooting and the concepts you train with end up getting implanted in your memory. If you consider the example of the mid-level shooter that wastes time aiming too much on close range targets, it is easy to see how the habit was built up. When this person started, they were probably having accuracy issues and they were initially ranked in D class.

Our example shooter is quick. He naturally felt comfortable shooting the gun quickly and was faithfully dryfiring every night for a few months. The draw and reload became quick and natural. The gun became an extension of this shooter's hands. The only problem was he would miss a lot at matches. He made some friends in shooting and they all gave him the same assessment. "You need to aim every shot and stop missing." Our shooter did that. Over the course of a year between matches and some casual shooting with his new friends he made sure he aimed every shot. He climbed from D class to B class. The regular dryfire and disciplined shooting was the key to their improvement.

As the bar gets raised, you have to adapt.

Our example shooter was able to instill good habits and it was enough he could move up in the rankings. However, if he wants to move up even more, some things still need to change.

You can get to B class by getting a hard-front sight focus for every shot. The problem is, you are going to have a hard time moving up to M or GM if you hold onto a concept like that. Say this person takes a class with some hotshot shooter and understands that he needs to have multiple aiming schemes they can call upon and use at will. That would be a big help in ranking up further.

After months of shooting and thinking about seeing the front sight, our shooter now needs to understand new aiming schemes, how to use them and when to use them. He needs to train himself to do that.

He decides to shoot close targets by reacting to the color of the fiber optic front sight. As soon as he sees that in the center of the target, he is going to shoot. He is not going to use the rear sight at all and is not going to change the focal depth to the front sight.

To make this habit an automatic, it might take weeks of training. It would take dryfire training to learn to look for the color of the sight on certain targets. He would need to do live training to check the times on shooting and get them up towards the Master level by using this technique. He would want to run drills where he changes between close targets and tough targets to make sure he can use the correct aiming scheme for the correct targets.

In order to move up in performance, our shooter would need to do specific work on their specific issue. They would need to understand what the problem is, then work on specific corrections until they become subconscious.

Human nature

The above example fits right into the theme of this book. It describes someone that came into practical shooting as their first serious gun sport and is predisposed to shoot quickly. They did some practice until they stalled out in B class and now they want to get better, but are not sure how. This is a common case and what this training manual is designed to address.

You might notice that this person's experience, mindset, practice and skills all helped build a picture of why they were in B class, how they got there and what it would take to move up. That case may not describe you, but it might describe someone you know.

Predictable

Even though we all are special and unique, you will tend to see the same patterns in people's behavior.

In my experience teaching classes, people tend to have specific inclinations. When you tell them to go faster they tense up. When people are pressed for time, they stop confirming with their sights. When people transition from distant target to distant target, they tend to stare at their sights. When people stare at their sights, they tend to transition imprecisely. This list goes on and on.

People generally work in a similar fashion when it comes to shooting. These issues tend to happen without regard for what technique a person *thinks* they are using. People tend to make the same mistakes, under the same circumstances, until they specifically train to correct those mistakes.

Tension problems

Tenison is one of the most common areas where people struggle against their natural inclinations. It might be arm/shoulder tension as they battle recoil. It might be upper body tension when they transition from target to target. It might be they are stiff legged when it would be better to be loose and ready to move. These things can all happen, but some problems are more common than others.

A common problem especially among lower-level shooters is a constant struggle with hand pressures. The main issue is that the normal tendency is to grip the gun extremely hard with your dominant hand. People are used to using their dominant hand to do all sorts of things. That normal human tendency becomes a problem when shooting pistols. The tighter you hold your pistol with your dominant hand, the more difficult it becomes to isolate your trigger finger and move it by itself. The faster you shoot, the more tightly your dominant hand will squeeze down. It is better to hold the gun tightly and do a lot of the recoil management with your support hand, but that requires that you be using different amounts of pressure with each hand. It takes time and training to perfect this skill.

As you work your way to a more advanced level, you will start to notice that as you change the target distance and difficulty it will influence how you are inclined to control your pistol. As you move your focus to aiming carefully or pressing the trigger oftentimes it will change the way you are gripping the pistol. You may get the sense that the more carefully you try to aim at difficult targets the less control you appear to have over your sights. As you move your focus around you will grip the gun less and less aggressively and the gun will not recover the same way from recoil.

The easiest way to summarize tension issues is this: the faster you go the more tense you will get. Releasing unnecessary tension is the key to going faster. Figuring out what tension is productive and what is not will take time and experimentation.

Vision problems

Your natural propensity will also cause problems as it relates to your vision. For better or worse, you hit where you look. This is a concept that is too simple for many people to accept. If you look at the outside shape of the target or the target's color, you will be less accurate than if you drive your vision to a specific point. If there is some reason (such as the placement of a no-shoot) where you would want to hit away from the center of the target, you need to account for that with where you drive your vision to when you engage the target. The core idea was quite simple, but the way it applies to a variety of circumstances becomes extremely complicated.

Another complicating factor when it comes to controlling your vision is focal depth. Most shooters are taught to focus on the front sight when they are using iron sights. Most shooters using a red dot know they are supposed to focus on the target. Both groups of shooters have problems as they develop. Iron sight shooters will soon figure out they are too slow shooting front sight focus all the time. Dot shooters may notice that under certain circumstances they start focusing on the dot itself and not the target. Both groups of people need to train to get their eyes doing what they are supposed to be doing at the time they are supposed to be doing it.

People have vision that needs to be corrected, issues changing focal depth brought about by age, cross-dominance, astigmatism and other issues. Many people never quite figure out how to get their vision and vision correction calibrated to work for them when it comes to shooting. It is a difficult problem, and one that you cannot stop working on.

Movement Problems

When it comes to moving around the stage quickly, there are even more problems caused by doing the thing you are naturally inclined to do. Early in your shooting career, people tend to believe raw foot speed matters a lot for putting up fast times. As you get better and better, you will notice that it comes down to developing good technique.

Moving around stages quickly brings issues to the other things that we have previously discussed. You might be inclined to stand a certain way that will induce you to have inefficiency in your technique. For example, most people want to stand comfortably for shooting. However, if you stand more like a shortstop with your knees bent and your feet spread apart in a wide stance, you will be able to launch yourself out of a position much faster. Something as simple as teaching yourself to stand like a shortstop can take weeks of training.

When it comes to efficient movement, one of the most important concepts is one of the most difficult to explain. You might hear people at a match talk about how a stage "flows." This concept is critical to competing at a high level. Flow is the ability to string together different shooting positions into an unbroken string of target engagements. It is impossible to win major matches without being able to make a stage flow.

Conceptual problems

At the core level, most people carry ideas that are counterproductive to shooting well.

People have the idea that you need to control the recoil of your gun. This is one idea that does not help people shoot well. It may seem crazy, but give it some consideration. What will work the best for most people is to hold onto their gun firmly with good grip technique and then let the gun do what the gun is going to do. You should not try to stop the recoil from happening, or to hold the gun perfectly still. Instead, accept the recoil will move the gun a little bit and you should allow it to happen.

Instead of trying to stop the gun from moving, ensure that the gun is returning to the same spot. Let the gun track up and down in recoil and see if it is a predictable pattern. If you insist on stopping the gun from recoiling at all, you will almost certainly push down on the gun as you shoot it and induce marksmanship errors.

The previous example should illustrate how ideas that are stuck in your brain can cause problems for you. The idea that you want to stop the gun from recoiling is logical and if you did not know better, it would make sense. I am hoping to convey that you should examine a lot of ideas you have in your head to make sure they make sense. As your skill grows and you learn more, you will undoubtedly discard a lot of ideas that do not serve you well any longer.

Other ideas that people believe that do not work as shooters try to improve:

- physical effort = speed
- aiming = accuracy
- I can trust my sense of time
- As I shoot faster, I will drop more points

Technical Hitches

Technical differences are not important when it comes down to this process. An example of this is a "scoop" draw as opposed to a "conventional" draw. Conventionally, you get a firing grip on your pistol while it is in the holster and pull it out and present it to the target. With a "scoop" technique, you grab the pistol and pull it from the holster immediately and sort your grip on the pistol out as you bring it up into position to fire. This technique is .1 or .2 seconds faster depending on a lot of factors, but also a lot more error prone.

While some would be interested in a virtually endless discussion of the merits of one technique vs the other, the fact is that it is not productive. By the time you get good enough that the .1 seconds matters one way or the other to you, you will be equipped to make the right decision for yourself.

In most matters of technique, you will see a similar pattern. You can get exceptional results with most reasonable technique choices. The driving factor to your success is going to be training and skill level.

Confounded by crutches

There is one technique issue that bears highlighting and that issue is crutches.

An example of a technical crutch is trigger prepping. This is the idea you should press your trigger back to the "wall" prior to a shot being fired. By preloading the trigger this way, the theory is when you fire the shot, the effort is minimal. The hope is, it will be less likely you will move the gun when you press the trigger the rest of the way back. Trigger prepping is a common technique that many shooters would report they use and are successful with.

The problem with trigger prepping is it is slow. Pressing the trigger back to the wall obviously takes time to do. However, if you are to consciously recognize that you have prepped the trigger, this will add a lot of time to the shot. It would be about .2 seconds for your brain to be able to process that you have pressed the trigger back to the prep point and the shot is ready to go when you get the right sight alignment.

Adding .2 seconds to a shot means if you are prepping the trigger and know you have done so, you will be shooting shots every .4 or .5 seconds at the fastest. The math speaks for itself. It simply adds time due to needing to prep the trigger and know you have done so.

There are many adherents to the "trigger prep" technique that believe they do this technique and will tell you to do it too. Someone can adopt this technique and have good success with it, but get to a point where the technique no longer works for them. Imagine prepping the trigger works well for you on challenging shots until you get to about the Master level, then you find you are not fast enough. Prepping the trigger then pressing it is taking too much time on the mid-range targets and you are falling behind.

Prepping the trigger worked well for you because it was a technical crutch. The thing about the technique that worked well for you is that it made you pay attention to pressing the trigger straight. The rest of the technique created a speed barrier for you without you realizing. You might be afraid to abandon this technique because it does make you accurate, but not for the reason you thought it does.

This is a complex and technical example, but that is what a technical crutch is. You adopt a technique; you get good results for a while, but when it is time to move on from that technique, it is difficult for you. You created a crutch for yourself to lean on because you did not have your focus in the right spot to begin with.

You are your own enemy

If you take nothing else from this section, take this:

In order to improve, you will be battling your own habits, predispositions and self-limiting ideas.

Early on in your shooting journey, pay close attention to how you grip the gun and make sure you build up discipline. Your body will be screaming at you to "go faster," but as you build the confidence to aim (even though you are on the clock) you will get to a fairly good place skill wise.

To move to the middle of the pack (around B class), you will need to work on gun handling skills dry. You will need to shoot your gun as fast as you can pull the trigger and learn some semblance of control while you do it.

To move to M or GM, you need to dryfire like it is a part time job. You need to understand scoring. You need to be able to apply different aiming schemes to different targets.

Training at level 4 in this book will press you to seamlessly blend different techniques and concepts together. It will challenge you to develop your predictive shooting ability to such a level that you are confident shooting aggressively even though you are often off balance or moving.

No matter where you are right now, or where you are trying to go, you will need to make serious and difficult changes to substantially improve. The main thing holding you back is you.

PREDICTIVE VS REACTIVE

This book contains a lot of concepts, ideas and drills that are going to be new for most of the people. One of the most key new concepts deserves a very detailed explanation is that of predictive shooting vs reactive shooting.

Reactive Shooting:

Shooting every shot as a result of reacting to visual information coming from the sights.

Example: You see the front sight or dot return back down to the center of the target before firing your second shot. This is "reactive" to your sights.

Predictive Shooting:

Leveraging your knowledge of your technique and equipment to shoot without getting explicit confirmation from the sights of every shot.

Example: After confirming your sights are in alignment on the center of the target you fire a rapid fire pair, as fast as you can pull the trigger. The second shot in the pair is not aimed in the conventional sense. Instead, you are counting on your strong grip and your shooting platform to take care of recoil mitigation so the second shot will still hit in a desirable location.

How it works:

When you start out in your shooting career you do not attempt to utilize predictive shooting. In this text, this idea is expressed by level 1 training simply not including any sort of advice to do predictive shooting.

Reactive shooting ties every single round you fire to your own human reaction time. This means every shot you will be adding about .2 seconds to perceive your sights return and then decide to fire the next shot. There is not any way around the math. Reaction takes time.

Think about it. The goal for level 1 is to become able to safely get through a match and hit all the required targets. This requires the knowledge to move safely, learn muzzle discipline, learn trigger control and actually be able to do those things under the pressure of a real match. To learn predictive shooting at this phase of your training does not make a lot of sense.

For those training at level 2, predictive shooting starts to be valuable. Level 2 training is designed to get you to B class. One of the primary things you need to do to get to B class is to learn to shoot aggressively at close ranged targets. This means that you should learn how to shoot fast "hammer" pairs inside of 10 yards. This also means that you will start to train predictive shooting on Doubles drill and on classifier style challenges. If the targets are 10 yards and closer, I recommend you see your sights in the center of the target and then fire two shots.

You should not do this if you are moving. You should not do this if the target is moving. It only works when conditions are perfect and you can start really hammering the targets.

It is at this point in the explanation that people start to get confused. "Is he saying you see the sight once and then just rip two shots?" Yes and no.

Yes, when you see the sight where it is supposed to be, I want you to shoot two shots. What I want to add into that is that you should be continually aware of what the sights are doing. You should keep both eyes open. Try not to flinch or blink. See everything as much as you can.

What you should develop is continual awareness of what your sights are doing. How are they moving in recoil? Do you see the dot dip down below the point of aim after the first shot, but before the second shot? What EXACTLY are you seeing? You need to know.

The concept of continual sight awareness is intertwined with predictive shooting. The power of this is simple. As you train your way to B class and you start doing predictive shooting under those perfect conditions, only when you are stopped and stable and the range is minimal, you will hop on the learning curve.

As you move to level 3 and 4 training the opportunities for predictive shooting are only going to grow.

Do you think the top open shooters in the world, with a heavy race gun, a compensator on the muzzle, a red dot sight and years of training can get away with pretty insane feats of predictive shooting? Do you think they could shoot fast predictive pairs on 20-yard partial targets? You bet they can. They do this through years of training and exploring their limits. They can intuitively know how much control they are going to have over their gun under all sorts of circumstances.

Good training requires some bad shots

This text is going to push you more and more towards predictive shooting as you develop. There is a major hang up with this that many people have.

When you train predictive shooting, you are going to have errant shots. You are going to have shots sail over the target. You will tense up occasionally and press bad shots down low. This is bound to happen. Do not feel bad about this or even consider it a mistake. It is all part of the process. You need to find the limits in your training. Open up your thinking to allow for some experimentation and it is going to pay off for you. Given time, training, and awareness of what your sights are doing in recoil, you can accomplish some amazing feats of predictive shooting. It is ok to make mistakes in training. It is ok to fire bad shots on occasion if it gets you closer to firing more and more good shots as you develop your skills.

MEASUREMENT

Competitive shooting is very much about measurement. It is about measuring the skills of one person against another so you can make judgements about what technique or equipment works better. By understanding the results, everyone can get better.

We measure things by points and time. There is a hit factor. There is a stage winner. This is how we measure ourselves in competition.

At a match we know there will be a score and meaning will be attached to the score. You shoot each stage one time. There is no chance to practice. Your competitors shoot the same match, at the same time so the weather conditions should generally be equal.

There is a disconnect for most people between match measurement and practice measurement. Simply put, people do not do as well at matches as they think they ought to. This is very common. There tends to be lots of mistakes come match day.

If you are reading this, you have certainly walked away from a match disappointed about how poorly you did. It never feels the same as the practice range, does it? When you are shooting "for real," things happen that are hard to quantify. You start making mistakes or chasing unrealistic scores. Matches reveal the flaws in your shooting.

This disconnect between matches and practice is not really a disconnect at all. It is an indication that the *measurement* of your shooting in practice is the problem. You are not reading the situation properly and do not get a good understanding of your skills.

Let me give you an example:

You are out training on El Prezidente. This is a well-known drill that is described in detail in the drill section of this text. 6 seconds is fast. 5 seconds is awesome. 4 seconds is legendary. Most of you know how all this works. During your training you do repetition after repetition. You make a lot of mistakes. This is training, and you need to push yourself.

After lots of messed up reloads and misses on the target, you get a score under 5 seconds with only a few points down. This is what you are capable of. Now you just need to manifest this capacity in a match setting.

The next week you go to your local match and El Prez is set up as a classifier. You just trained on this! You can do it in under 5 seconds! As you step up to the line to shoot you feel the pressure mount. Your hands are slightly shaking. This is a physiological change that takes place when you are under stress. You know you can run this under 5, you just need to pull it off in the match.

You know how the story ends. There is no reason to continue telling it. The bottom line is, going to a controlled training environment with unlimited attempts is in no way, shape, or form the same sort of thing as shooting in a scored competition. It does not work like that. The real problem here is on the training range.

Let's go over some conditions that affect your shooting:

Match

A match is where you feel pressure while people watch you shoot. This is where you will find out where you stack up relative to the other competitors. If you do not care about how you do in club matches, you may not feel pressure. The pressure tends to find you when you go to a club you do not normally attend or go to a big match.

Big Match

A "big" match means that it is big for *you*. If your goal in life is to win your class at your annual State Sectional, there will be pressure at the event. This match pressure comes from your own experiences and perceptions. You bring it with you. If the match matters to you, there will be pressure.

Pushing

"Pushing" is when you are making a conscious effort to get a better result. It usually manifests in more speed and tension. It also results in more mistakes. To push or not to push is something you should consciously control. Pushing is needed in training and can be useful in matches.

Shooting Safe

Shooting safe is when you confirm your aim more than you think necessary. It is when you press the trigger a bit more slowly and carefully than you otherwise would. Shooting "safe" helps ensure an "okay" score, but mitigates the risk of a terrible one.

Why does any of this matter?

When you are shooting you are always measuring and assessing. Oftentimes that assessment is happening subconsciously. You will start to form thoughts and beliefs about your shooting. Ideas about what your strong and weak points are will work their way into your consciousness. This will affect your training and match results.

The reason the above ideas about what type of conditions you are shooting under and the assessment matters is that you need to be your own coach. You need to decide what you need to work on, how long to work on it, and what the goal is. This book guides you in some ways, but it is on you to get better.

Your training is going to take place largely in friendly environments. You will need a home dry fire area. You will have a range or two that you regularly visit. These environments will become safe for you. You will be loose and relaxed and likely do your best shooting. This is where you need to be on guard.

It is very easy to have incredible results in that safe environment and then believe you have abilities you do not have yet. This mistake can cost you big as you start pushing in matches to make the same scores happen. Do not fall for that; do not give into that.

The Instagram effect is a real thing. People will often bend technique to the breaking point and score any hits on brown to get a run that looks good for the 'gram. There is nothing wrong with getting that one smoker run on video, but there might be a problem if you think you will be able to do that on demand.

Remember, you are training to shoot juiced up on adrenaline. You are training to shoot under pressure. You are training to place well at matches you care about. Make sure your training mindset reflects that.

Training Measurement

To assist with measurement of your abilities, I have highlighted a few ideas you want to pay attention to.

You need to understand par times are and what they mean. The idea for a par time is that it gives you a good idea about what someone of a certain ability level can generally do.

Do I expect that a top tier shooter can shoot an El Prezidente in under 4.5 seconds?

Yes.

Do I expect that they will do it in their first attempt?

No.

This book uses 5 seconds as the 10 yard par time for a level 4 shooter. That means that I expect in roughly **9/10** attempts a **trained up** and **warmed up** level 4 dude is going to nail that. Let's break it down some more.

9/10 means you will often have mistakes. The nature of practical shooting is it needs to be fast. It needs to be right on the edge of out of control. If you are going too slowly, you will never make mistakes. You will not be in contention for winning anything.

Trained up means the guy has been training recently. Do I expect a deathstalker level shooter to strap on a rig and nail a hot run if they have not trained in a month? No, I do not.

Warmed up means you have been shooting enough during the season that you feel you are shooting at your normal level. Does being warmed up help you shoot better? Yes, it does.

Expectations should always be changing based on conditions.

To cut through the noise and get to the signal, I recommend that you generally do aggregate scoring. Most of the time you are training, you should be shooting the drill you are working on with several attempts in succession. After the attempts are done, you should score the targets and assess the hit patterns. You will find answers to questions if you look at the big picture and score in aggregate.

DRYFIRE TRAINING

Dryfire training is training using your equipment (gun, magazines, holster, etc.) without ammunition. This means you can train an unlimited amount without needing to spend money on ammo or go to a range. It is the process of going through the motions. You perform the exact same actions, the exact same way. During dry training you can draw the pistol 200 times in a matter of minutes. Each repetition burning into your subconscious. After repeated sessions and time doing the same training, you will not need any conscious direction to be able to do that action the way you were doing it.

It is essential for your advancement that you develop the habit of regular in-home dryfire training. With very few exceptions, top level shooters use regular dry training as part of a regimen to attain a high level of skill. This section will help familiarize you with the basics and give you some drills to practice from the convenience in your own home, on your own schedule.

These drills can and should be done at the shooting range as well. Dryfire isn't just for home training. It will help you save ammunition, learn faster and increase the total amount of repetition you can perform in you training session.

How dryfire works may seem self-explanatory to you, but there are some important aspects to dryfiring that can make you better at shooting. It is useful to consider these ideas, so think about what you are trying to accomplish when dryfiring.

Dryfire is a powerful idea with a definite upside, as with anything though, there is a bit of downside as well that you should also be paying attention to.

If you have done any dry training at all, you understand there is a big change in mindset once the gun is unloaded and you have switched to dry training. You can relax yourself because you know there will not be any shooting. There is no blast, recoil, or brass kicking out of your pistol. Everything will be relatively benign during the dry training. When you know you cannot get hurt or have an accident because you took away the live ammo, you can train yourself at the limits of your body. That is an incredibly positive thing for your development. Your window of comfort can rapidly expand.

There are negative psychological effects to this phenomenon as well. When you know that there will not be live ammo coming out of your gun, the normal habit of bracing for that recoil will not happen the same way. You can see this very clearly with a new shooter. As soon as they are sure their gun is unloaded and they are handling the gun dry, you see a total change in their posture and attitude towards the gun. This also affects higher level shooters to a much lesser degree.

Dryfiring the gun with this relaxed posture/grip can be counterproductive to being a good shooter. Remember, dryfire works because you do the same things the exact same way as live fire training. If you subconsciously relax your grip while you do dry training, you are not training yourself to do what you want to do in competition.

On top of the subtler things like mental attitude and grip pressure there are some more obvious drawbacks to dry training as well. With dry training you will not be getting feedback from holes you put into targets and the accuracy assessment part of your shooting training will be left to you getting visual feedback from your sights. You will never know if you are being accurate until you go out and do some live shooting.

In the end, dryfires greatest asset is training without the sound of ammo. The greatest drawback of dryfire is the same. The lack of noise can allow you to train yourself incorrectly. To have dryfire work for you, you must constantly be on guard against doing training that would be counterproductive with live ammo.

Just to recap the two important points here:

Dryfire works because you do the exact same actions the exact same way so you can train them to be subconscious.

When you do things during dryfire instead of live fire, there is a shift in your mindset and approach that is difficult to overcome. You want to continually assess whether your repetitions are "real" or not.

Live/Dry Loop

Dryfire is a powerful and essential tool; it is also a double-edged sword. You have the means for unlimited in-home training so you can become incredibly proficient with your firearm. At the same time, if you are not extremely careful with the particulars of how you are dryfiring you can build some bad habits by using repetition of incorrect technique.

To get maximum effectiveness from your dry training, you want to regularly go out and do live training. Dryfire is your practice, live fire is your test. If you adopt this mindset it will allow you to maximize the efficiency of the dryfire you are doing.

Imagine doing hundreds of repetitions for an hour a night. You can work on drawing the gun fast, reloading, trigger control, or any other skill. This training is sitting there waiting for you whenever you care to do it. This is a powerful tool to have.

Consider this scenario: after you have been training for an entire week, it is finally Saturday. You go to the range for a couple hours and work on the same sorts of skills you were working on dry. This time you get the noise and blast of the gun firing. You get acclimated to the recoil and you get to train. Your gun behaves as it would during an actual match. As you work through some set of drills or tests with your live shooting you can see how your dryfire has been serving you. Is your grip pressure what you trained it to be? Are you aiming properly when you shoot? There are an endless number of questions you can ask yourself, but the important thing is that you get feedback on how your training has gone.

After returning from the range and reflecting on your experience, your dry training the next week gets refocused and intensified. If you had some failing in your dry training, you start working on fixing it.

Imagine the power this cycle of training has when you faithfully engage in it over a period of years. Train, shoot, assess and train some more. It is an endless loop of productive training for as long as you want it to be.

Create Mistakes

One part of dry training that is generally lost on the shooting community is the idea of creating mistakes. This might seem insane after reading the previous section. All of the discussion is on how to do correct repetition and avoid the pitfalls of gripping the gun softly or whatever else you might be doing wrong. This might seem like a contradiction to many.

It is a common situation for a shooter to be shooting inaccurately. Often after doing a lot of fast shooting on a target, but having some problem, the shooter will get frustrated and switch to doing dryfire to correct the issue. The dryfire will then intentionally be slow. After doing technically correct, but slow repetition, our shooter will return to live shooting often with similar results.

This scenario is common and it is exactly what I mean by "creating mistakes." You are going to learn, improve and get better by seeing incorrect technique and correcting it. You do this by creating the circumstances that are causing problems. For example, if you have a problem pulling the trigger back fast and straight, it is likely that you can pull it straight *slowly*. Doing it slowly is not your problem. You need to learn to do it quickly. It is the speed component of the technique that is the issue. If you remove the requirement for it to be fast, you are not addressing the problem.

It is essential that you control the circumstances of your training. If you have a problem with your technique, you need to recreate the problem in dryfire so you can fix it. The best way to know you have created the circumstances that cause mistakes is, you start observing exactly the mistake you are trying to fix. Once you see that, you know your training is hitting on the right note and you can start working towards correcting the problem.

Honesty/Assessment

For all the above reasons that have been discussed, your honesty with yourself is of the utmost importance. A big driving force behind this book is the hundreds of seminar style classes I have taught with competitive shooters from around the world. As part of those classes, I will set up and demonstrate training exercises, then have the class do them. In my estimation, less than 1 in 4 students do the dryfire they are instructed to do the way they are instructed to do it without frequent corrections.

You need to be hard on yourself to get better. You need to watch your sights, assess your grip, pay attention to the way your gun transitions from target to target and check your footwork when you move. You cannot do all these things all the time, but you need to be doing something with your attention. You need to be watching what is going on in order to get better.

Nobody else can relieve you of this burden. Even if you hire a full-time coach to watch you and evaluate you, it will not get you off the hook. You will learn more and learn faster by paying close attention to every single repetition and trying to refine your technique as you go along.

It is also important that you are honest with yourself when it comes to using the timer for dryfire. When you set the par time pay attention to the stop beep. Were you done with the drill in the time you set out? Just setting an aggressive par time does not make you fast. You need to strictly enforce it.

Boredom

The number one complaint about dryfire is that it is boring. It is a fact of the human condition that we like to be continuously stimulated in some way or we get bored. Dryfire does not stimulate your senses. Instead, you need to engage your senses during dryfire and find those inputs to assess your training. Some suggestions to curb the boredom and engage your senses are to listen to music while you do it or you can change drills frequently. You can also train with a buddy to minimize boredom. Standing around endlessly practicing reloads can get boring. When you are bored and no longer engaged with the process, you should stop for a while. At this point it is no longer productive.

What you need to effectively dry fire:

Match Equipment

You need to have all the gear you would normally need for a match. Gun, belt rig, magazines, etc. I recommend dressing in a similar fashion to what you would wear in a match. Wear the type of pants you wear at a match and get rid of loose-fitting clothing that can foul your gun handling.

Secure space

You want to have a place where you dryfire.

The most sensible thing is to have is an area where an accidental discharge is less likely to cause injury or escape the area. A basement or other type of area is ideal. You would also be wise to remove any live ammunition from your dry training space. This reduces the probability of an accident.

You can affix scaled targets to the walls or have targets on stands. You can even put down floor mats or gym mats to reduce damage to magazines when they are dropped on the ground.

This may not feasible for everyone, but consider it a wish list. Not everyone even has a basement, let alone a partner that is going to stand for targets semi permanently affixed to walls. Compromise is a part of life, do the best you can to create a good space for productive dry training.

Targets

I strongly recommend using scaled targets for dry training. 1/3rd scale is quite common and allows you to simulate distance inside a normal indoor space. You can use a smaller or larger scale as your space allows.

Timer

You should have a proper shot time for dry training. Having a timer you can quickly change the par setting on will help you train the most efficient way possible.

Quality of Life Items

These items are strongly recommended.

Dummy rounds (ammo with no powder or primer) are an excellent tool to get your gun and magazines to feel the same as they will in competition. Filling your mags with this dummy ammo will make things feel much closer and more realistic. If you do not do this step already, you should consider it.

Many people go so far as to have a dryfire set of magazines permanently loaded with dummy ammo. This is a good step to take if you have the money for it. It will speed up your training by eliminating the setup time of filling mags with dummy rounds.

You should consider using grip enhancers such as "Pro Grip" during your dry training if you use it in competition. This gives your training that more realistic feel and it should help you build a more consistent grip. Many people always use a grip enhancer at a match, but not during their dry training.

Have dedicated gear

Along the same lines of a dedicated space, it is good to have dedicated gear. For the more serious competitors that have backup guns and backup belt rigs, this means that you leave a backup set of gear in/near your dryfire area and use that to train with. This allows you to get started in the time it takes to strap your gear onto your inner belt. The easier it is to get started training, the more training you are going to do.

Other tools

You can use laser modules, SIRT pistols, gas pistols, airsoft guns, or any other similar tool that is currently on the market to aid in your shooting training. These tools are each a bit different and can help with certain problems, but none of them are required. While you can benefit in some way from most of them, you should do the majority of your dryfire with your match gear. The other tools are a bonus.

EFFICIENT TRAINING

Many of you have heard Malcolm Gladwell discuss how it takes 10,000 hours to master something. He is not wrong. It will take mountains of time and energy for you to climb to the top and maximize your potential.

Many people get this confused. They think if they put in 10,000 hours, they will get where they want to go. This sort of thinking is prevalent in the shooting community. Many people will ask "how long has he been shooting?" There seems to be some unspoken expectation that as the number of years you participate in matches goes up, so do your skills.

Occasionally someone new comes into shooting and gets good, fast. It is not all that uncommon to have someone achieve M class after trying USPSA for the first time less than 12 months prior. How is this possible? How is this happening?

Many people want to dismiss such cases. They say talent, age, or even luck is responsible for someone getting to a high level quickly. There is no doubt all these factors exist to some extent. The thing that propels people to the top of the game is spending the time they do put in wisely and putting in lots of time.

The bottom line is, if you think you are going to "go through the motions" of doing serious training over several years and get better because you put in the time, you are kidding yourself. You need to pay attention to your practice.

With all that preamble out of the way, the point of this section is to discuss *specific* techniques for reducing the number of hours you are putting in and still give you the same result, or an even better result. You can learn the shortcuts to excellence that many other people have already proven work.

Know your limits

Everybody has limits. You have only so much time in the day. You can only do so much physical exertion. You only have a certain amount of money to buy ammo. The list of limiting factors when it comes to your training is extensive.

If you are looking to maximize your skills, it is imperative that you understand what your limitations are. You know yourself better than anyone else knows you. Use that knowledge of yourself to set yourself up for success, not for failure and frustration.

As an example, some new shooters have the idea they are going to dryfire four hours a day, every day and get insanely good in a short amount of time. The problem with this is very few people have the mental focus or physical ability to do such an intense amount of training. It is not that they are weak, it is that everyone has limits.

Oftentimes, these personalities force themselves to train to this standard they set for themselves. They pick a number and are going to force themselves to do it. It may be four hours a day of dryfire. It may be 100k rounds of live fire a year in training. The point is, by picking some arbitrary number and forcing themselves to train to that standard, they will burn out, get tired and start performing bad or incorrect repetitions of skills. They will develop bad habits instead of good habits.

I have even seen these same personalities enter a "death spiral" in their shooting ability. They keep focusing on the input of their training. They pour more and more energy into training even when they are exhausted and unable to focus. This leads to poor skill development. Poor skill development leads to unsatisfactory competition results. This often becomes a negative feedback loop that results in a rage quit from the sport, or at least demotivation from training.

Listen to yourself. If you are tired, stop. If the ammunition is breaking the bank, shoot less. If you do not feel like you are learning, stop. Come back fresh later. Know your limits and work within them.

Accountability

There is one important note of caution that simply cannot be ignored. Many of the techniques to make yourself more efficient come at a cost. For example, one common technique to speed up training is to not restore hits to the A zone, only hits that land outside the A zone. Under certain circumstances this is a good way to speed up training. Under other circumstances it can lead to creating bad habits.

Before we get into detailed discussion of the specifics for how to speed up your training, we need to make this point. You need to know where your shots are going. You cannot guess. You cannot assume. You NEED to know.

Live Training Efficiency

The number one thing you can do to speed up your live fire training is structuring the training session properly. If you put in a little bit of forethought you can save yourself tons of hassle. Here are a few rules that we use in our training to speed things up.

1. Set up the range one time - If possible, structure your training so you only need to move around equipment once. This will minimize the amount of work you need to do.

   Example: You intend to train on Accelerator and Mounted Movement. You could quite easily set up Accelerator as one side of your Mounted Movement drill. Then you add position markers and a couple more targets. If you set things up properly, you can successfully train on both your intended drills and you do not need to spend time or energy rearranging things.

2. Use a brass net/chute - If you are one of the many of us that relies on picking up and reloading brass to be able to afford ammunition, consider using a tool to assist you with that. Brass nets that you lay on the ground or brass chutes that catch brass as it ejects from your gun are a valuable tool. Consider trying one out if you have not. These will save your time and energy.

3. There is an important cautionary note here when it comes to brass nets. They can often have an undesirable psychological effect in that they anchor you to having the desire to shoot all from one

location. If that is what your training needs and what your training calls for, then fine, shoot from one spot. However, if you need to do more dynamic shooting and training and you find the net making you lazy you might want to discontinue using it for a while. The net needs to be a tool to help and not an anchor to hold you in place.

4. Use a paster gun - Paster guns will dramatically reduce the amount of time it takes to restore a target during practice.

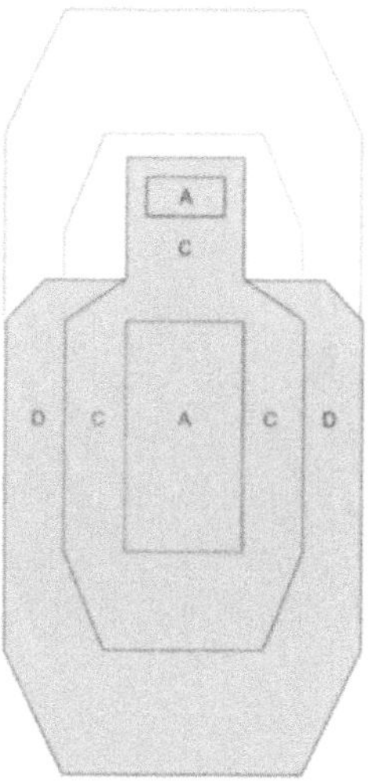

5. Use aggregate scoring - I recommend using aggregate scoring. For a typical drill you shoot it three to six times consecutively without pasting or resetting. Look at the average hits and time. Not only does this give you a more accurate measurement of what is happening, it also helps you identify patterns in the scoring while simultaneously saving a lot of time. I cannot advocate aggregate scoring more forcefully. It is an excellent practice that you should be undertaking. If you are doing aggregate scoring on a target that you are likely to miss, such as a USPSA headbox at distance, consider placing a no shoot behind that target. This way, the no shoot will catch the bullets that miss the target, and you will have more data about where exactly your hits are going.

6. Paste only outside the A zone - A big-time saver is pasting only what lands outside of the A zone. This means C and D hits get restored and the A's remain holes in the cardboard. If you are a skilled shooter and doing high round count training at close range, this is certainly a valid idea. If you ever have any doubt about where your hits are going, you should not do this. This is recommended for level 3 or 4 training at ranges inside of 10 yards. Other than that, you should make sure you are restoring everything so you are confirming you know where everything went.

LEVEL 1

Level 1 Goal: Complete a Club Match without a Penalty

The 1st level in this book is designed to make you competent, safe, accurate and able to shoot under pressure. This level contains no time *Standards* of any kind. It does not have any advanced shooting concepts such as different aiming schemes for different targets. This level is designed to take you from no practical experience doing competitive shooting and get you through a club match without shooting misses.

To reach the goal of getting through a match without a miss, there are quite a few things that need to be accomplished and understood. This starts with safety rules for the sport of practical shooting and if you are new to guns, you need to understand safe gun handling habits as well. This section contains the procedures you should follow in training that will keep you safe and keep you in compliance with safety rules.

You will need to practice and become comfortable with the procedures for loading, firing, reloading and clearing malfunctions with your firearm. After a bit of time spent working with the drills, you will make these procedures become a habit.

You will learn about dryfire training. You can work with your equipment at home, on your own schedule, to build the base of your shooting skills. You can draw the gun to your grip. You can practice transitioning the gun around from target to target. Eventually you will develop the "index" ability where you can intuitively aim your gun anywhere you put your vision.

You will teach yourself good habits for your live fire training. You will learn to grip the gun properly and manage the recoil. With diligent practice, you can shoot very consistently and accurately.

The important thing you learn in level 1 is discipline. If you instill good technique, train with good habits, and shoot with discipline you will very quickly be getting through matches with very few penalties.

Level 1 Training Standards

The Destination:

This training level is designed to get you through matches with no penalties for misses or no-shoot hits. This may not sound like a lofty goal, but I assure you it requires work and dedication to make that happen.

The idea is to understand marksmanship fundamentals, safety habits and training discipline. This training level should get you familiar with the concepts and training format that will be built on later in your shooting career.

If those things are taken on board, you will be in an excellent position to advance to level 2.

Input:

This level will require that you do dryfire training on a regular or semi-regular basis. It will also necessitate occasional trips to the range for live training.

What Comes Next:

Using the good habits built in this section you should be able to quickly advance to level 2 training where you will introduce tight time *Standards* and more advanced technical concepts.

Specific Standards:

Level 1 training does not have a specific set of *Standards* as it relates to numbers. You do not need to draw at X speed or shoot splits at Y pace. Those concepts do not exist at this training level. It is to your advantage at this level to NOT have specific time standards. In my experience from training, lower-level shooters worrying about time *Standards* causes them to focus on the wrong things and slows down improvement.

Knowledge/mindset:

What you should be getting out of level 1 training are the habits that make you successful later. This level is defined by going to and completing a match without shooting a penalty. Most members of USPSA have never done this in their shooting career. This goal requires that you learn how to hit the targets in the context of practical shooting and have the discipline to do it when you are under pressure. It is not a small task.

In addition to the shooting ability and technique, you need to learn about how to safely load and unload your pistol. You should understand how to use your holster safely. You need to know how your pistol functions and be able to clear malfunctions. These things are needed to get to the starting line at a practical shooting match.

It is important to establish productive habits when it comes to safety, especially if you are new to guns. Make sure you do the things to ensure you have a long career with no accidents. Things like checking your gun to see if it is loaded every single time you pick it up will keep you safe. Once you establish the habit, you will be able to shift some focus to getting better at shooting.

Once you can handle your gun and shoot safely, you can start working on getting better. You should learn to make the shots in a practical setting. A practical setting means you are shooting a variety of courses under competition pressure. Your training should be focused on simple concepts like a strong support hand grip and careful trigger presses. You want these things to be reflexive and happen under pressure. If your training is good, you will soon be able to shoot a stage without being worried about missing a shot.

Standard Practice Setup

In later levels, the standard practice setup will become an invaluable tool to specifically measure your performance. At this level, you should familiarize yourself with the drills and shoot them a little bit, to get a sense for how the drills feel to shoot and what kind of performance you can expect.

Shooting impressive times is not something you need to do at this level. It is counterproductive to spend energy on these highly specific exercises before getting a handle on the broader concepts that will propel you forward in terms of skill.

Try these drills. Learn these drills. Understand these drills. They are going to be with you for a while.

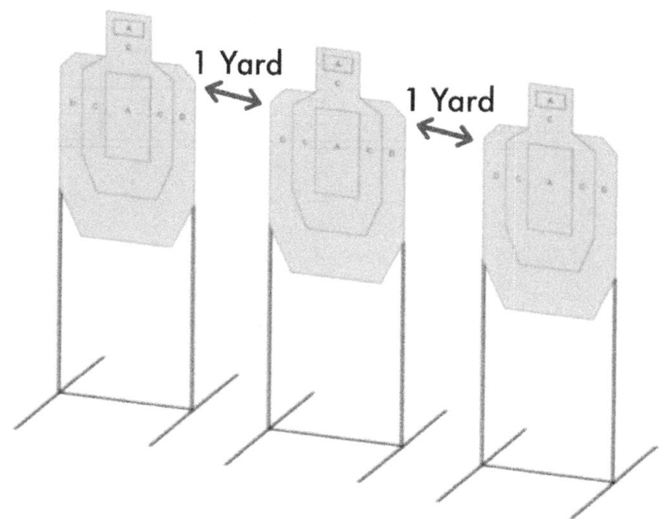

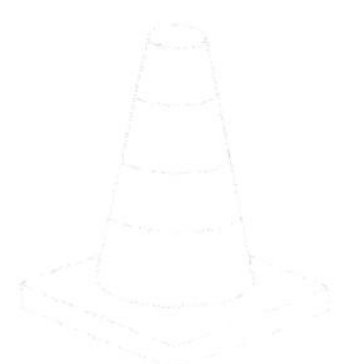

Livefire Level 1

Drill Name	Procedure	goal draw/reload times	3 yards	7 yards	10 yards	15 yards	25 yards	add time for: surrender	facing uprange	unloaded start
One Per Target	Engage each target with 1 round	na	na	na	na	na	na	na	na	na
Pairs on One Target	Engage one target with 2 rounds	na	na	na	na	na	na	na	na	na
4 Aces	Engage 1 target with 2 rounds, reload, reengage w/ 2 rounds.	na	na	na	na	na	na	na	na	na
Bill Drill	Engage one target with 6 rounds	na	na	na	na	na	na	na	na	na
Bill/Reload/Bill	Engage one, 6 rounds, reload, 6 more	na	na	na	na	na	na	na	na	na
Blake Drill	Engage each target with 2 rounds	na	na	na	na	na	na	na	na	na
El Prez	Turn, draw, engage each target w/2, reload, reengage each w/2	na	na	na	na	na	na	na	na	na
Criss Cross	Engage each of the 6 A zones in a criss cross pattern	na	na	na	na	na	na	na	na	na
Stong Hand Only	Engage each target w/ 2 rounds Strong hand only	na	na	na	na	na	na	na	na	na
Weak Hand Only	Engage each target w/ 2 rounds weak hand only	na	na	na	na	na	na	na	na	na

Dryfire Training 1

Training Focal Points

Your focus should be to build familiarity and comfort with your firearm and gun handling skills.

You should have a developed index and subconscious gun handling skills. This means that you can look to any spot and bring your gun to that spot. The sights should show up roughly in alignment on that spot. You should be able to draw, reload and clear malfunctions without conscious thought.

Training Schedule

To facilitate developing the required skills, you will need regular training until your index/gun handling skills reach the requisite place. Commonly, someone will train five days a week for a month or so and those skills will be in place. After that point, occasional training will maintain these skills.

Level 1 Drills

In addition to the standard dry drills, listed below are dryfire versions of all the other level 1 drills. Construct the drill to scale as described in the dryfire training section in the general information section of this book.

Standards

In later levels, the standard practice setup will become an invaluable tool to specifically measure your performance. At this level, you should familiarize yourself with the following drills and train on them.

What is important is that you learn "the language" of drills and training. Simply learning what the drills are and learning to execute them will make you more effective later in your shooting. For example, many people in classes struggle to draw the pistol and shoot six shots into a target. I do not mean they are not capable of doing this, I mean they must actually think through the process step by step. If I introduce anything for them to pay attention to (such as trigger control), they cannot do the drill properly. They end up shooting the wrong number of rounds or getting confused in some other way.

Your dry training on these drills will prepare you to test yourself on them with live ammunition without wasting ammunition learning the drill itself.

Dryfire Level 1

Drill Name	Procedure	goal draw/reload times	3 yards	7 yards	10 yards	15 yards	25 yards	add time for: surrender	facing uprange	unloaded start
One Per Target	Engage each target with 1 round	na	na	na	na	na	na	na	na	na
Pairs on One Target	Engage one target with 2 rounds	na	na	na	na	na	na	na	na	na
4 Aces	Engage 1 target with 2 rounds, reload, reengage w/ 2 rounds.	na	na	na	na	na	na	na	na	na
Bill Drill	Engage one target with 6 rounds	na	na	na	na	na	na	na	na	na
Bill/Reload/Bill	Engage one, 6 rounds, reload, 6 more	na	na	na	na	na	na	na	na	na
Blake Drill	Engage each target with 2 rounds	na	na	na	na	na	na	na	na	na
El Prez	Turn, draw, engage each target w/2, reload, reengage each w/2	na	na	na	na	na	na	na	na	na
Criss Cross	Engage each of the 6 A zones in a criss cross pattern	na	na	na	na	na	na	na	na	na
Stong Hand Only	Engage each target w/ 2 rounds Strong hand only	na	na	na	na	na	na	na	na	na
Weak Hand Only	Engage each target w/ 2 rounds weak hand only	na	na	na	na	na	na	na	na	na

Marksmanship Fundamentals

Group Shooting

Purpose/Goal:

The ability to shoot A zone hits without any time pressure. Shooting all A's at 15 yards.

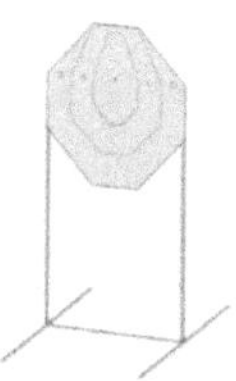

Instructions:

With no time limit, engage the target with as many rounds as desired. Shooting at least a five shot group is a good test of consistency.

Cues:

The most important cue to pay attention to is the tactile feel of your firing hand. Paying attention to the feel of your hands instead of the visual component of sight alignment may not feel natural. In most cases you will get better results by focusing on the feel inside your hands.

Corrections:

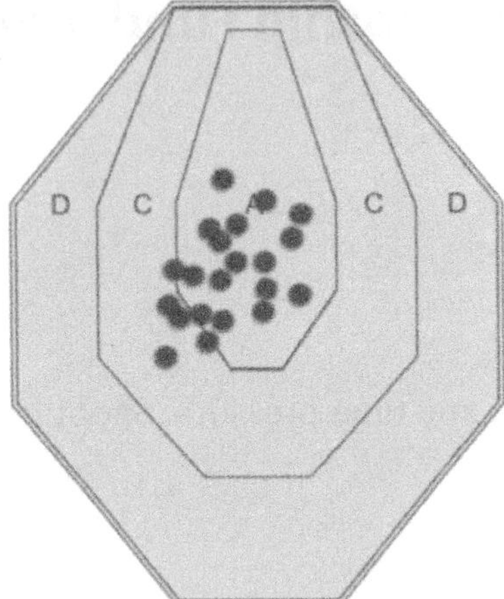

Hitting low/left is the classic sign of pushing down into the anticipated recoil. Focus on holding your firing hand still while you press the trigger straight.

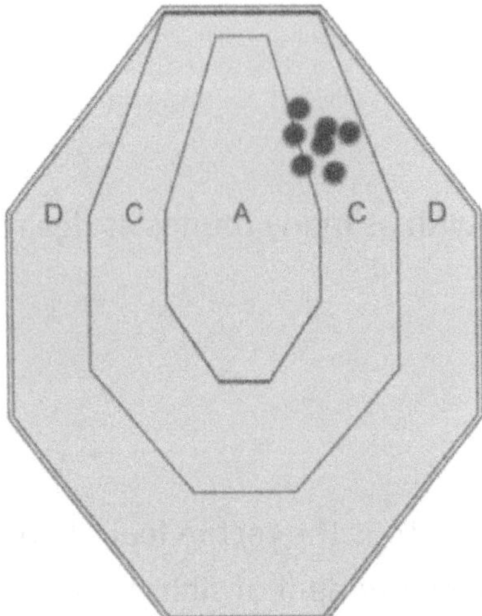

If you are forming a small group but in the wrong spot of the target, consider adjusting your sights. If you are unsure if you or the sights are the issue, have a friend shoot your gun to confirm your zero.

Evolution:

Be sure to vary the target configuration. Try using no-shoots or hardcovers to block off part of the target. Forcing yourself to work around the obstruction will help you learn what your sights should look like when engaging a target that is partially obstructed.

Tips:

Shooting tight groups is an important skill to develop for any practical shooter. This skill will allow you to make sure that your pistol is mechanically accurate and able to hit any reasonable target at a reasonable distance.

The best results during group shooting are typically going to be had when you are focused on the feel of your hands rather than the visual component of aiming. The most common error that we observe during group shooting training is when the shooter sees a desirable sight picture, they immediately want to press the trigger. Typically, this is accompanied by pushing down into the anticipated recoil. If this shooter accepts a little bit of "wobble" in the sight picture and focuses on smoothly and cleanly releasing that shot, they will get a much better result.

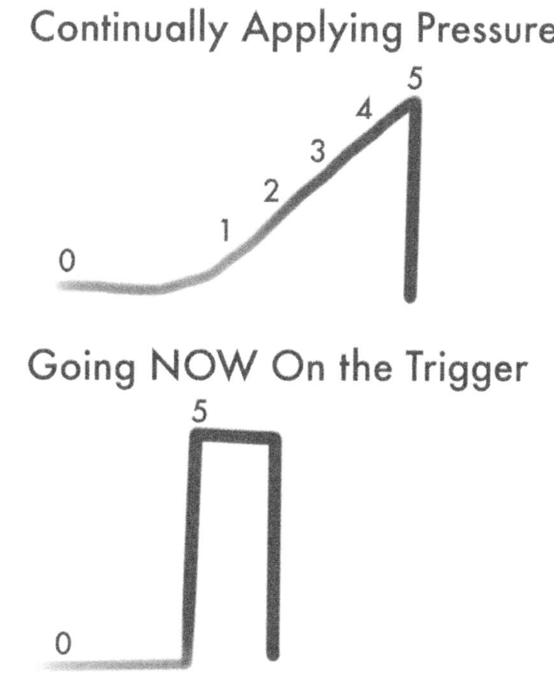

Try applying pressure slowly and continually until the trigger breaks opposed to going NOW on the trigger. Focus on your hands and how you hold the gun as you slowly increase pressure in one continuous motion. For example, slowly apply one pound, then two pounds, then three pounds, then four pounds, in one continuous press and at some point, the hammer will fall and the gun will fire. Fight the urge to apply all four or five pounds of pressure instantly when you get the sights where you want them. Going NOW on the trigger will often move your sights off target.

Drill Progress Tracker			
Date	Drill Time	Hit Factor	Notes

Notes:

Practical Accuracy

Purpose/Goal:

Shoot the gun with acceptable accuracy at practical pace. Learn to grip your gun properly. Shooting all A hits at 15 yards is a good initial goal.

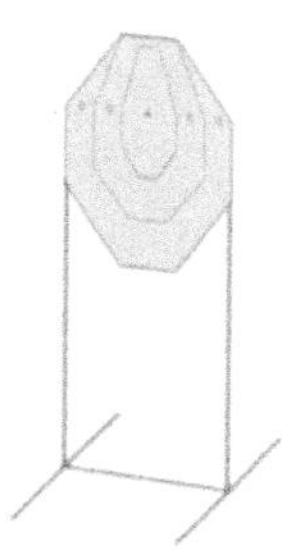

Instructions:

At the start signal, draw and engage the center of the A zone with six rounds and no time limit. Six strings at a time is recommended.

Cues:

Pay close attention to the feel of your gun in your hands. Once you feel yourself making some sort of mistake with your grip or trigger control you are going to be able to correct it much more easily.

Corrections:

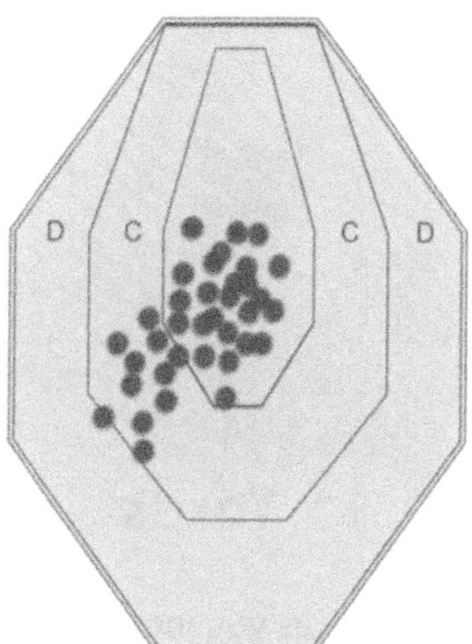

Low/left hits are almost always caused by moving the gun with the firing hand while shooting.

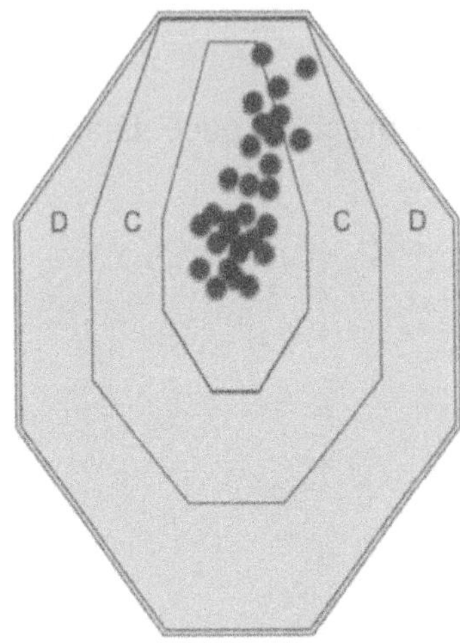

High hits generally come from insufficient support hand pressure.

Evolution:

Try to draw and shoot A's from any desired distance or on any target configuration.

Try this exercise one handed.

Tips:

It is important to think of this exercise as a grip exercise first and foremost. If you are gripping the gun correctly and consistently then you are going to get very good results. Pay attention to the feel of your hands as you are shooting. When you feel an errant shot happen because you pushed the gun sideways or some similar mistake then you will generally stop making that mistake so frequently. It is counterintuitive, but important, focus on your hands and don't worry so much about the way the sight picture looks.

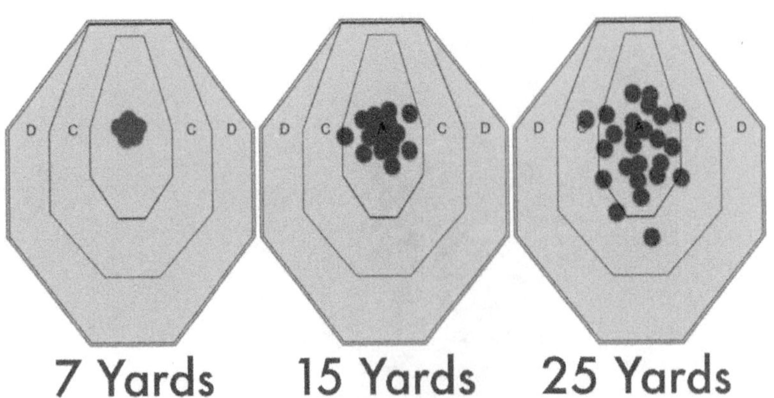

The goal is for your group to open concentrically as you increase the distance to the target. Flyers can, and will, still happen. Be looking at where the majority of the hits are going and be looking for any patterns. Compare any patterns you see to how your hands feel as you are breaking the shot. Connecting the dots from a feeling you have to where the shots are going will be go a long way towards being able to eliminate marksmanship errors.

Drill Progress Tracker			
Date	Drill Time	Hit Factor	Notes

Notes:

Single-handed Shooting

Purpose/Goal:

Developing the ability to make shots using only one hand on the gun. Both dominant hand only and non-dominant hand only need to be trained.

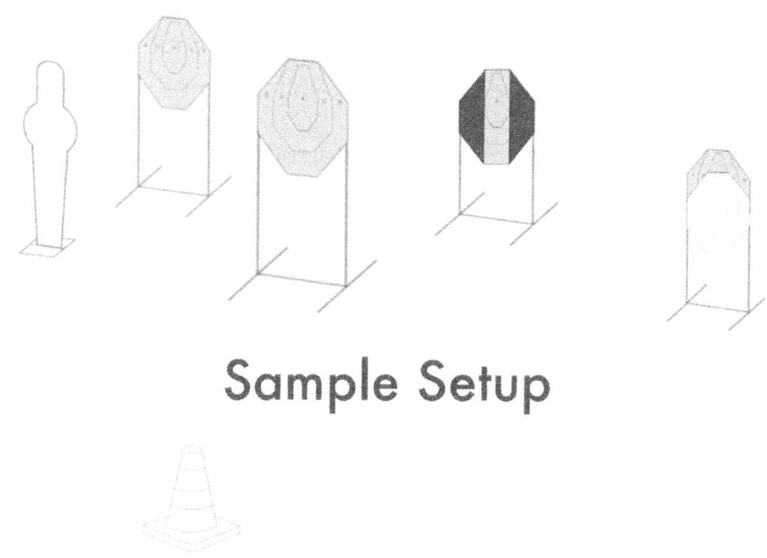

Random Target Set

Setup notes:

Set up any target scenario you desire.

Instructions:

At the start, draw and engage the targets with a single hand. If you are using your non-dominant hand, draw the gun, transfer it to the correct hand and engage the targets.

Cues:

Pay attention to your firing hand. The most common issue you are going to run into is pushing down into the gun sympathetically as you press the trigger. Paying attention to your hand during the course of that drill is going to mitigate that issue.

Corrections:

Low/left shots when shooting right handed or low/right shots when shooting left handed are going to be very common, especially as you increase your speed. This issue is the primary one you should be focused on eliminating.

Evolution:

Try out a variety of start positions. "Gun on table" to start is fairly common when you come to a single-handed shooting stage in a match. Make sure that you don't run into stuff that causes you to be nervous because the first time you have ever done it is in a match.

Tips:

If you are aiming, you will feel slow. A big part of most people's training is teaching themselves the discipline to aim and press the trigger properly no matter how long it *feels* like it is taking. Believe me, you will feel slow.

It is critical that you do a lot of single-handed repetition dryfire. If you are using a dot this becomes even more important. You will need to develop a whole new index for your non-dominant hand to be able to bring the sight to where it needs to be to be able to make hits. Do not neglect your dry training.

If the situation allows, holding your gun vertical is preferred. Canting your gun can cause your point of impact to shift, especially at longer ranges.

Drill Progress Tracker			
Date	Drill Time	Hit Factor	Notes

NOTES:

Transition /Vision Drills

Target Transitions

Purpose/Goal:

Move the gun smoothly and precisely from one target to the next.

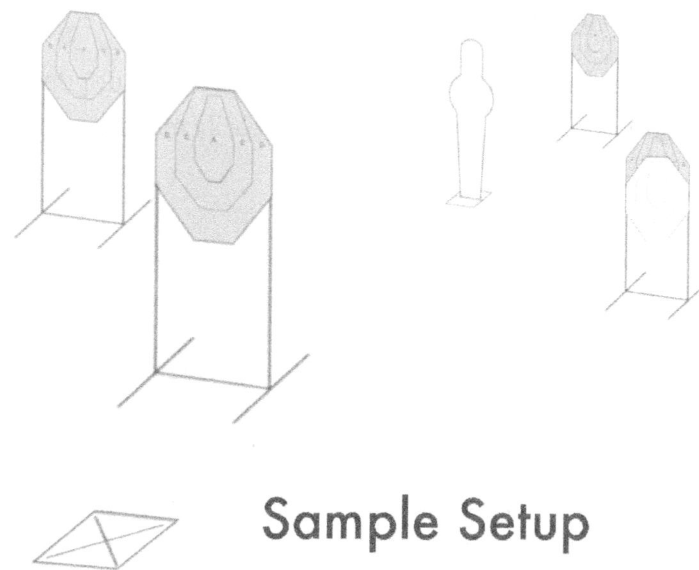

Instructions:

Set up targets of mixed distance and shot difficulty. Mixing in steel plates or poppers are optional if you have them available. Try to create a very plain cross section of the targets you expect to encounter at matches. At the start signal, engage each target. Keep the engagement order the same for a few repetitions. Shoot the drill at your practical match pace to begin and increase your speed as you feel comfortable doing so. Restore the targets after you assess them and change the engagement order if you wish for subsequent sets of repetitions on the exercise.

Cues:

Lead with your eyes. Look exactly where you wish to hit. You should not be looking at a big brown target, but picking an exact spot to move the gun to. Putting a mark or paster on the perforated letter A of your targets can be helpful in training your eyes to find the center. Some shooters like tracing the A zone with a marker to help with their initial training. These methods should only be used like a set of training wheels to help you get used to finding the center of the targets.

Do not muscle the gun around because it will cause the sights to stop imprecisely.

Corrections:

Relax your shoulders. Look exactly where you want the bullet to go and allow the gun to follow your vision to that spot.

Evolution:

Do dry aiming on each target at your full speed before doing live training. Move your vision from aimpoint to aimpoint on each target and learn to have the gun follow you. Make sure that you are not focusing on the sighting system as you move the gun from one target to the next but instead your vision is out on the target. When you are consistently performing these skills dry then begin live training. After each set of runs on the drill then return to dryfire before the next set of runs.

Develop the sense that your gun is a part of your body. As soon as your gun feels like an extension of your hands that you are not fighting with, you will much more easily move the gun from target to target.

Tips:

This training at an early stage of your development is not intended to make you extremely fast. It is only intended to develop your ability to index the gun precisely where you look.

Try to minimize technical errors as you do the drill. These errors include, but aren't limited to, following your sight in between targets, closing an eye, squinting, hunching down onto the gun and so on. These things are common and will not prevent you from being proficient as a shooter. As you develop your skills and attempt to go faster and faster, negative habits you have developed will become a problem. The best way to do business is both eyes open, target focused and looking for very specific aimpoints on each target.

Drill Progress Tracker

Date	Drill Time	Hit Factor	Notes

Notes:

STAGE SKILLS/ MOVEMENT

Movement

Purpose/Goal:

Move around a stage/scenario while keeping the gun pointed in a safe direction.

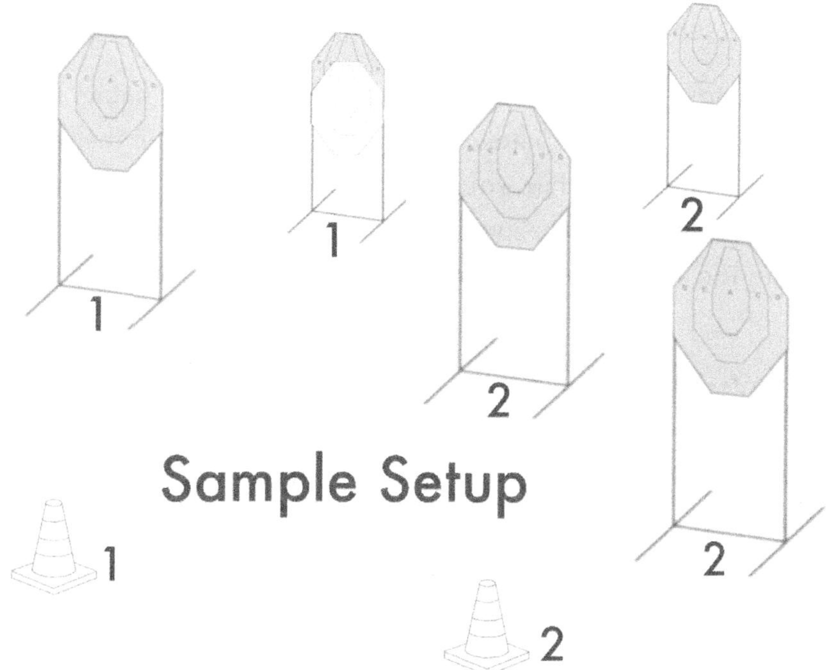

Setup notes:

Set the target scenario in a fair representation of what you expect to see in matches.

Instructions:

At the start signal, engage the required targets from position:

1. Move to position.
2. Engage the required targets.

Cues:

Remember the "laser" rule. Imagine a laser emanating from the muzzle of your pistol. You NEVER allow that laser to cross anything you do not want to shoot. Be mindful of your support hand when you run around and keep it out of the way of your muzzle.

Remove your trigger finger from the trigger guard as you dismount your pistol and get moving. Establish an index point on the frame of your pistol that you affirmatively move your finger to. This index point will ensure you keep your finger away from the trigger when you move.

Check to make sure you are not violating any other safety rules. Predominantly this will be the "180" rule that restricts you from pointing your gun in any way up range. Make sure you build the habit to stay away from the 180 as much as possible.

Corrections:

The place you want to get to in your training is when you are comfortable moving around and staying safe while you do it. There are essentially only two worthwhile corrections in this phase of your training.

Firstly, if you are running afoul of a safety rule, or in any way building habits that will cause you to be unsafe, you must correct that issue immediately. If you notice your finger in the trigger guard, or you swing your muzzle right on the safe angle while you run, act immediately. As you ramp up the speed and aggression level in your training the habits you build now are going to be what keeps you safe and keeps you *appearing* to be safe. The appearance of safety is going to matter a lot when you get to high pressure situations in matches.

Secondly, if you are comfortable moving around and are properly observing all the necessary safety precautions, start moving more aggressively. You can start this exercise off at a walking pace. After some training sessions, you will be comfortable running around at full speed and doing so safely. You will be well positioned to go to matches.

Evolution:

Initially, your primary concern should be learning to move laterally and down range. These are your typical directions of movement in competition and will not present much of a challenge to someone who has done the most rudimentary safety training. After you are comfortable, start working in up range movements. It is important that you actively think through how to keep the gun safe during your training so when you have the occasional up range movement during competition, you are not thrown off by it.

Tips:

Use a buddy or a camera to check out your movement. Make sure that what you are seeing on the camera playback or what your buddy reports to you is consistent with what you think is happening. It is exceedingly difficult to assess your own shooting in the moment so make sure you get verification from a 3rd party.

Drill Progress Tracker			
Date	Drill Time	Hit Factor	Notes

Notes:

Mock Stage Training

Purpose/Goal:

Learn to smoothly navigate a stage.

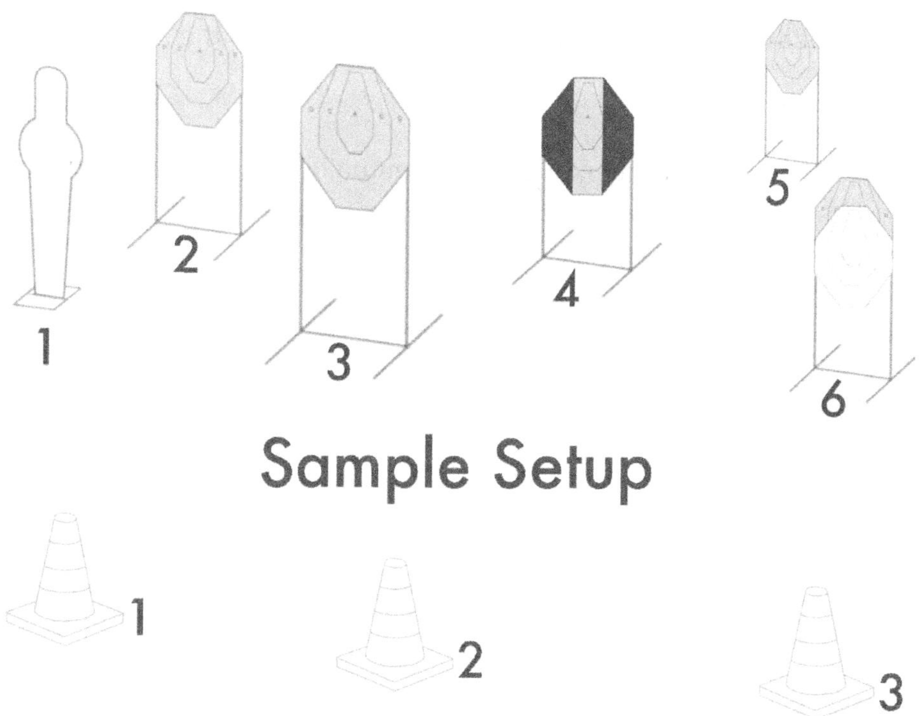

Setup notes:

Construct a multi position "stage." Using markers such as cones on the ground to denote shooting positions. Setting up non-falling steel and multiple paper targets is ideal to give target variety. Stipulate an order to engage the targets and what position to engage them from. Feel free to use the same target from more than one position.

Example: Engage Target 1-4 from position one. Engage Targets 3-6 from position 2. Engage targets 2-3 from position 3.

Instructions:

Shoot the stage to the best of your ability. Make sure that the stage is executed without needing to consciously think about what the next step is. Ensure that your shooting is accurate and disciplined.

Cues:

You should shoot your mock stage just like a match stage. Do not focus on training cues during your stage run.

Corrections:

If you find yourself hesitating or not remembering what to do, you need to visualize the entire stage. When you can see a first person "Go Pro" video of your stage run without needing to specifically think the stage through, you are ready to shoot it. Do frequent walk-through passes just like you would in competition.

Be on guard for undisciplined shooting. Make sure you are not squirting bullets hoping for good results. Instead, calmly punch out hits in the center of each target and move to the next one.

Evolution:

As your execution improves, start changing the stage. Eventually, you should be able to change the order of targets/positions every single run and be able to hold a good performance. Once you can pick an order, visualize it, and execute it without hesitation you are in excellent shape.

Tips:

The main reason to do full stage training is to ensure that you can go through a complex shooting scenario without falling apart.

Consider the "Training Philosophy" section at the front of this book. The way you shoot, your style, your inclinations and your habits are what you are assessing when doing this exercise. You are not trying to accomplish anything specific by doing this training. The larger goal here is to see what happens and spot the "big picture" trends.

Ask yourself the following:

- What mistakes am I making repeatedly?
- What specific exercises should I do to mitigate these mistakes?
- Am I confident that I can perform to an acceptable level on a random set of competition stages?

The above questions are examples of the sorts of questions you should be interested in. The best way to summarize the mindset for this type of training is, you spot the patterns in your shooting that are holding you back as a shooter. Look at the big picture.

Drill Progress Tracker			
Date	Drill Time	Hit Factor	Notes

Notes:

Special Drills

Classifier Training

Purpose/Goal:

Train on and experiment with USPSA classifier stages in order to expand your knowledge and skill set.

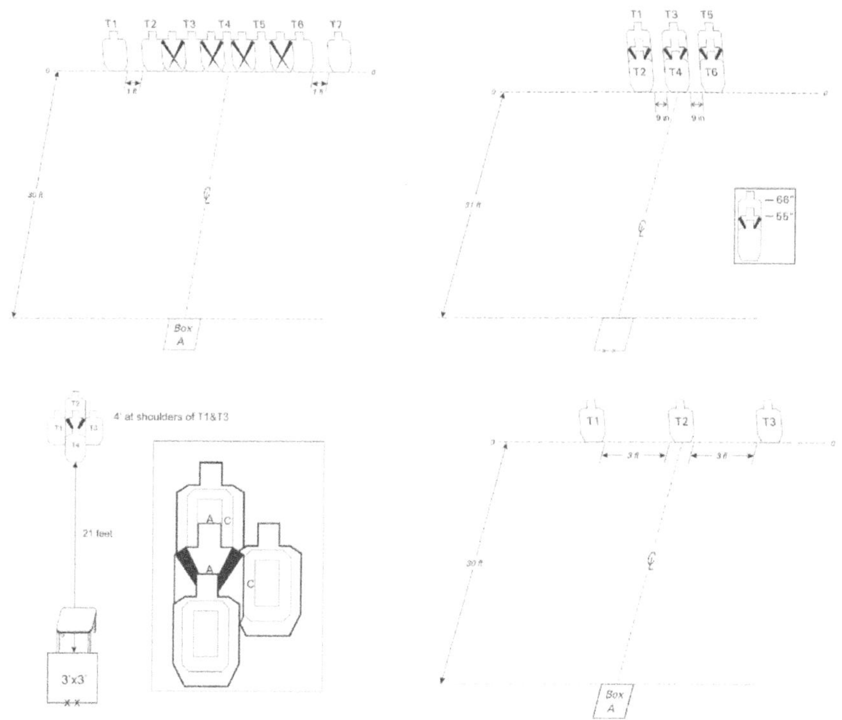

ANY DESIRED CLASSIFIER

Setup notes:

Setup any desired USPSA classifier.

Instructions:

Set up any desired USPSA classifier.

Shoot the classifier stage the desired number of times. Note time, points and hit factor. Your goal is to competently execute the skills required. You should be able to consistently execute the classifier without incurring penalties.

Drill Progress Tracker			
Date	Drill Time	Hit Factor	Notes

Notes:

Special Challenges

Purpose/Goal:

Become comfortable with non-standard scenarios that may present themselves in matches. Things like off body start positions, shooting in awkward positions, shooting one handed and so on.

Make sure that you get comfortable shooting accurately in a variety of positions and circumstances.

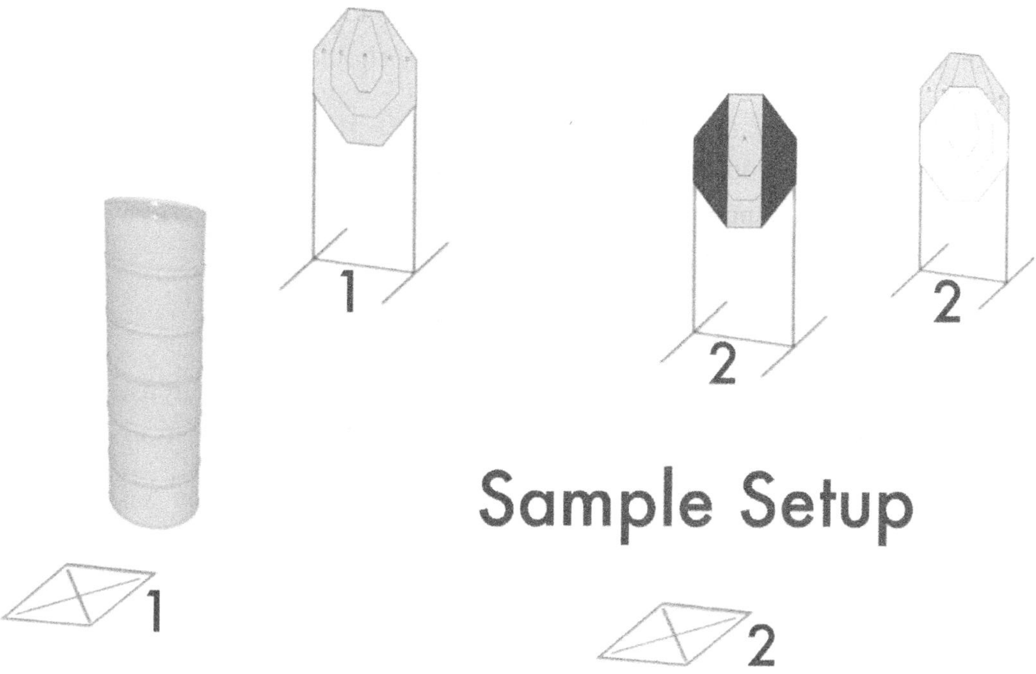

Setup notes:

Construct challenges that you expect to see in future matches. Keep the scenarios small, simple and focused.

Things like leans, crouches, one handed, prone and other types of shooting positions and circumstances can be experienced in training so you don't have your first time occur at a match.

Instructions:

At the tone, engage the targets in your setup while observing the special conditions you have set for yourself.

Example: Engage the targets while kneeling would be the procedure if you are working on kneeling shooting.

Cues:

When the shooting is awkward or difficult, remember shooting fundamentals. Confirm sight alignment and carefully stack pressure onto the trigger for each demanding shot and you will get the best chance at a good score you could possibly have that day.

Corrections:

Pay close attention to the sight pictures you are seeing. As the shooting gets more awkward or difficult your gun will not behave the same as when you are standing comfortably in your preferred stance. If you sense the gun is not properly aimed where it needs to be you should have the discipline to hold off on shooting until it is.

If the gun is not returning to your point of aim as quickly as it normally does then you will need to resist the temptation to force that to happen. It is quite common for shooters to aggressively over return the gun back to the target and induce even more errors.

Evolution:

As you get comfortable with whatever challenge you are working on, simply increase the difficulty of the challenge. Move the targets further away, add partials, make the position more demanding, or do whatever else makes sense to increase the difficulty for the given challenge.

Tips:

The best piece of advice to remember for special challenges is that you do not need to be the best at everything. You need to be able to hit the targets under pressure. Shooting from an awkward position is a challenge for everyone and nobody is going to be comfortable doing it. Suppress the feelings you have about being too slow and execute the shots.

Drill Progress Tracker			
Date	Drill Time	Hit Factor	Notes

Level 2

Goal: Get to B class

If you understand USPSA safety rules and how to shoot your gun accurately, the next goal is to get into USPSA B class or a similar skill level. This level introduces basic time *Standards* for many exercises. It also discusses the concept of different aiming schemes based on different targets. By taking these concepts on board and adjusting your training, you should be able to quickly get to USPSA B class or an analog level of skill.

You have likely heard about super quick times on a variety of exercises. You can see plenty of people reloading in under a second on social media. You have probably seen a video of someone performing El Prezidente in under four seconds. It is probably a good thing to set that aside at this point. The bottom line is these times come after exorbitant amounts of practice. Measuring yourself against top level shooters best efforts on drills is a recipe for demotivation.

Instead, pay close attention to the time *Standards* that are introduced in this level of training. I have laid down training times that are fast enough to get you to B class. These times are achievable with a few weeks of regular dry training for most people. Once you get up to speed, making sure your technique is correct at speed is a much easier thing to do.

One concept this level will ask you to learn is different aiming schemes based on the target, or the circumstances. Instead of reading your sights all one way, you will be encouraged to learn to start trading away a perfect sight picture for a "good enough' sight picture.

In addition to changing how you aim; this section will start you down the road to excellent predictive shooting ability. For most shooting applications you aim the gun and shoot in a reactive mode. You react to seeing the sights return to the target you are shooting from recoil and press the trigger. Predictive shooting is the method by which you shoot faster than that. As you improve, you will need to learn to shoot faster than you can consciously make decisions.

To recap, this level builds on level 1 by adding time *Standards* for your training. These *Standards* will get you to B class if you follow them. You will also learn to shoot faster by learning when you can bend or outright break the conventional rules of marksmanship.

Level 2 Training Standards

The Destination:

This training level is designed to take you to USPSA B class or an equivalent rating in your sport or organization.

By utilizing challenging time *Standards* for gun manipulation, you will be able to very quickly develop the skill to shoot targets at a practical pace.

Input:

This level will require that you do dryfire training on a regular or semi-regular basis. It will also necessitate occasional trips to the range for live training.

What Comes Next:

Using the drills in this section you should be able to quickly advance to level 3 (master level).

Specific Standards:

Level 2 training requires the following:

Fast/Competent gun handling: Using a 1 second draw time and 1.2 second reload time you should be able to get fast and confident with gun manipulation in dryfire.

With live ammunition learn to control the gun when shooting as fast as you can pull the trigger (about .2 splits). You should be able to hold the A zone at 5 yards.

The target time for El Prezidente is seven seconds.

Knowledge/mindset:

The important thing to develop at this level is a sense of what "fast" shooting looks and feels like. Your perception will depend on your background.

If you are a traditionally trained shooter then the speed requirements are likely to make you feel uncomfortable. The fact that you will be required to shoot with imperfect sight pictures will probably frustrate you. The time *Standards* should force you to go quickly. After enough repetition you will start to feel comfortable and controlled at your aggressive pace.

Some people are naturally comfortable going very quickly and need to worry more about being disciplined. The time *Standards* in this case might help calm you down. If you are easily making the time *Standards* in this section, but you are not yet a B class shooter then you need to work on consistency and control.

Standard Practice Setup

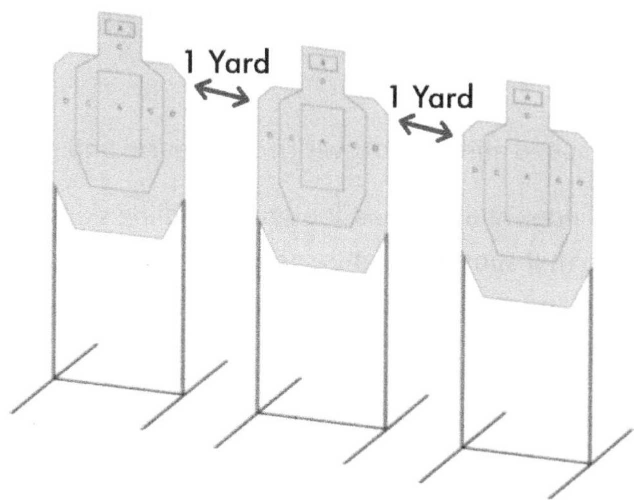

Livefire Level 2

Drill Name	Procedure	goal draw/reload times	3 yards	7 yards	10 yards	15 yards	25 yards	add time for: surrender	facing uprange	unloaded start
One Per Target	Engage each target with 1 round	1.2/na	2.3	2.5	3	4	5	0.2	0.2	2
Pairs on One Target	Engage one target with 2 rounds	1.2/na	1.4	1.5	1.8	2	2.5	0.2	0.2	2
4 Aces	Engage 1 target with 2 rounds, reload, reengage w/ 2 rounds.	1.2/1.5	3.5	3.5	4	4.5	6	0.2	0.2	2
Bill Drill	Engage one target with 6 rounds	1.2/na	2.3	2.5	2.8	4	5	0.2	0.2	2
Bill/Reload/Bill	Engage one, 6 rounds, reload, 6 more	1.2/1.5	5.5	6	7.5	9	10	0.2	0.2	2
Blake Drill	Engage each target with 2 rounds	1.2/na	2.8	3	3.5	4	6	0.2	0.2	2
El Prez	Turn, draw, engage each target w/2, reload, reengage each w/2	1.5/1.5	6	6.5	7.5	9	12	0.2	0.2	2
Criss Cross	Engage each of the 6 A zones in a criss cross pattern	1.2 (1.5 head)/ 1.5 (2.0 head)	6	10	12	15	n/a	0.2	0.2	2
Stong Hand Only	Engage each target w/ 2 rounds Strong hand only	1.5/na	4	6	7	10	n/a	0.2	0.2	2
Weak Hand Only	Engage each target w/ 2 rounds weak hand only	2.5 w/transfer/na	6	8	10	12	n/a	0.2	0.2	2

This is a set of standards designed to give a rough idea about general ability. The par times are set so you should be able to do a proper repetition 9/10 times to demonstrate proficiency. A single attempt does not mean much; you are looking for consistency. If you are using a red dot sight, subtract 5% from the times as you simulate distances of 15 yards or greater. If you are scoring major, subtract another 5% from the times at 15 yards or greater. These two conditions "stack," so open guns subtract 10% in total.

Dryfire Training 2

This is a brief primer on how to do the dry training component of your preparation.

Training Focal Points

Your focus should be to build speed and comfort with your firearm and gun handling skills.

You should have a developed index and subconscious gun handling skills. This means that you can look to any spot and bring your gun to that spot. The sights should show up roughly in alignment on that spot. You should be able to draw, reload and clear malfunctions without conscious thought.

Make sure you are getting your dry draw time down to 1 second and your dry reloads are less than 1.5 second. You will need this speed to accomplish the live training standard times.

Training Schedule

To facilitate developing the required skills, you will need regular training until your index/gun handling skills reach the requisite place. Commonly someone will train five days a week for a month or so and those skills will largely be in place. After that point, occasional training will maintain these skills.

Level 2 Drills

The drills you should train on, in addition to the standard dry drills with par times listed below are dryfire versions of all the other level 2 drills. Construct the drill to scale as described in the dryfire training section in the general information section of this book.

Dryfire Level 2

								add time for:		
Drill Name	**Procedure**	**goal draw/reload times**	**3 yards**	**7 yards**	**10 yards**	**15 yards**	**25 yards**	**surrender**	**facing uprange**	**unloaded start**
One Per Target	Engage each target with 1 round	1.2/na	2	2.2	2.5	3	3.5	0.2	0.2	2
Pairs on One Target	Engage one target with 2 rounds	1.2/na	1.2	1.4	1.5	1.8	2.2	0.2	0.2	2
4 Aces	Engage 1 target with 2 rounds, reload, reengage w/ 2 rounds.	1.2/1.5	3	3.5	3.8	4	5	0.2	0.2	2
Bill Drill	Engage one target with 6 rounds	1.2/na	2	2.2	2.5	3	3.5	0.2	0.2	2
Bill/Reload/Bill	Engage one, 6 rounds, reload, 6 more	1.2/1.5	5	5.5	6.5	7	8	0.2	0.2	2
Blake Drill	Engage each target with 2 rounds	1.2/na	2.5	2.8	3	3.5	5	0.2	0.2	2
El Prez	Turn, draw, engage each target w/2, reload, reengage each w/2	1.5/1.5	5	5.5	6	8	10	0.2	0.2	2
Criss Cross	Engage each of the 6 A zones in a criss cross pattern	1.2 (1.5 head)/ 1.5 (2.0 head)	5	7	10	12	n/a	0.2	0.2	2
Stong Hand Only	Engage each target w/ 2 rounds Strong hand only	1.5/na	3.5	5	6	8	n/a	0.2	0.2	2
Weak Hand Only	Engage each target w/ 2 rounds weak hand only	2.5 w/transfer/na	5	7	9	10	n/a	0.2	0.2	2

This is a set of standards designed to give a rough idea about general ability. The par times are set so you should be able to do a proper repetition 9/10 times to demonstrate proficiency. A single attempt does not mean much; you are looking for consistency. If you are using a red dot sight, subtract 10% from the times as you simulate distances of 15 yards or greater.

Marksmanship Fundamentals

Group Shooting

Purpose/Goal:

The ability to shoot A zone hits without any time pressure. Shooting all A's at 25 yards is a good goal.

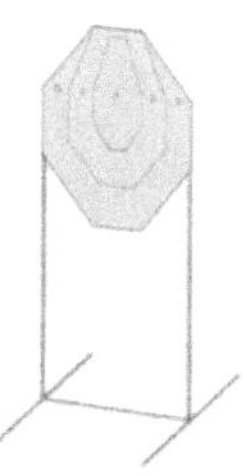

Instructions:

With no time limit, engage the target with as many rounds as desired. Shooting at least a five shot group is a good test of consistency.

Cues:

The most important cue to pay attention to is the tactile feel of your firing hand. It is counter intuitive in many respects to pay attention to the feel of your hands instead of the visual component of sight alignment. In most cases you will get better results by focusing on the feel inside your hands.

Corrections:

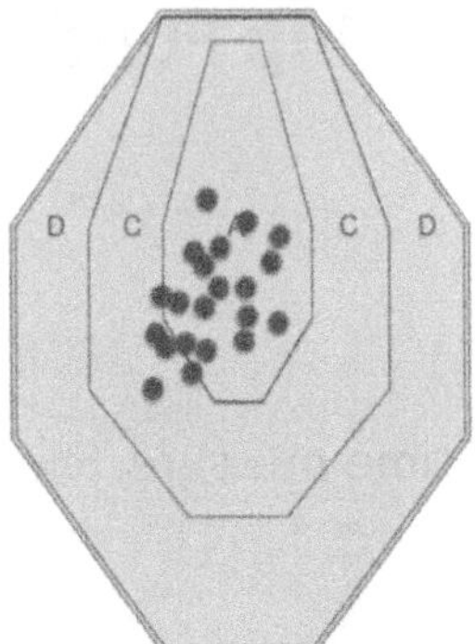

Hitting low/left is the classic sign of pushing down into the anticipated recoil. Focus on holding your firing hand still while you press the trigger straight.

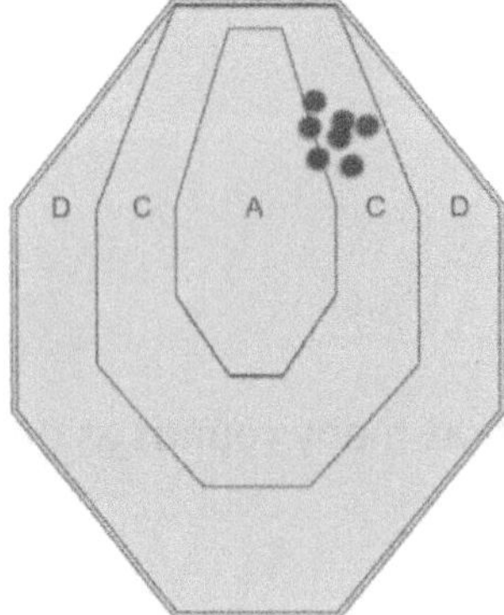

If you are forming a small group but in the wrong spot of the target, consider adjusting your sights. If you are unsure if you or the sights are the issue, have a friend shoot your gun to confirm your zero.

Evolution:

Be sure to vary the target configuration. Try using no-shoots or hardcovers to block off part of the target. Forcing yourself to work around the obstruction will help you learn what your sights should look like when engaging a target that is partially obstructed.

Tips:

Shooting tight groups is an important skill to develop for any practical shooter. This skill will allow you to make sure that your pistol is mechanically accurate and able to hit any reasonable target at any reasonable distance.

The best results during group shooting are typically going to be had when you are focused on the feel of your hands rather than the visual component of aiming. The most common error that we observe during group shooting training is when the shooter sees a desirable sight picture, they immediately want to press the trigger. Typically, this is accompanied by pushing down into the anticipated recoil. If this shooter accepts a little bit of "wobble" in the sight picture and focuses on smoothly and cleanly releasing that shot, they will get a much better result.

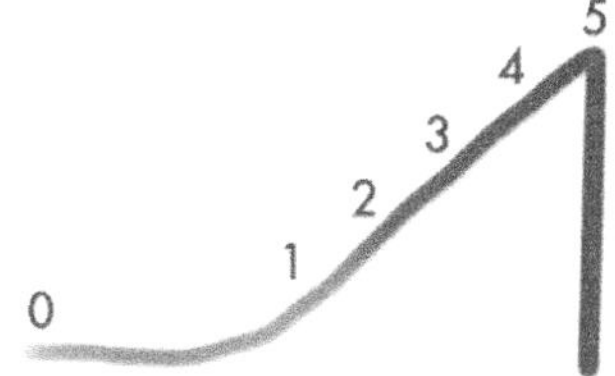

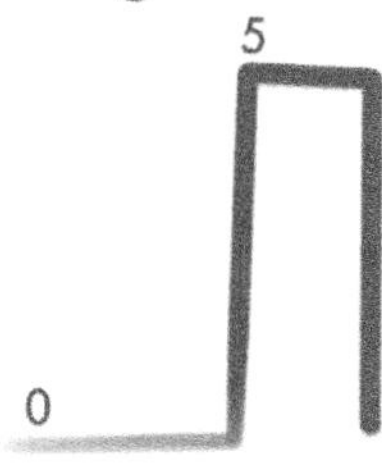

Try applying pressure slowly and continually until the trigger breaks opposed to going NOW on the trigger. Focus on your hands and how you hold the gun as you slowly increase pressure in one continuous motion. For example, slowly apply one pound, then two pounds, then three pounds, then four pounds, in one continuous press and at some point, the hammer will fall and the gun will fire. Fight the urge to apply all four or five pounds of pressure instantly when you get the sights where you want them. Going NOW on the trigger will often move your sights off target.

Drill Progress Tracker			
Date	Drill Time	Hit Factor	Notes

Notes:

Trigger Control at Speed

Purpose/Goal:

Learn to press the trigger straight.

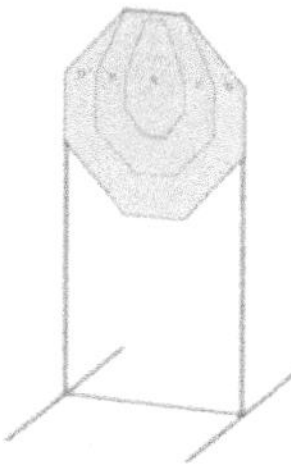

Single target

Setup notes:

Use a single target at any desired distance.

Instructions:

Start with the gun mounted, and a perfect sight picture on your target. Your finger should be just out of contact with the trigger. At the tone, fire a shot. The shot should come in under .25 seconds or it is a "fail" for the drill.

Cues:

Your hand tension is going to tell you a lot. If your firing hand tenses up, or you have sympathetic movement in your fingers, the shot will not hit precisely on your intended impact point. Pay attention to your hands and you will learn quickly.

Corrections:

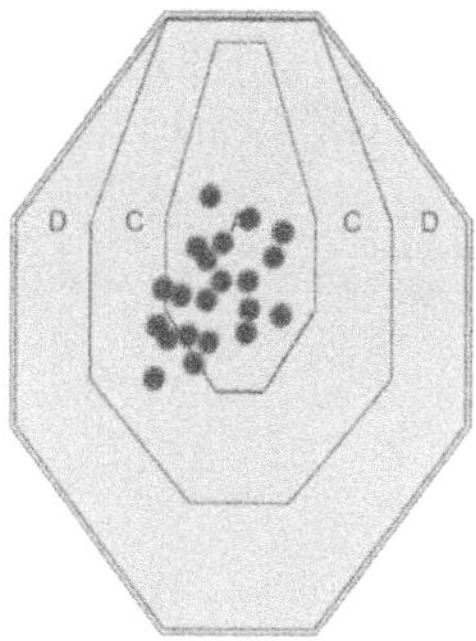

Most commonly shots will be pressed down and left for a right-handed shooter. Hold your hand still. Isolate your trigger finger. Putting more attention on the sights will not help.

Evolution:

This is an excellent drill to try single-handed as well. You can master dominant hand only shooting. You can work on weak hand trigger control as well.

You can also start the drill with your finger out of the trigger guard and try to match the same time it took to get the shot off with your finger in the trigger guard. By doing this you stress pressing the trigger straight on back.

Drill Progress Tracker			
Date	Drill Time	Hit Factor	Notes

Notes:

Practical Accuracy

Purpose/Goal:

Shoot the gun with acceptable accuracy at practical pace. Learn to grip your gun properly. Shooting all A's at 15 yards in under four seconds consistently is a reasonable goal.

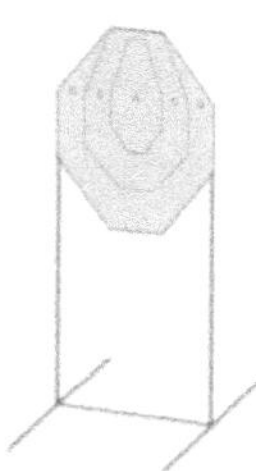

Instructions:

At the start signal, draw and engage the center of the A zone with six rounds. Fire a follow on shot as soon as your sights recover. There is not a specific time limit, but the idea for the exercise is to shoot as soon as the sights recover.

Six strings at a time is recommended.

Cues:

Pay close attention to the feel of your gun in your hands. Once you feel yourself making some sort of mistake with your grip or trigger control you are going to be able to correct it much more easily.

Look to the spot on the target you want to hit. Do not look for the target's outline or at the color of the target. Look at a specific point.

Corrections:

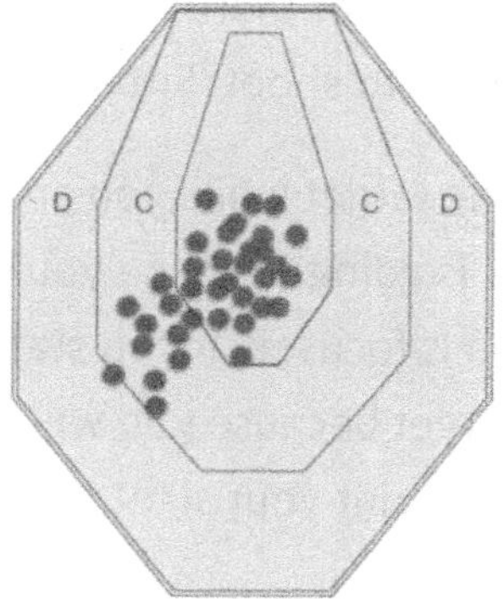

Low/left hits are almost always caused by moving the gun with the firing hand while shooting.

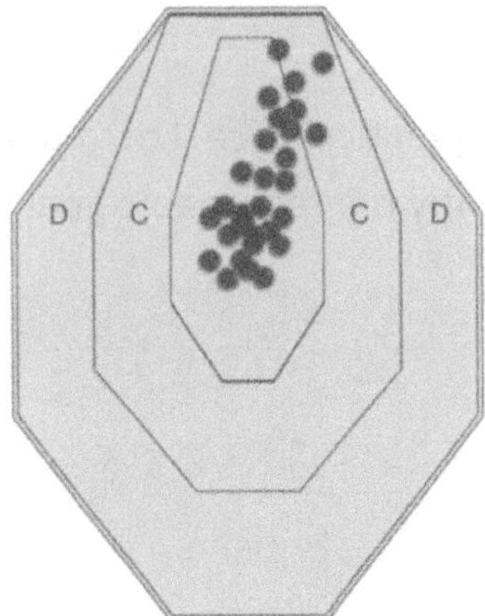

High hits generally come from insufficient support hand pressure or from shifting your vision onto the sights themselves instead of the target.

Evolution:

Try to draw and shoot A's from any desired distance or on any target configuration.

Try this exercise one handed.

Tips:

It is important to think of this exercise as a grip exercise first and foremost. If you are gripping the gun correctly and consistently then you are going to get very good results. Pay attention to the feel of your hands as you are shooting. When you feel an errant shot happen because you pushed the gun sideways or some similar mistake then you will generally stop making that mistake so frequently. It is counterintuitive, but important. Focus on your hands and do not worry so much about the way the sight picture looks.

Make sure you are in control of the pace of your shooting. You want to develop the ability to shoot reacting to a sight picture for each individual shot. This means follow up shots should be in the range of .3 to .6 seconds between shots. If follow up shots get to be much faster than .3 seconds it is quite likely that you did not see the sight return and consciously make a choice to fire. You are likely shooting to a rhythm. If your follow up shots start to get long, .6 seconds or more then it is likely you are over confirming your sight picture. When the sights come back you need to shoot. Sitting on that sight picture will not help you.

Make sure to look at a particular spot on the target while you are shooting. The spot you look at should be the size of a coin. Just staring at that spot is going to make you more accurate and likely to hit near that small spot. Be mindful of where your vision is focused. If you start to focus on your front sight or dot, your shots will tend to climb up higher on the target because you will not be resetting the sight back down onto the aimpoint. If your vision stays on the aimpoint your sight will tend to come back to that point.

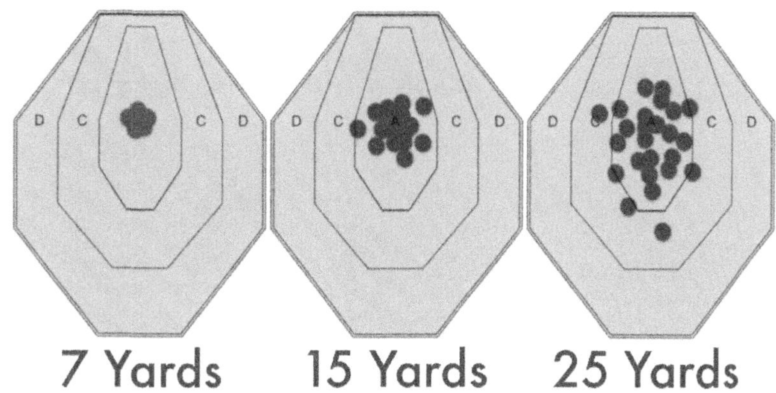

The goal is for your group to open concentrically as you increase the distance to the target. Flyers can, and will, still happen. Be looking at where the majority of the hits are going and be looking for any patterns. Compare any patterns you see to how your hands feel as you are breaking the shot. Connecting the dots from a feeling you have to where the shots are going will go a long way toward being able to eliminate marksmanship errors.

Drill Progress Tracker			
Date	Drill Time	Hit Factor	Notes

Notes:

Doubles

Purpose/Goal:

- Refine grip and marksmanship.
- Learn predictive shooting.

Hold the A zone at 7 yards while firing your pistol at practical pace. Splits should be under .25 seconds.

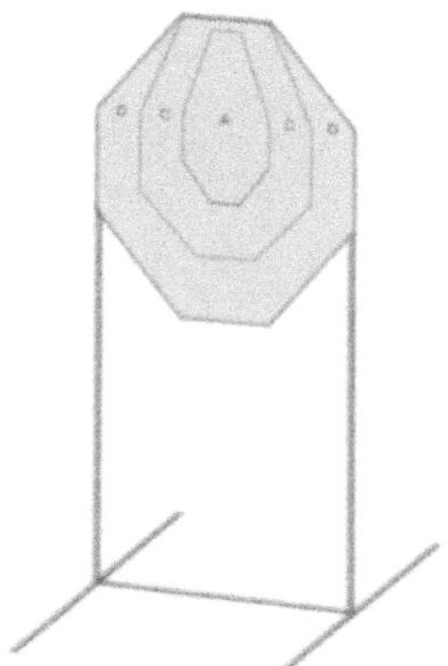

Instructions:

At the start signal, engage the target with four pairs of shots. Each pair should be fired as fast as you can pull the trigger. Allow the gun to completely quiet down from recoil before firing the next pair. Return your trigger finger to a relaxed position between pairs of shots.

Repeat this procedure for multiple strings.

Cues:

Pay close attention to the feel of your gun in your hands. Once you feel yourself making some sort of mistake with your grip or trigger control you are going to be able to correct it much more easily. Isolate the trigger finger. Make sure your firing hand fingers are not curling due to an over tense firing hand.

Observe the movement of the sights in recoil. This will provide clues for how to improve your technique moving forward.

Corrections:

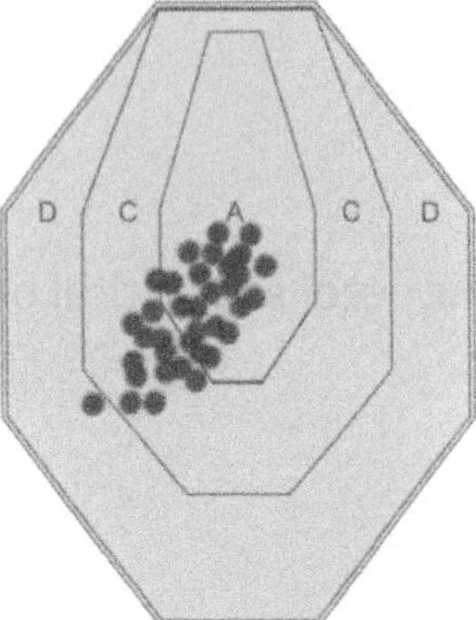

Low/left hits are almost always caused by moving the gun with the firing hand while shooting.

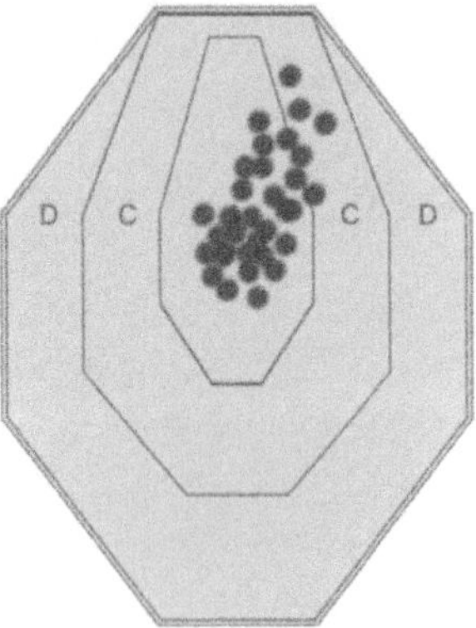

High hits generally come from insufficient support hand pressure.

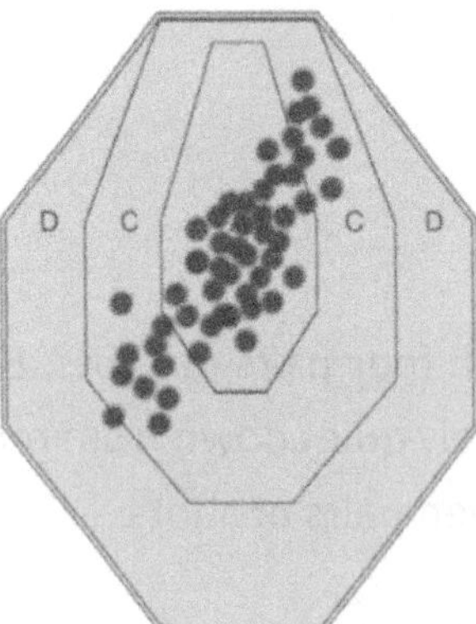

This is a quite common target for level 2. This is typically caused by changing your grip as you are shooting. The result is a mix of pushing on the gun as it fires and not maintaining support hand pressure on the gun as it fires.

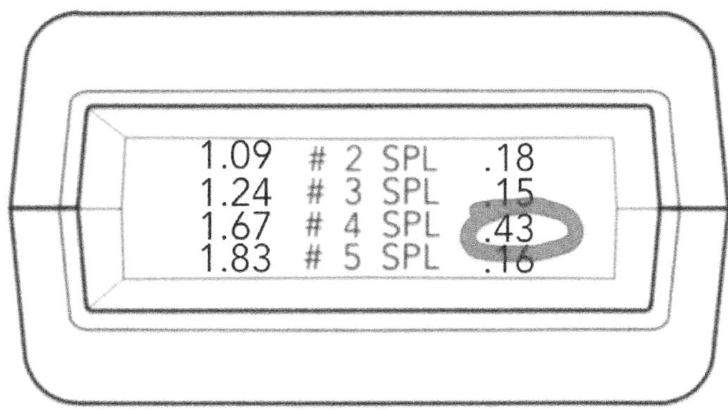

"Trigger Freeze" (the inability to reset the trigger for a second shot) is caused by an over tense firing hand in most cases.

Evolution:

As your control grows you can adjust the distance to the target and adjust your pace. This will give you a good idea of what sort of expectations are realistic in a match setting. As the range increases you will need to accept some points being dropped.

Tips:

It is important to think of this exercise as a grip exercise first and foremost. If you are gripping the gun correctly and consistently then you are going to get very good results. Pay attention to the feel of your hands as you are shooting. When you feel an errant shot happen because you pushed the gun sideways or some similar mistake then you will generally stop making that mistake so frequently. It is counterintuitive but important, focus on your hands and don't worry so much about the way the sight picture looks.

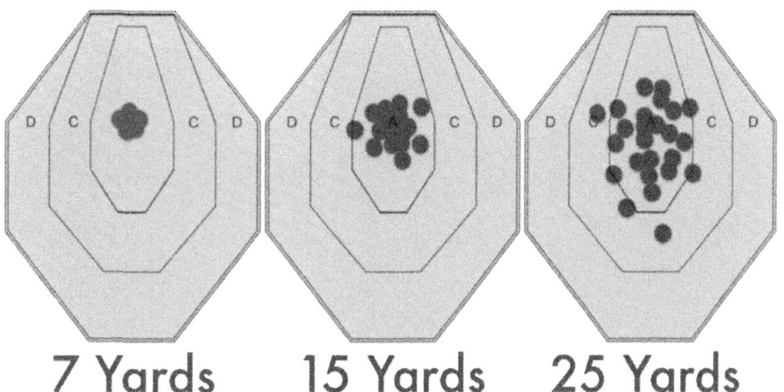

The goal is for your group to open concentrically as you increase the distance to the target. Flyers can, and will still happen. Be looking at where the majority of the hits are going and be looking for any patterns. Compare any patterns you see to how your hands feel as you are breaking the shot. Connecting the dots from a feeling you have to where the shots are going will go a long way towards being able to eliminate marksmanship errors.

Drill Progress Tracker			
Date	Drill Time	Hit Factor	Notes

Notes:

Single-handed Shooting

Purpose/Goal:

Ability to make shots using only one hand on the gun. Both dominant hand only and non-dominant hand only need to be trained.

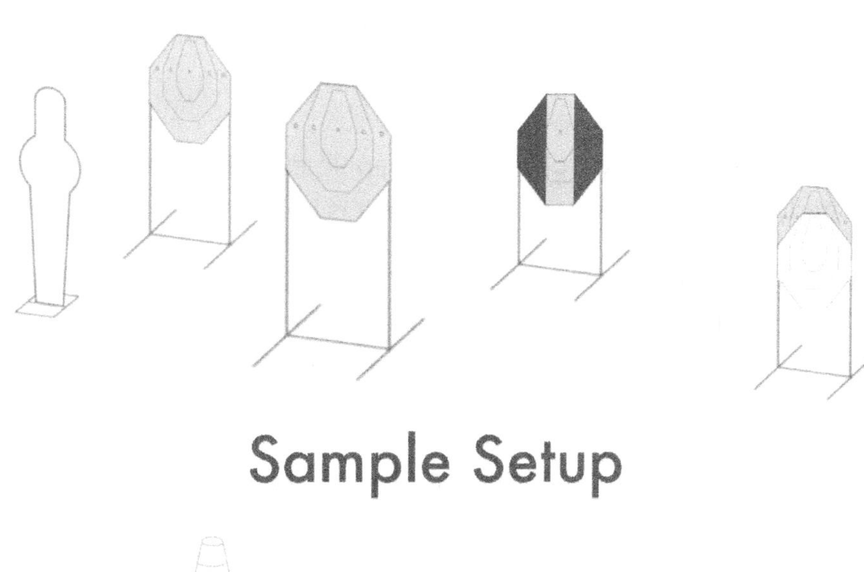

Random Target Set

Setup notes:

Set up any target scenario you desire.

Instructions:

At the start, draw and engage the targets with a single hand. If you are using your non-dominant hand, draw the gun, transfer it to the correct hand, engage the targets.

Cues:

Pay attention to your firing hand. The most common issue you are going to run into is pushing down into the gun sympathetically as you press the trigger. Paying attention to your hand during the course of that drill is going to mitigate that issue.

Corrections:

Low/left shots when shooting right handed or Low/right shots when shooting left handed are going to be very common, especially as you increase your speed. This issue is the primary one you should be focused on eliminating.

Evolution:

Try out a variety of start positions. "Gun on table" to start is fairly common when you come to a single-handed shooting stage in a match. You want to make sure that you don't run into stuff that causes you to be nervous because the first time you have ever done it is in a match.

Feel free to do a bit of single-handed shooting on any training scenario you set up and work with. It isn't a bad idea to try a few runs of single-handed shooting on any drill you have set up. This will help ensure that your training is well rounded. Also, getting good with one hand never hurts the two-handed shooting.

Tips:

If you are aiming, you will feel slow. A problem most people experience is lack of discipline to aim and press the trigger properly no matter how long it *feels like* it is taking. Believe me, you will feel slow.

It is critical that you do lots of single-handed repetition dryfire. If you are using a dot sight this becomes even more important. You will need to develop a whole new index for your non-dominant hand to be able to bring the sight exactly to where it needs to be for you to be able to make hits. Do not neglect your dry training.

If the situation allows, holding your gun vertical is preferred. Canting your gun can cause your point of impact to shift, especially at longer ranges.

Drill Progress Tracker			
Date	Drill Time	Hit Factor	Notes

Notes:

Transition /Vision Drills

Target Transitions

Purpose/Goal:

Move the gun smoothly and precisely from one target to the next. Learn to change between reactive and predictive shooting.

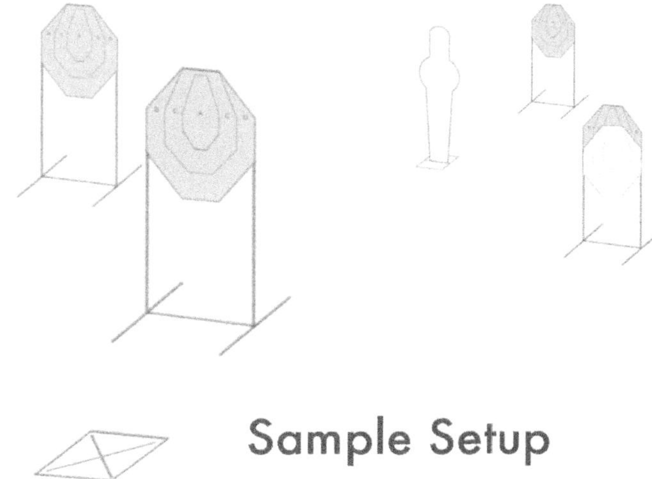

Sample Setup

Instructions:

Set up targets of mixed distance and shot difficulty. Mixing in steel plates or poppers are optional if you have them available. Try to create a very plain cross section of the targets you expect to encounter at matches. At the start signal, you will engage each target. Keep the engagement order the same for a few repetitions. Shoot the drill at your practical match pace to begin and increase your speed as you feel comfortable doing so. Restore the targets after you assess them and change the engagement order if you wish for subsequent sets of repetitions on the exercise.

Cues:

Lead with your eyes. Look exactly where you wish to hit. You should not be looking at a big brown target, but picking an exact spot to move the gun to.

Do not muscle the gun around because it will cause the sights to stop imprecisely.

Make sure you understand where each shot is going and adjust aiming strategies as needed.

Corrections:

If the gun is not moving quickly or precisely to your aim point, make sure you are leading with your eyes.

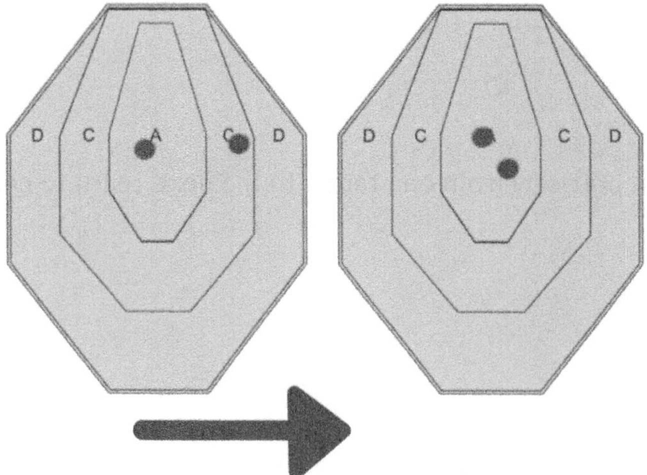

Moving your eyes off a target before you are done shooting it will drag the hits off the target. This usually happens with targets perceived as low difficulty. Notice how your gun follows the path your eyes take. Train yourself to keep your eyes on the target as long as you are shooting it.

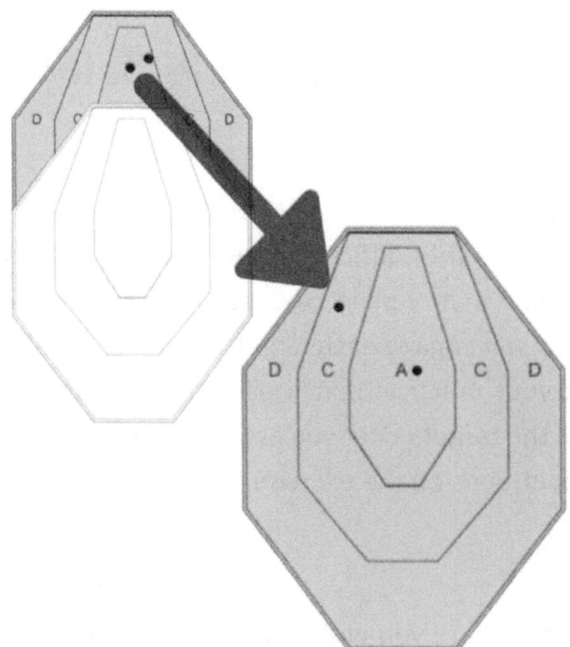

Pressing the trigger before the gun gets to the intended aimpoint will drag hits onto the target. The severity will vary from shooting between the targets, to a hit just outside of the A zone.

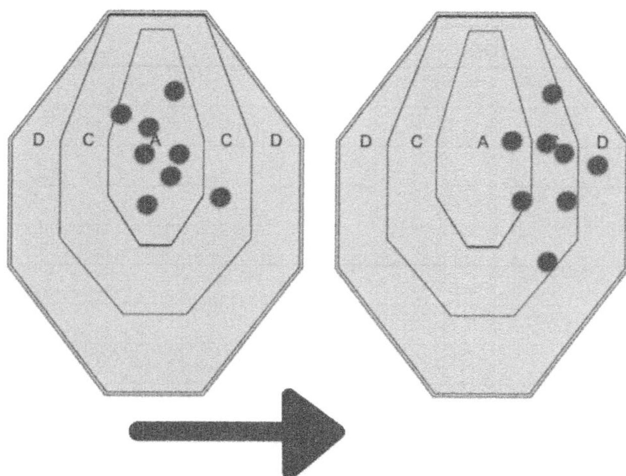

If you are overswinging/overdriving the gun relax your shoulders. A telltale sign this is happening is if you feel very tense as you transition the gun. Your shoulders should not be any more raised or tense than if you were standing normally. Commonly, the hits will all trend on one side of the target.

Do not over aim or over confirm on close-ranged, open targets. Shoot immediately when you recognize the gun is on target. While training ask yourself, "Could I have been shooting sooner?"

Evolution:

Do dry aiming on each target at your full speed before doing live training. Move your vision from aimpoint to aimpoint on each target and learn to have the gun follow you. Make sure that you are not focusing on the sighting system as you move the gun from one target to the next, but instead your vision is out on the target. When you are consistently performing these skills dry then begin live training. After each set of runs on the drill then return to dryfire before the next set of runs.

Try to instill a sense that your gun is a part of your body. As soon as your gun feels like an extension of your hands, you will be able to easily move the gun from target to target.

If your shooting performance is going well, systematically push yourself to go faster. Understand that this will eventually induce you to make mistakes such as shooting too early when coming onto the target, overrunning the intended target by pushing the gun too aggressively, swinging the gun to the wrong spot on target and so on. Pay attention to what is happening and apply the right corrections in order to improve. After you feel you are back on solid ground again, push yourself to go faster.

Tips:

Get in the habit of recalling what you observed as you were shooting. As you learn to recall flashes of the sight pictures you were seeing, the hits on targets will not be anywhere near as mysterious.

Watch out for technical errors throughout the drill. These errors include, but aren't limited to, following your sight in between targets, closing an eye, squinting, or hunching down onto the gun. These things are common and will not prevent you from being proficient as a shooter. As you develop your skills and attempt to go faster and faster, negative habits you have developed will become a problem. The best way to do business is both eyes open, target focused and pinpointing an exact aimpoint on each target.

Drill Progress Tracker			
Date	Drill Time	Hit Factor	Notes

Notes:

Spot to Spot Transitions

Purpose/Goal:

Accurate and precise transitions.

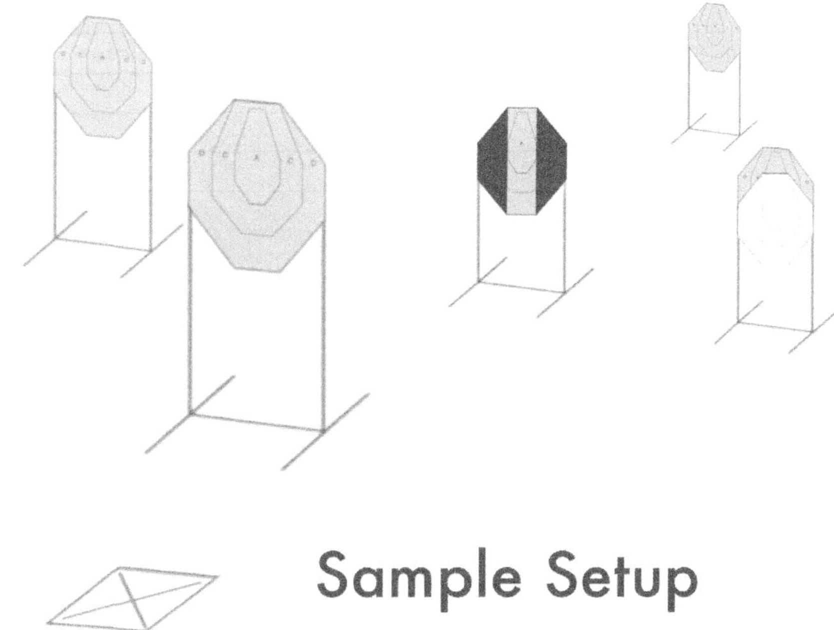

Random target setup

Setup notes:

This is a dry drill done during training. Do it on whatever target setup you are working on.

Instructions:

Practice moving your vision to exactly where you want the rounds to go on each target, in sequence.

Cues:

Look at the exact spot where you want to hit.

Corrections:

There are two corrections that are normally needed.

First, make sure you are finding a spot on the target and not just looking at the color. Oftentimes people are satisfied by aiming at the brown blob and not finding a specific spot. Do not look for the shape or the color of the target, look exactly where you want to hit.

Second, do not "sweep" or "drag" your gaze through the target. Find a spot and aim.

Evolution:

After you master the sequence, work in dry gun movement from spot to spot. Make sure you apply the correct aiming scheme.

Tips:

This drill should be done on a regular basis, both on the training range and in matches. What you are doing is practicing the transitions from spot to spot using just your eyes. This will help you memorize the specific focal points that you need to be paying attention to.

Drill Progress Tracker			
Date	Drill Time	Hit Factor	Notes

Notes:

Transition Exit/Entry

Purpose/Goal:

Break down the target transition technique into its most basic parts to understand it better.

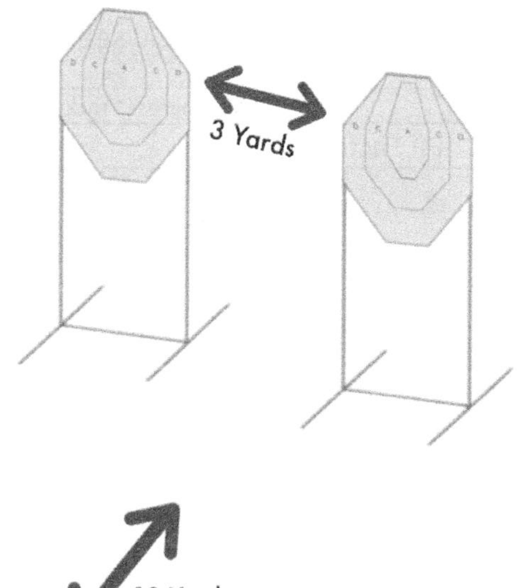

2 targets 3 yards apart. 10 yards distance.

Instructions:

Drill 1 (exit): Start with your pistol aimed at one of the targets. Your visual focus should be on the target you are aimed at. At the tone, engage the target with one round only, transition the gun to the other target. Get a good sight picture on that target, but do not fire.

Drill 2(entry): Start with your pistol aimed at one of the targets. Your visual focus should be on the target you are aimed at. At the tone transition the gun to the other target. Get a good sight picture on that target and fire the shot.

Cues:

Your vision drives everything. Look exactly where you want the gun to go and allow it to go there smoothly.

Relax your back and shoulders as much as you can. This will make the target transitions more exact.

Corrections:

Focus on the target while you transition, never the sight. If you have an excessively bright fiber or dot setup, this will be difficult. You need to get your vision out to the target.

Be aware of overswinging the gun or under swinging the gun. Look exactly where you want the gun to go and be extremely critical of any excess movement you see.

Drill Progress Tracker			
Date	Drill Time	Hit Factor	Notes

Notes:

Accelerator

Purpose/Goal:

Learn to employ different aiming schemes.

Par time 8 seconds

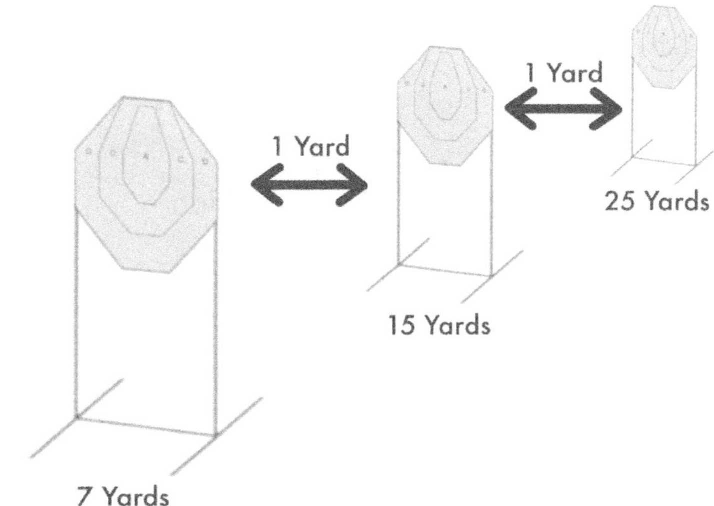

Setup notes:

Targets should be set so there is minimal transition laterally between the targets.

Instructions:

At the tone, engage each target with two rounds. Reload and re-engage each target with two more rounds.

Cues:

React immediately on the close target when your gun arrives in the center of it. Shoot right away without over aiming.

Allow the sight to settle on the far target for each shot. Press the trigger carefully and with discipline. You have time to fire a reactive pair of shots on the far target.

Corrections:

If you are struggling to hover near the par time for this drill you should look at draw and reload times. Drawing around 1.2 seconds and reloading around 1.5 seconds on the close ranged target is fast enough to make par time. If you are lagging behind those times by a substantial amount you should look to dry training to improve those times.

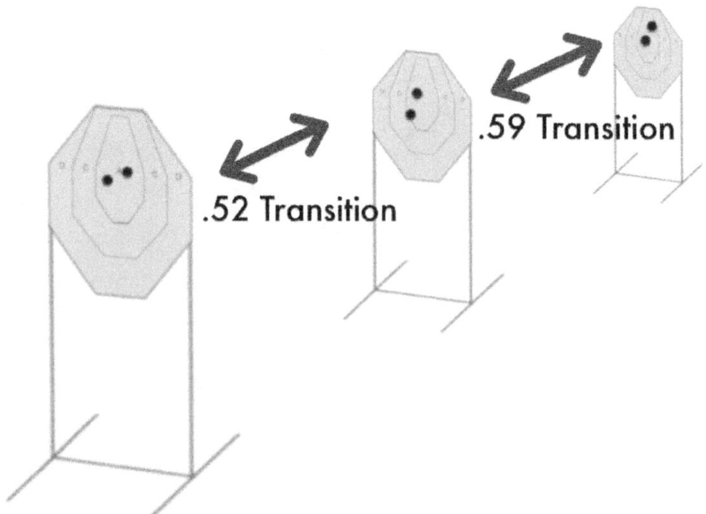

If your draw/reload times are on point, but you are struggling to meet the par then ensure you are not delaying your movement off the target you are shooting as soon as you finish shooting it. Oftentimes people have a fast pair of shots on the target, but they delay moving their eyes off the target as soon as they finish it. This will cause the gun to settle back down on a target that they should be transitioning away from. If you are seeing transition times between the targets longer than .5 seconds this is a likely cause.

Evolution:

Shoot this drill back to front and front to back. Make sure you are comfortable working either direction.

Feel free to shoot a "goofy" order on this drill as well. A goofy order is one that makes no sense in a match setting. This would be starting or finishing on the middle target and forcing yourself to transition the gun around more.

Tips:

The most important advice to take from this drill is to shoot with your eyes, not your ears. You should be shooting the drill where you address each target with the correct aiming scheme for you. The close ranged target should be shot using predictive shooting and a rapid-fire pair. The distant target should be shot in a disciplined manner. Make sure you see the sight return for the follow up shot. It is frequently the case that less experienced shooters will try to "go fast" on the close stuff and "slow down" on the longer shooting. The recipe for success on this drill is to be process focused and not worried at all about how you think the drill is sounding.

Drill Progress Tracker			
Date	Drill Time	Hit Factor	Notes

Notes:

Distance Changeup

Purpose/Goal: Get used to "changing gears" between different target types. 5 second par time.

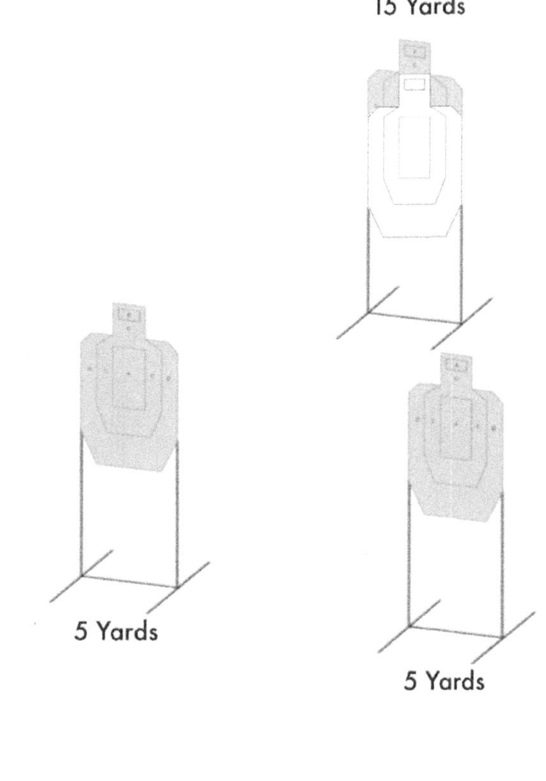

2 targets at 5 yards. A headbox or similar target should be set in between, 15 yards distance.

Setup notes:

Be sure you do not have a shoot through situation.

Instructions:

At the start, engage each target with two rounds.

Cues:

Aim! Make sure you confirm each shot. The tough shot in the back will require two distinct sight pictures. You may even need to switch your attention to your firing hand to ensure you are not pushing the pistol off target.

The close-up targets generally induce a bit of dragging on/off the targets. You hit where you look, so make sure you keep your attention in the center of the close ranged targets to ensure you are actually done shooting them when you transition off.

Corrections:

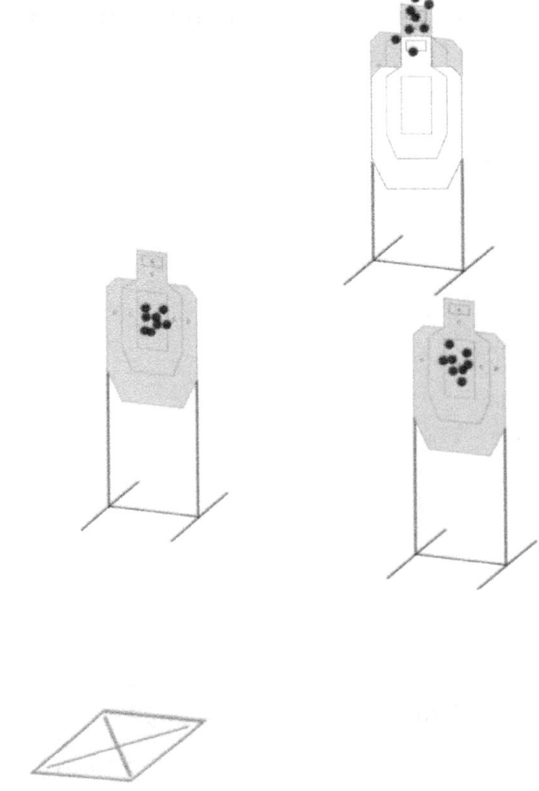

Watch your sights. The most common problem on this drill is inconsistent hits on the partial target. The main point of this exercise is for you to develop discipline on that target. You need to learn to "take your time in a hurry." Shoot quickly, but don't rush. Aim carefully, but don't waste time. It is not an easy thing to learn.

Evolution:

Change between different target orders. You can shoot left to right, right to left, near to far, or far to near. Each order will present the same sorts of challenges in slightly different ways. At the end of the day, this drill is about developing discipline.

Tips:

Make sure your sights are set up to work for you and not against you. Your dot or fiber front sight should not be so bright/overpowering that it is difficult for you to transition to the partial target. If you find your eye being focused on the dot or fiber, you should make an adjustment to the brightness level of your sight.

Drill Progress Tracker			
Date	Drill Time	Hit Factor	Notes

Notes:

MXAD
(Matt Xray Alpha Drill)

Purpose/Goal:

Get all A zone hits in under 4 seconds with some regularity.

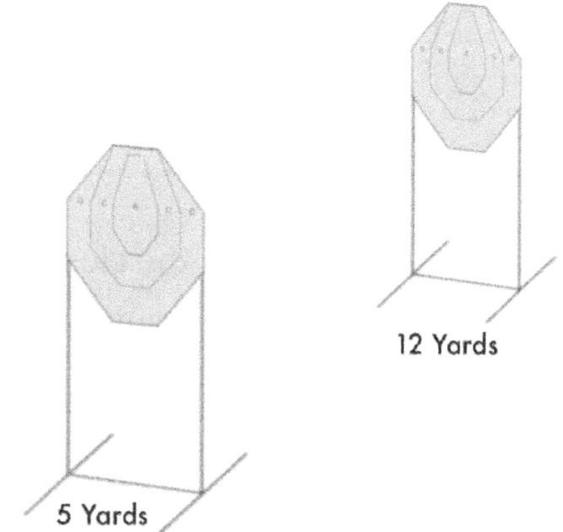

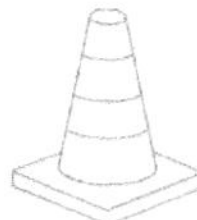

Target at 5 yards and target at 12 yards.

Setup notes:

This drill should be set up so that there is almost no swing of the gun from one target to the other. The transition is almost entirely in depth.

Instructions:

At the start signal, engage the close target with six rounds, then engage the other target with two rounds.

Cues:

Relax. This is a close range, high speed drill that will induce tension in your shoulders. If your upper body gets overly tense, you will overswing the transition and get a poor result. Just hold the gun with your hands, do not try to fight it with your entire body. If you release that unnecessary tension, the drill only gets easier.

Corrections:

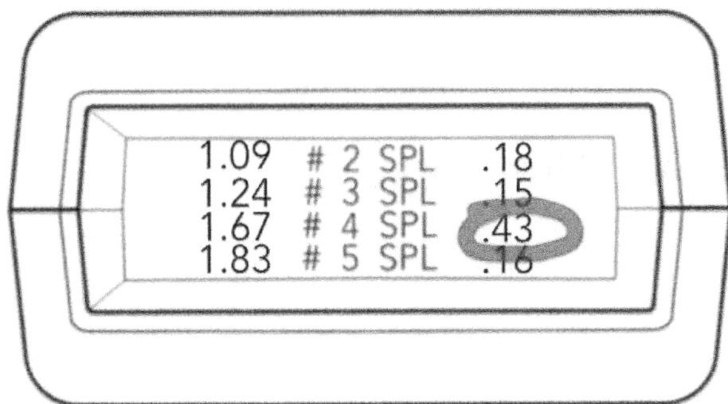

Relax your firing hand. If you experience trigger freeze on the close target or are having a hard time running the gun aggressively, the fix is likely to be relaxing your firing hand a bit. Death gripping the gun or over tension will induce trigger freeze.

Evolution:

Shooting the far target first is an interesting evolution that I recommend you try. Doing this often tempts people to start staring at their front sight or dot during the transition to the close target. This is counterproductive and you can start on the far target to work it out.

Tips:

You can learn a lot on this drill if you become hyper aware of what you are doing with your vision. Ideally, you want your vision to go from the center of one target to the center of the other target. Due to the close swing of the transition, it makes it difficult to keep from getting "tunneled into" the sights while you are shooting the drill. Do your best to get your vision out to the targets where it needs to be.

Drill Progress Tracker			
Date	Drill Time	Hit Factor	Notes

Notes:

Moving Targets

Purpose/Goal:

Learn to shoot moving targets.

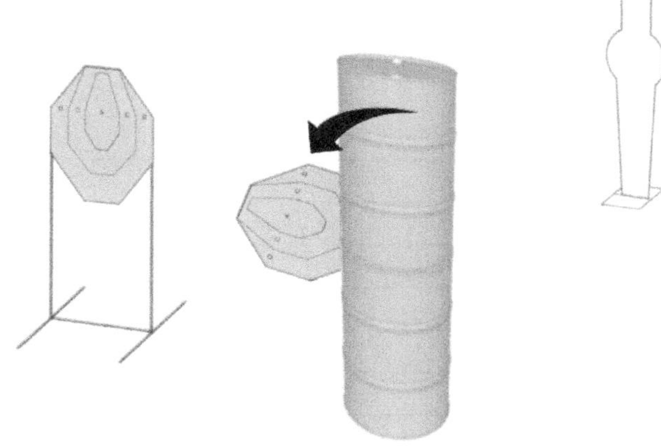

Setup notes:

Setup a simple scenario utilizing whatever props/targets you have at hand. If you wish to train on it, set it up. Utilize swingers, drop turners, max traps, windmills, or any other activated target type you want to use.

Instructions:

At the start, engage each target in your scenario.

Cues:

Track the target. The most important thing to remember when you are shooting a mover is your vision should be in the spot on the target that you wish to hit. Your gun will naturally track that spot if you keep your vision and attention focused there.

Corrections:

It is extremely common on swinging targets for the target be hit low. The low part of the swinger will attract your vision because it moves slower. Remember, you hit where you look. Make sure you lock your vision on the part of the target you want to hit.

Evolutions:

Make sure you set up and test yourself against any available activated target you have access to train on.

Drill Progress Tracker			
Date	Drill Time	Hit Factor	Notes

Notes:

STAGE SKILLS/MOVEMENT

Movement

Purpose/Goal:

Move around a stage/scenario while keeping the gun pointed in a safe direction.

Move as aggressively as possible, set up ready to move again, be ready to shoot when you arrive in position.

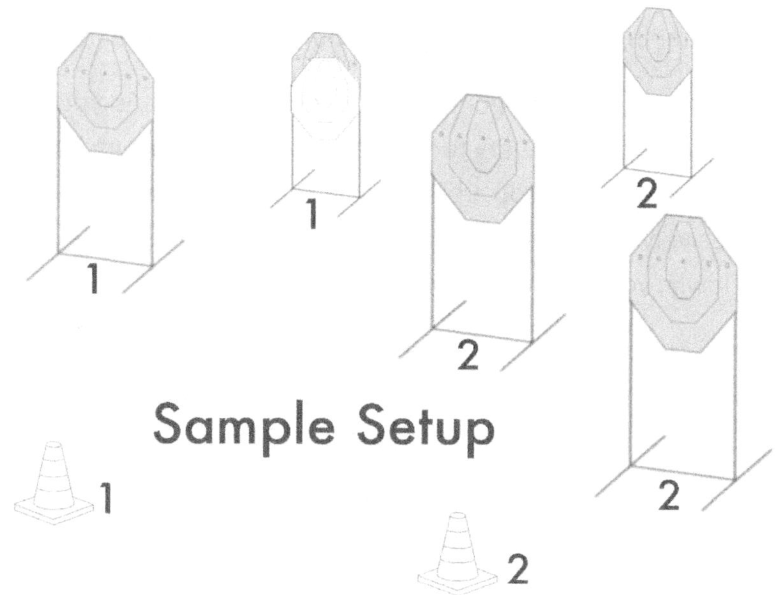

Setup notes:

Set the target scenario such that it is a fair representation of what you expect to see in matches.

Instructions:

At the start signal, engage the required targets from position

1. Move to position.
2. Engage the required targets.

Cues:

Have the gun mounted and ready to shoot as you are approaching the next shooting position.

Run aggressively enough that you get winded quickly.

After stopping in position ensure you are ready to move to the next position.

Remember the "laser" rule. Imagine a laser emanating from the muzzle of your pistol. You NEVER allow that laser to cross anything you do not want to shoot.

Corrections:

The place you want to get to in your training is where you are comfortable moving around and staying safe while you do it.

Firstly, if you are running afoul of a safety rule, or in any way building habits that will cause you to be unsafe, you must correct that issue immediately. If you notice your finger in the trigger guard, or you swing your muzzle right on the safe angle while you run, act immediately. As you ramp up the speed and aggression level in your training the habits you build now are going to be what keeps you safe and keeps you *appearing* to be safe. The appearance of safety is going to matter a lot when you get to high pressure situations in matches.

After you are certain you are being safe, start checking yourself against the other important training cues.

Make sure when you are training, you are going full power/full speed. As you go faster and faster it will change the nature of your movement at a very fundamental level. Faster running means, you need to apply the brakes and slow yourself down to a stop a bit sooner. You cannot learn everything you need to unless you are truly going aggressively. Doing proper movement training will cause you to tire quickly for this reason. If you are going slowly, you are not training yourself correctly.

Make sure that every time you stop you are ready to move. This means your feet should be spread apart, knees bent, 50/50 weight distribution, ready to spring to the next place you need to go. Consciously check each movement to make sure you are getting the outcome you want.

If it feels like it is taking ages to get started shooting when you get to a new position, you might be late to get the gun mounted and pointed where you want it. If you get to your second shooting position and notice that your gun is not yet up in front of you ready to go, make a point to get the gun gripped properly and mounted a step or two sooner as you come into position.

Evolution:

Initially, your primary concern should be learning to move laterally and downrange. These are your typical directions of movement in competition and will not present much of a challenge to someone who has done the most rudimentary safety training. After you are comfortable, start working in up range movements. It is important that you actively think through how to keep the gun safe during your training so when you have the occasional up range movement during competition, you are not thrown off by it.

Be sure to work through this exercise dry, without using ammunition. This will allow you to carefully assess whether you are getting yourself stopped properly when you move. It will also take all the shooting out of the equation so you can focus very clearly on the specifics of your movements.

Tips:

Use a buddy or a camera to check out your movement. Make sure that what you are seeing on the camera playback or what your buddy reports to you is consistent with what you think is happening. It is exceedingly difficult to assess your own shooting in the moment so make sure you get verification from a 3rd party.

Drill Progress Tracker			
Date	Drill Time	Hit Factor	Notes

Notes:

Mock Stage Training

Purpose/Goal:

Learn to smoothly navigate a stage

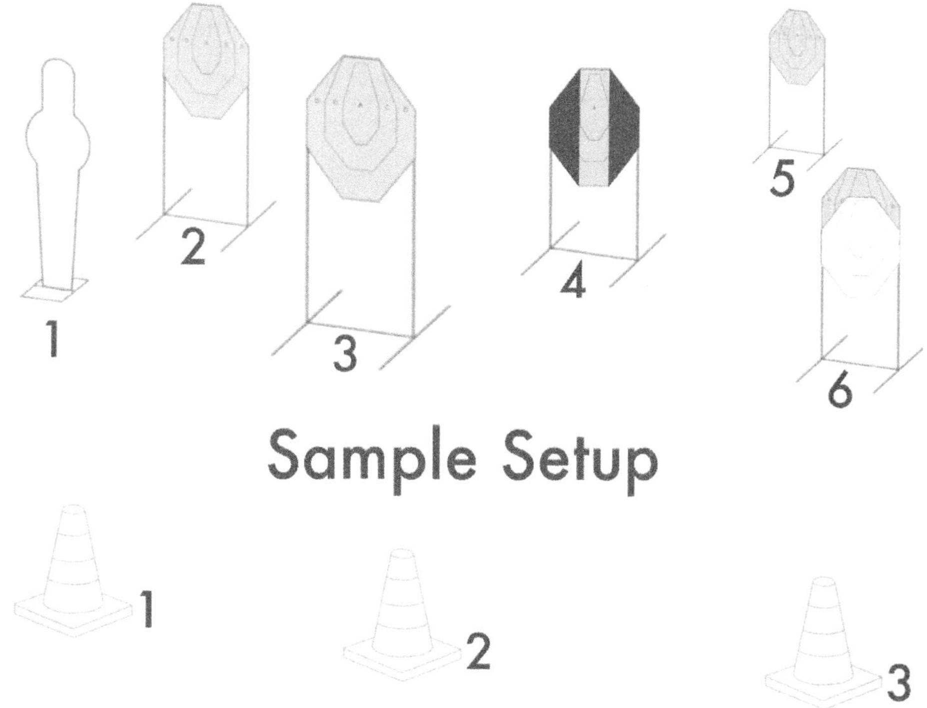

Setup notes:

Construct a multi position "stage." Using markers or cones on the ground to denote shooting positions. Setting up non-falling steel and multiple paper targets is ideal to give target variety. Stipulate an order to engage the targets and what position to engage them from. Feel free to use the same target from more than one position.

Example: Engage Target 1-4 from position one. Engage Targets 3-6 from position 2. Engage targets 2-3 from position 3.

Instructions:

Shoot the stage to the best of your ability. Make sure that the stage is executed without needing to consciously think about what the next step is. Ensure that your shooting is accurate and disciplined.

Cues:

You should shoot your mock stage just like a match stage. Do not focus on training cues during your stage run.

Corrections:

If you find yourself hesitating or not remembering what to do you need to visualize the entire stage. When you can see a first person "GoPro" video of your stage run without needing to specifically think the stage through, you are ready to shoot it. Do frequent walk-through passes just like you would in competition.

Be on guard for undisciplined shooting. Apply the correct aiming scheme for each target. Do not over or under confirm.

Evolution:

As your execution improves, start changing the stage. Eventually you should be able to change the order of targets/positions every single run and be able to hold a good performance. Once you can pick an order, visualize it and then execute it without hesitation you are in excellent shape.

Tips:

The main reason to do full stage training is to ensure that you can go through a complex shooting scenario without falling apart.

Consider the "Training Philosophy" section at the front of this book. The way you shoot, your style, your inclinations and your habits are what you are assessing when doing this exercise. You are not trying to accomplish anything specific by doing this training. The larger goal here is to see what happens and spot the "big picture" trends.

Ask yourself the following:

- What mistakes am I making repeatedly?
- What specific exercises should I do to mitigate these mistakes?
- Am I confident that I can perform to an acceptable level on a random set of competition stages?

The above questions are examples of questions you should be interested in. The best way to summarize the mindset for this type of training is, you spot the patterns in your shooting that are holding you back as a shooter. Look at the big picture.

Drill Progress Tracker			
Date	Drill Time	Hit Factor	Notes

Notes:

SPECIAL DRILLS

Confirmation Drill

Purpose/Goal:

Build an understanding of how different methods of confirmation/aiming scheme affect the outcome on the target.

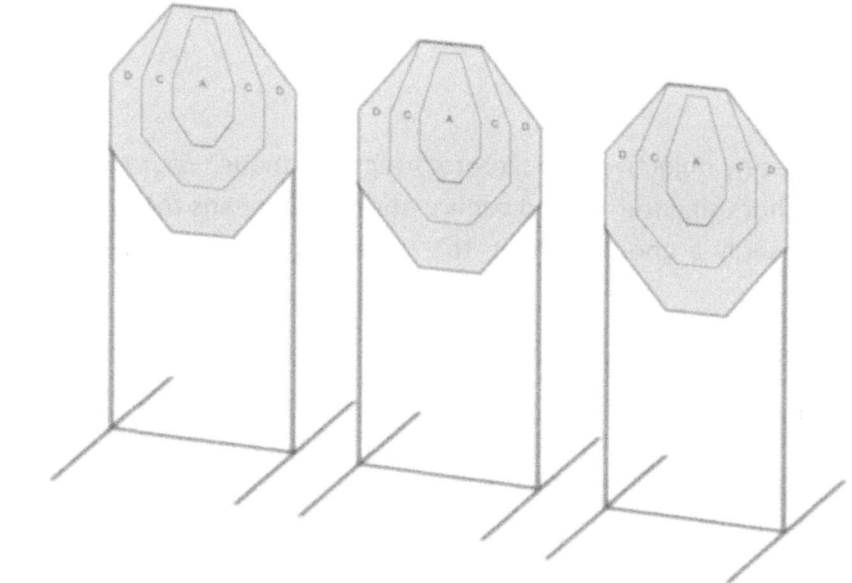

Setup notes:

Set up targets for comparison at 5 yards distance.

Instructions:

This drill will consist of many repetitions for each aiming scheme you are testing.

The start position for the drill is a two-handed grip on the gun, aimed at the bottom of the target stand of the target you are shooting.

At the tone, engage the very center of the A zone using the aiming scheme you are testing on that target. Fire one round only. Note the time.

Do the correct number of repetitions on each target. For example: Engage target 1 using confirmation 1 for 10 repetitions. Engage target two with confirmation 2 for 10 reps. Engage target 3 with confirmation 3 for 10 reps.

At the end of this test you should have a good sample of data that gives you an idea of the time and accuracy difference between different levels of confirmation. Check out the "tips" section of this drill if this is unclear to you.

Cues:

Make sure you use the confirmation you intend to.

Corrections:

This drill does not have any objective to build or correct technique. Your only job is to ensure that you actually execute each shot using the desired confirmation. This means that you need to create good data for yourself, not necessarily a good result on the target. Make sure you rigidly enforce your desired confirmation level.

Make sure you use the confirmation you intend to.

Evolution:

Feel free to attempt any confirmation/aiming scheme on any target type. This will give you more data and a good sense for what outcome you can expect given the particular aiming strategy.

This drill was developed using the following scheme:

Confirmation 1:

Kinesthetic alignment only. You "feel" your arms are pointed in the correct place and then you shoot. NO VISUAL CONFIRMATION

Confirmation 2:

You react to the color of your sight crossing your intended aiming area. With an optic you shoot as soon as you see the optical color. With a fiber optic iron sight setup, you shoot when you see the color of your front sight.

Confirmation 3:

Your dot is stopped and stable in your intended aiming area. Your dot should appear as a dot and not as a streak. With iron sights you see the front sight stopped through the rear notch.

This is a near perfect sight picture sort of setup.

As you move up in confirmation it will take more time, but the result on the targets will be much cleaner.

Shooting iron sights you might find it useful to distinguish between a perfectly aligned sight picture and seeing the front sight through the rear notch, but perhaps a bit misaligned. You might think of the sights slightly misaligned as confirmation 2.5.

There is no limit to what you can experiment with on this drill. Just remember, your goal with the drill is to put in a specific aiming scheme and then assess your outcome. You are not trying to get a "good" or "bad" outcome. You just want to see how it all works. Once you get a sense of this, it should be easy to apply these concepts to your other training.

Tips:

This drill was developed by Hwansik Kim in order to isolate the effect of the aiming strategy, confirmation level and aiming scheme on the target.

The component of target acquisition and engagement where you have a lot of control over speed is how you aim the gun at the target. More specifically, it is the reference you are using to confirm the gun is aimed. Traditionally, the expectation is that every sight picture looks the same on every target. People are generally trained in non-practical shooting context to get a "perfect" sight picture for each and every shot. As soon as you move beyond level 1 in this text that is no longer the advice or expectation.

Learning how much "perfect" sight picture you can trade away in order to go faster is one of the most important things that a practical shooter can do. As soon as you understand what sort of sight picture will produce what sort of outcome all you need to do is train yourself to address each target with the optimal strategy and your results will be excellent.

This exercise exists to strip away every other layer and show you the effect of the aiming strategy on the target outcome.

Drill Progress Tracker			
Date	Drill Time	Hit Factor	Notes

Notes:

Measurement Drill

Purpose/Goal:

Build an understanding of how much energy it requires to return your pistol to point of aim after firing a shot.

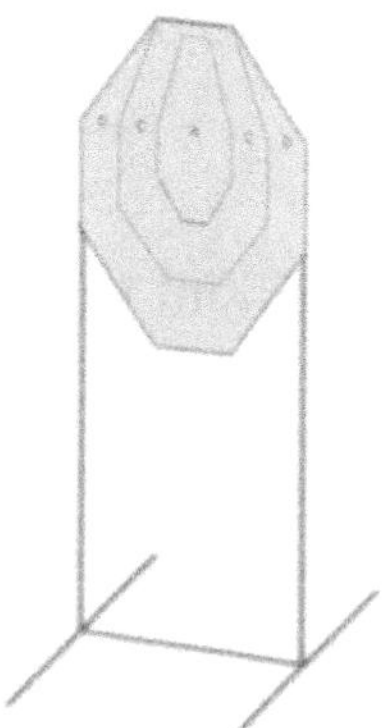

Setup notes:

This drill requires only one target. 5 yards is a good distance to use.

Instructions:

Grip your pistol properly. Engage the very center of the A zone of your target with one carefully fired shot. DO NOT PUSH THE GUN BACK DOWN AFTER FIRING THE SHOT. Fire a second shot at the point the gun recoiled to without re-aiming to your aimpoint. The distance between the two shots is the information you are looking for. This will measure how much the muzzle rises and thus how much it should be returned. Repeat this until you have a good sense of the distance the muzzle rises.

After you understand the distance of muzzle rise, start returning the muzzle back down to the original point of aim between the first and second shots. Start going slowly (1 or 2 seconds between shots). As you continue to train and understand, increase your speed until you are shooting as fast as you can pull the trigger.

Cues:

Learn how much energy it requires to return your pistol to point of aim after firing a shot.

Corrections:

This drill does not have any objective to build or correct technique.

Evolution:

Feel free to attempt this drill in unusual circumstances. Consider trying leans, awkward positions, or one-handed shooting in order to build more understanding.

Tips:

This drill was developed by Hwansik Kim to work on the concept of recoil control. Most people have an incorrect concept of recoil control. They believe that it will take a lot of muscle mass, force and effort to control the recoil of their pistol. The point of this drill is to facilitate you demonstrating to yourself that this isn't true. At least it isn't as true as you might think. You do not need to work that hard in order to bring your pistol down out of recoil. The muzzle of your pistol should only marginally rise when you fire a shot. The main issue you will have as you learn to shoot faster and faster is battling your tendency to overcorrect or overcontrol that recoil. Once you internalize how little force is required to return the gun it should improve your concept of recoil control.

Drill Progress Tracker			
Date	Drill Time	Hit Factor	Notes

Notes:

Sight Tracking

Purpose/Goal:

Learn to watch your sights. Test the cause and affect relationships related to your grip.

No targets needed

Setup notes:

Do not use a target. Fire the rounds in a safe direction into the backstop. Do not even aim at a particular spot on the backdrop.

Instructions:

Aim your gun in a safe direction. Watch the sights closely as you fire your gun. Assess how the sights move.

Cues:

Pay attention to your hands. Notice how the sights track differently as you adjust your hand pressure.

Corrections:

Keep your eyes open. If you are not sure what you just saw, you did not see enough. The gun is telling you a story as it moves in recoil, you need to keep your eyes open to be aware of the story.

Drill Progress Tracker			
Date	Drill Time	Hit Factor	Notes

Notes:

Classifier Training

Purpose/Goal:

Train on, and experiment with, USPSA Classifier stages in order to expand your knowledge and skill set.

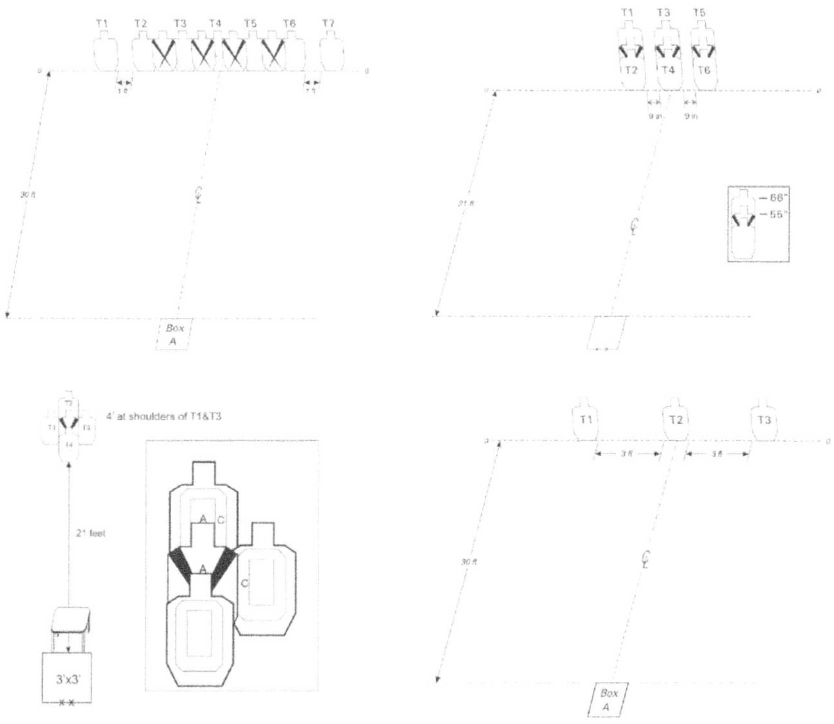

ANY DESIRED CLASSIFIER

Setup notes:

Setup any desired USPSA Classifier.

Instructions:

Set up any desired USPSA Classifier.

Shoot the classifier stage the desired number of times. Note time, points and hit factor. Your goal is to competently execute the skills required. You should be able to consistently execute the classifier without incurring penalties. Your goal is to consistently shoot over 60% of the national high hit factor.

Drill Progress Tracker			
Date	Drill Time	Hit Factor	Notes

Notes:

Special Challenges

Purpose/Goal:

Become comfortable with non-standard scenarios that may present themselves in matches. These include, but are not limited to, off body start positions, shooting in awkward positions and shooting one handed.

Make sure that you get comfortable shooting accurately in a variety of positions and circumstances.

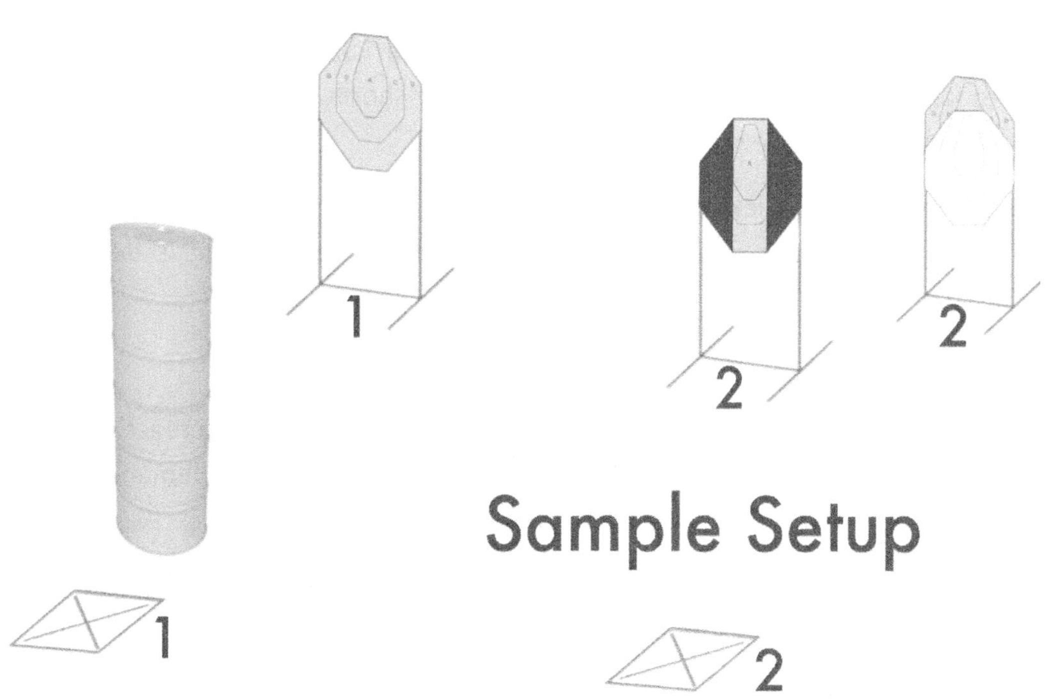

Setup notes:

Construct challenges that you expect to see in future matches. Keep the scenarios small, simple and focused.

Things like leans, crouches, one handed, prone and other types of shooting positions and circumstances can be trained on outside of matches, so you are faster and more comfortable dealing with them on the clock.

Instructions:

At the tone, engage the targets in your setup while observing the special conditions you have set for yourself.

Example: Engaging the targets while kneeling would be the procedure if you are working on kneeling shooting.

Cues:

When the shooting is awkward or difficult, remember shooting fundamentals. Confirm sight alignment and carefully stack pressure onto the trigger for each demanding shot and you will get the best chance at a good score you could possibly have that day.

Corrections:

Pay close attention to the sight pictures you are seeing. As the shooting gets more awkward or difficult your gun will not behave the same as when you are standing comfortably in your preferred stance. If gun is not properly aimed where it needs to be, have the discipline to hold off on shooting until it is.
If the gun is not returning to your point of aim as quickly as it normally does then you will need to resist the temptation to force that to happen. It is quite common for shooters to aggressively over return the gun back to the target and induce even more errors.

If you are getting erratic results, make sure you are not doing predictive shooting. It is not productive to get a marginal time advantage, but have spotty results. Predictive shooting is best done when the circumstances are more normal.

Evolution:

As you get comfortable with whatever challenge you are working on, simply increase the difficulty of the challenge. Move the targets further away, add partials, make the position more demanding or do whatever else makes sense to increase the difficulty for the given challenge.

If you are working on shooting from an awkward position and you are successful, you can modify the exercise to require you to start, get into your shooting position and shoot. This will make the training similar to what you should expect to see in a match setting.

Tips:

Remember for special challenges, you do not need to be the best at everything. You need to be able to hit the targets under pressure. Shooting from some awkward position is a challenge for everyone and nobody is going to be comfortable doing it. Suppress the feelings you have about being too slow and execute the shots.

Drill Progress Tracker			
Date	Drill Time	Hit Factor	Notes

Notes:

LEVEL 3

Goal: Get to Master/Grand Master

Once you are competent, accurate and you have some measure of speed, the next challenge is to become one of the best shooters in your club and achieve a high rank inside your shooting sport. For most people reading this book, that means USPSA Master class, or Grand Master class. Making Grand Master was my first goal when I started doing USPSA.

This level has advanced concepts like dynamic movement, predictive shooting, multiple aiming schemes, and GM time limits for basic exercises.

With this level you start to pay a lot of attention to time limits. You need to be able to draw and reload your pistol quickly and consistently. These training times are about as fast as you can physically perform these actions. You need tens of thousands of repetitions of these at high speed in order to get comfortable doing what you need to do.

This section will encourage you to learn and utilize a broader spectrum of aiming methods to cut down time from your stages. You need to understand target focused shooting vs sight focused. You need to pay attention to exactly what your vision is doing during your training. Learning different aiming schemes and getting your eyes to cooperate with you is immensely helpful to ranking up.

When it comes to moving around stages more efficiently, this section has you covered as well. Instead of a simple suite of basic movement drills, we start breaking things down and giving a larger, more detailed set of drills where you can work on your technique.

Getting a Master card in your shooting sport is not an easy thing. You need to master your technique and apply that mastery to the game properly. This section will show you how.

Level 3 Training Standards

The Destination:

This training level is designed to take you to USPSA M or GM class or an equivalent rating in your sport or organization.

By utilizing challenging time *Standards* for gun manipulation, you will be able to quickly develop the speed required to rank up.

You will need to use different aiming schemes and predictive shooting in order to be accurate at speed.

Input:

This level will require that you do dryfire training on a daily or near daily basis. It will also necessitate regular trips to the range for live training. Expect to train with about 20k rounds per year in most cases.

What Comes Next:

Using the drills in this section you should be able to advance to a high level given moderate physical talent, intelligent training and sustained effort over a long period of time. Once you reach a high level of shooting it becomes a personal choice for how serious you want to get. If you are chasing big matches then you would advance to level 4, if not you would stay at this level.

Specific Standards:

Level 3 training requires the following:

- Fast/Competent gun handling. Using a .8 second draw time and 1 second reload time you should be able to be fast and confident with gun manipulation in dryfire.
- With live ammunition, learn to control the gun when shooting as fast as you can pull the trigger (about .2 splits). You should be able to hold the A zone at 10 yards.
- The target time for El Prezidente is 6 seconds.
- If you are using an optic you should expect to have to shoot even faster.

Knowledge/mindset:

This level requires you to leverage your good training habits over a longer period of time.

Sometimes shooters with age on their side and/or a high level of talent in some way can rank up very quickly. It can even happen in a matter of a few short months.

Most people will not have things come quite so fast. It will take sustained effort over a long period of time, lots of ammunition and patience in order to achieve mastery at this level.

You will benefit from carefully paying attention to the training cues and corrections at this level. Unsophisticated thinking like "go faster" or "slow down" that works at lower levels is too non-specific to fix complex problems that you will encounter as you ratchet up your speed in level 3. Take a careful look at your targets when training and do a good assessment of your issues. It will speed your development.

Standard Practice Setup

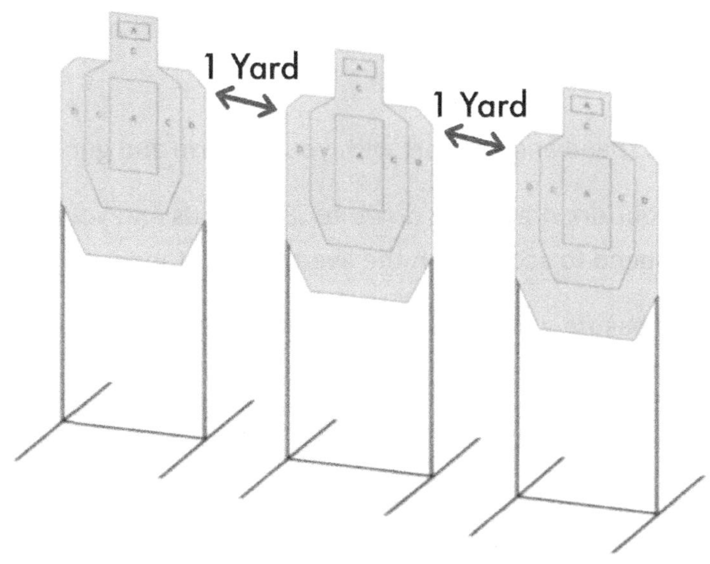

Livefire Level 3

Drill Name	Procedure	goal draw/reload times	3 yards	7 yards	10 yards	15 yards	25 yards	add time for: surrender	facing uprange	unloaded start
One Per Target	Engage each target with 1 round	1.0/na	1.6	1.8	2	2.5	3	0.1	0.2	1
Pairs on One Target	Engage one target with 2 rounds	1.0/na	1.2	1.4	1.6	1.8	2	0.1	0.2	1
4 Aces	Engage 1 target with 2 shots, reload, 2 shots.	1.2/1.2	2.3	2.5	3	3.5	4	0.1	0.2	1
Bill Drill	Engage one target with 6 rounds	1.0/na	1.8	2	2.2	2.8	3.5	0.1	0.2	1
Bill/Reload/Bill	Engage one, 6 rounds, reload, 6 more	1.2/1.2	3.8	4.3	5	6	7.5	0.1	0.2	1
Blake Drill	Engage each target with 2 rounds	1.0/na	2.2	2.5	3	3.5	4	0.1	0.2	1
El Prez	Turn, draw, engage each target w/2, reload, reengage each w/2	1.2/1.2	5	5.5	6	8	10	0.1	0.2	1
Criss Cross	Engage each of the 6 A zones in a criss cross pattern	1.0 (1.3 head)/ 1.2 (1.5 head)	5	6	7	8	n/a	0.1	0.2	1
Stong Hand Only	Engage each target w/ 2 rounds Strong hand only	1.5/na	3	3.5	3.8	5	n/a	0.1	0.2	1
Weak Hand Only	Engage each target w/ 2 rounds weak hand only	2.2 w/transfer/na	3.5	3.8	4	5.5	n/a	0.1	0.2	1

This is a set of standards designed to give a rough idea about general ability. The par times are set so you should be able to do a proper repetition 9/10 times to demonstrate proficiency. A single attempt does not mean much; you are looking for consistency. If you are using a red dot sight, subtract 5% from the times as you simulate distances of 15 yards or greater. If you are scoring major, subtract another 5% from the times at 15 yards or greater. These two conditions "stack," so open guns subtract 10% in total.

Dryfire Training 3

This is a brief primer on how to do the dry training component of your preparation.

Training Focal Points

Your focus should be to build speed and comfort with your firearm and gun handling skills.

Make sure you are getting your dry draw time down to .8 seconds and your dry reloads are less than 1.2 seconds. You will need this speed to accomplish the live training standard times.

The most difficult thing to measure will be gun movement when you transition or move. Be sensitive to how the gun arrives on target and when you move it onto a new target.

Training Schedule

To facilitate developing the required skills, you will need regular training. Commonly someone will train five days a week for a period of a few years to rank up.

Level 3 Drills

The drills you should train on, in addition to the standard dry drills with par times listed below are dryfire versions of all the other level 3 drills. Construct the drill to scale as described in the dryfire training section in the general information section of this book.

Standards

This level requires you to leverage your good training habits over a longer period.

Dryfire Level 3

								add time for:		
Drill Name	**Procedure**	**goal draw/reload times**	**3 yards**	**7 yards**	**10 yards**	**15 yards**	**25 yards**	**surrender**	**facing uprange**	**unloaded start**
One Per Target	Engage each target with 1 round	1.2/na	1.6	1.8	2	2.5	3	0.1	0.2	1
Pairs on One Target	Engage one target with 2 rounds	1.2/na	1	1.1	1.3	1.6	2	0.1	0.2	1
4 Aces	Engage 1 target with 2 rounds, reload, reengage w/ 2 rounds.	1.2/1.2	2.3	2.5	2.8	3.2	3.8	0.1	0.2	1
Bill Drill	Engage one target with 6 rounds	1.2/na	1.6	1.8	2	2.5	3	0.1	0.2	1
Bill/Reload/Bill	Engage one, 6 rounds, reload, 6 more	1.2/1.2	3.5	3.8	4	4.5	5	0.1	0.2	1
Blake Drill	Engage each target with 2 rounds	1.2/na	2	2.2	2.5	3	3.8	0.1	0.2	1
El Prez	Turn, draw, engage each target w/2, reload, reengage each w/2	1.2/1.2	4.5	5	5.5	6.5	8	0.1	0.2	1
Criss Cross	Engage each of the 6 A zones in a criss cross pattern	1.2 (1.5 head)/ 1.5 (2.0 head)	4.8	5.8	6.2	7.5	n/a	0.1	0.2	1
Stong Hand Only	Engage each target w/ 2 rounds Strong hand only	1.5/na	2.5	2.8	3	3.7	n/a	0.1	0.2	1
Weak Hand Only	Engage each target w/ 2 rounds weak hand only	1.7 w/transfer/na	2.7	3	3.5	4.2	n/a	0.1	0.2	1

This is a set of standards designed to give a rough idea about general ability. The par times are set so you should be able to do a proper repetition 9/10 times to demonstrate proficiency. A single attempt does not mean much; you are looking for consistency. If you are using a red dot sight, subtract 10% from the times as you simulate distances of 15 yards or greater.

MARKSMANSHIP FUNDAMENTALS

Group Shooting

Purpose/Goal:

Ability to shoot A zone hits without any time pressure. Shooting all A's at 25 yards is a good goal. Shooting 100% hits on a reduced target surface (like a USPSA Headbox) is also important.

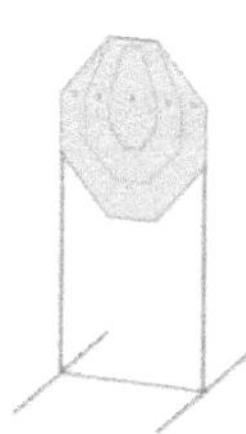

Instructions:

With no time limit, engage the target with as many rounds as desired. Shooting at least a five shot group is a good test of consistency.

Cues:

The most important cue to pay attention to is the tactile feel of your firing hand. It is logical in many respects to pay attention to the feel of your hands instead of the visual component of sight alignment. In most cases you will get better results by focusing on the feel inside your hands.

Corrections:

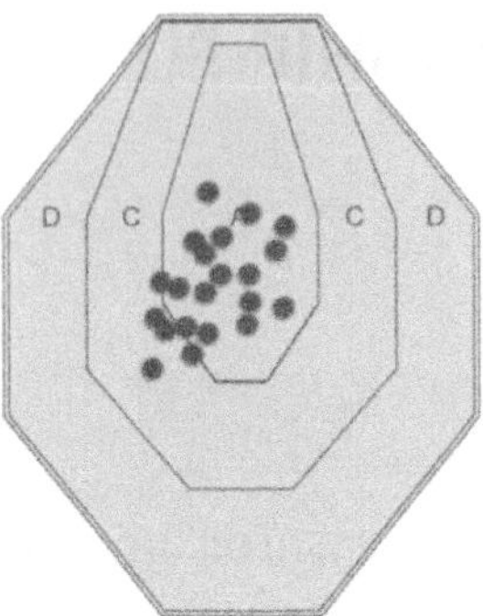

Hitting low/left is the classic sign of pushing down into the anticipated recoil. Focus on holding your firing hand still while you press the trigger straight.

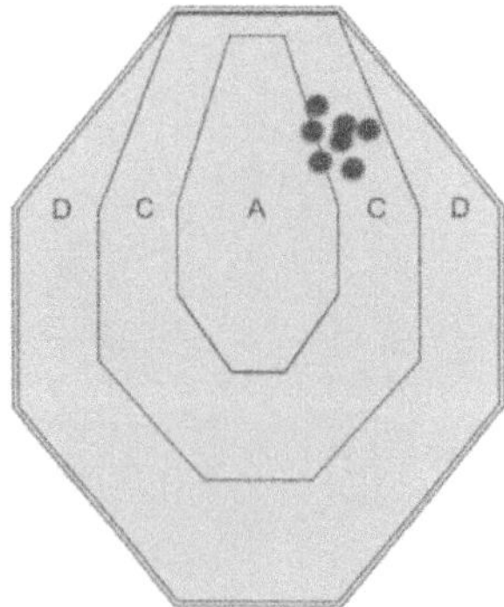

If you are forming a small group but in the wrong spot of the target, consider adjusting your sights. If you are unsure if you or the sights are the issue, have a friend shoot your gun to confirm your zero.

Evolution:

Be sure to vary the target configuration. Try using no-shoots or hardcovers to block off part of the target. Forcing yourself to work around the obstruction will help you learn what your sights should look like when engaging a target that is partially obstructed.

Tips:

Shooting tight groups is an important skill to develop for any practical shooter. This skill will allow you to make sure that your pistol is mechanically accurate and able to hit any reasonable target at any reasonable distance.

The best results during group shooting are typically going to be when you are focused on the feel of your hands rather than the visual component of aiming. The most common error that we observe during group shooting training is when the shooter sees a desirable sight picture they immediately want to press the trigger. Typically, this is accompanied by pushing down into the anticipated recoil. If this shooter accepts a little bit of "wobble" in the sight picture and focuses on smoothly and cleanly releasing the shot they will get a much better result.

Drill Progress Tracker			
Date	Drill Time	Hit Factor	Notes

Notes:

Trigger Control at Speed

Purpose/Goal:

Learn to press the trigger straight.

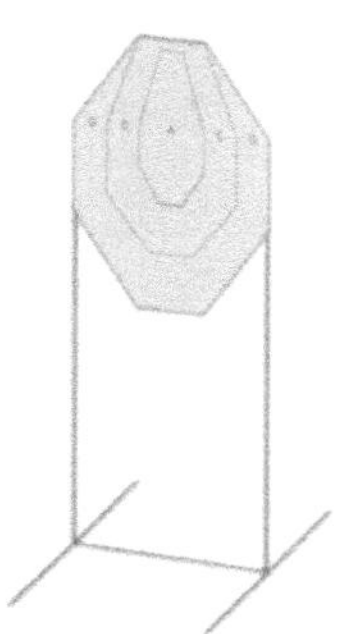

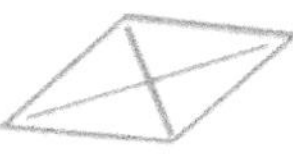

Single target

Setup notes:

Use a single target at any desired distance.

Instructions:

Start with the gun mounted and a perfect sight picture on your target. Your finger should be just out of contact with the trigger. At the tone, fire a shot. The shot should come in under .25 seconds or it is a "fail" for the drill.

Cues:

Your hand tension is going to tell you a lot. If your firing hand tenses up, or you have sympathetic movement in your fingers, the shot will not hit precisely on your intended impact point. Pay attention to your hands.

Corrections:

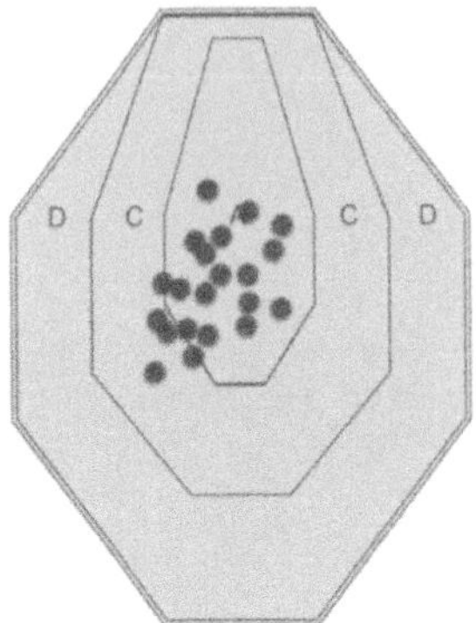

Most commonly, shots will be pressed down and left for a right-handed shooter. Hold your hand still. Isolate your trigger finger. Putting more attention on the sights will not help.

Evolution:

This is an excellent drill to try single-handed as well. You can master dominant hand only shooting. You can work on weak hand trigger control as well.

You can also start the drill with your finger out of the trigger guard and try to match the same time it took to get the shot off with your finger in the trigger guard. By doing this you stress pressing the trigger straight on back.

Drill Progress Tracker			
Date	Drill Time	Hit Factor	Notes

Notes:

Practical Accuracy

Purpose/Goal:

Shoot the gun with acceptable accuracy, at practical pace. Learn to grip your gun properly. Shooting all A's at 15 yards in under 3 seconds consistently is a reasonable goal.

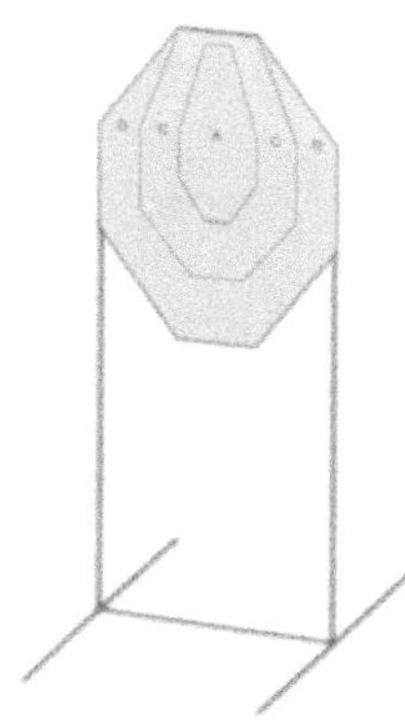

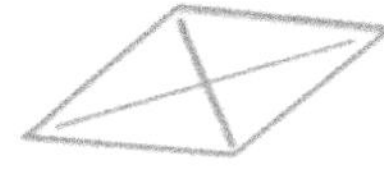

Instructions:

At the start signal, draw and engage the center of the A zone with six rounds. Fire a follow up shot as soon as your sights recover. There is not a specific time limit, but the idea for the exercise is to shoot as soon as the sights recover.

Six strings at a time is recommended.

Cues:

Pay close attention to the feel of your gun in your hands. Once you feel yourself making a mistake with your grip or trigger control you are going to be able to correct it easier.

Look to the spot on the target you want to hit. Do not look for the target's outline or at the color of the target. Look at a very specific point.

Corrections:

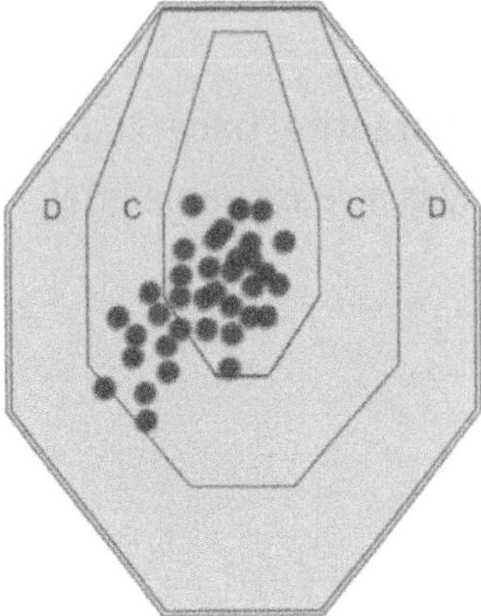

Low/left hits are almost always caused by moving the gun with the firing hand while shooting.

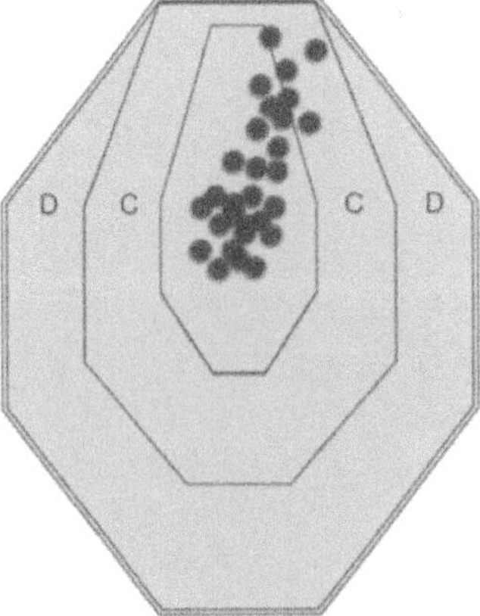

High hits generally come from insufficient support hand pressure or from shifting your vision onto the sights themselves instead of the target.

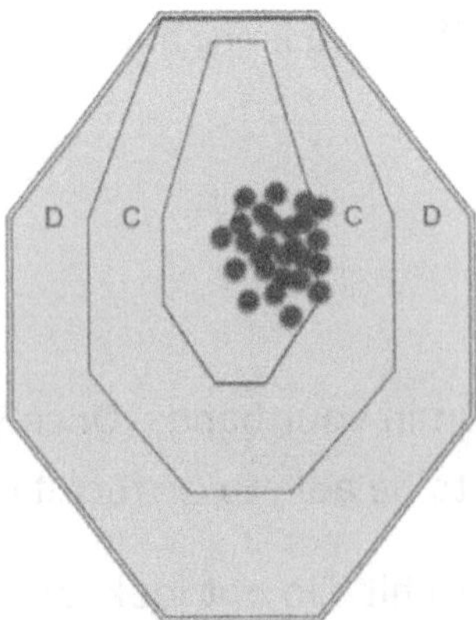

Hits trending in a small way to one direction or another can often be mitigated by small adjustments to grip pressure and trigger finger placement. Experiment to find what works best.

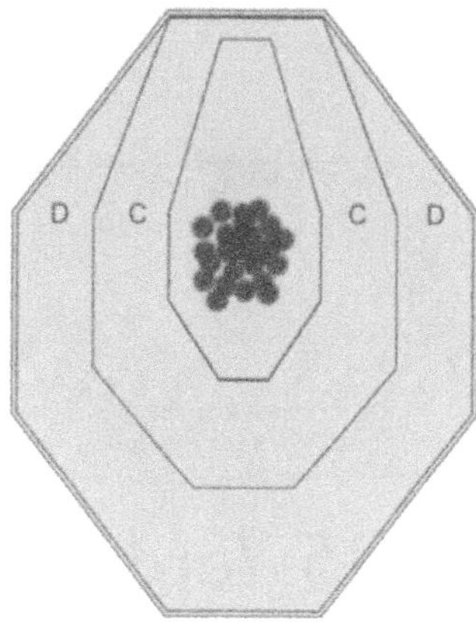

Even if your target looks great, constantly be assessing if you could have shot sooner or more aggressively.

Evolution:

Try to draw and shoot A's from any desired distance or on any target configuration.

Try this exercise one handed.

Tips:

It is important to think of this exercise as a grip exercise first and foremost. If you are gripping the gun correctly and consistently, you are going to get very good results. Pay attention to the feel of your hands as you are shooting. When you feel an errant shot happen because you pushed the gun sideways or some similar mistake, you will generally stop making that mistake so frequently. Focus on your hands and do not worry so much about the way the sight picture looks.

Make sure you are in control of the pace of your shooting. You want to develop the ability to shoot reacting to a sight picture for each individual shot. This means follow up shots should be in the range of .3 to .6 seconds between shots. If follow up shots get to be much faster than .3 seconds it is likely that you did not see the sight return and consciously make a choice to fire. You are shooting to a rhythm. If your follow up shots start to get long, .6 seconds or more, it is more than likely you are over confirming your sight picture. When the sights come back you need to shoot. Sitting on that sight picture will not help you.

Keep looking at a particular spot on the target while you are shooting. The spot you look at should be the size of a coin. Just staring at that spot is going to make you more accurate and likely to hit near that small spot. Be mindful of where your vision is focused. If you start to focus on your front sight or dot, your shots will tend to climb up higher on the target because you will not be resetting the sight back down onto the aimpoint. If your vision stays on the aimpoint your sight will tend to come back to that point.

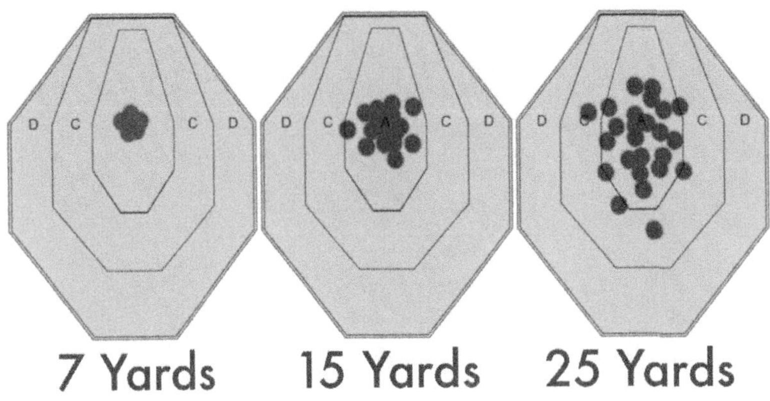

The goal is for your group to open concentrically as you increase the distance to the target. Flyers can, and will, still happen. Be looking at where the majority of the hits are going and be looking for any patterns. Compare any patterns you see to how your hands feel as you are breaking the shot. Connecting the dots from a feeling you have to where the shots are going will go a long way towards being able to eliminate marksmanship errors.

Drill Progress Tracker			
Date	Drill Time	Hit Factor	Notes

Notes:

Doubles

Purpose/Goal:

Refine grip and marksmanship

Learn predictive shooting

Hold the A zone at 7 yards while firing as fast as you can pull the trigger.

Develop the ability to shoot predictive pace out to 15 yards.

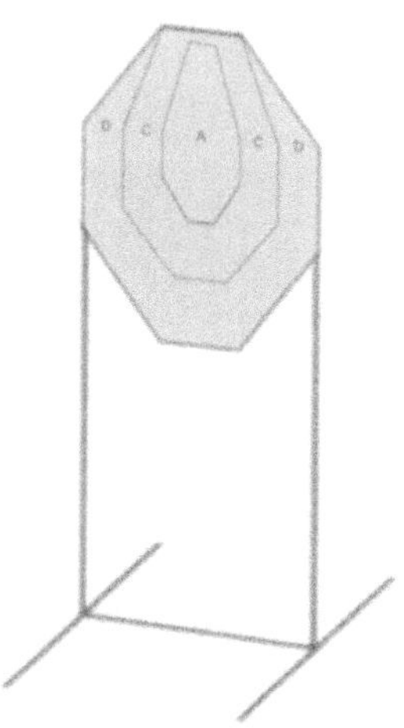

Instructions:

At the start signal, engage the target with four pairs of shots. Each pair should be fired as fast as you can pull the trigger. Allow the gun to completely quiet down from recoil before firing the next pair. Return your trigger finger to a relaxed position between pairs of shots.

Repeat this procedure for multiple strings.

Cues:

Pay close attention to the feel of your gun in your hands. Once you feel yourself making a mistake with your grip or trigger control you are going to be able to correct it much more easily. Isolate the trigger finger. Make sure your firing hand fingers are not curling due to an over tense firing hand.

Observe the movement of the sights in recoil. This will provide clues for how to improve your technique moving forward.

Corrections:

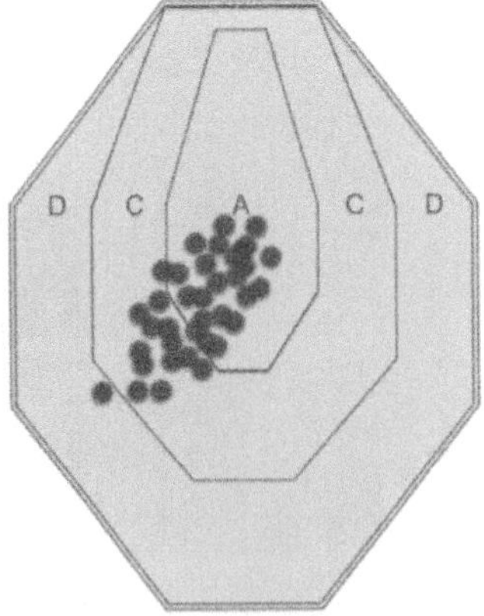

Low/left hits are almost always caused by moving the gun with the firing hand while shooting.

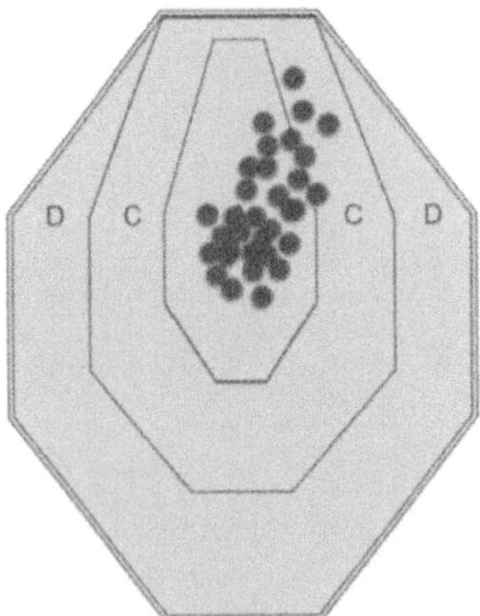

High hits generally come from insufficient support hand pressure.

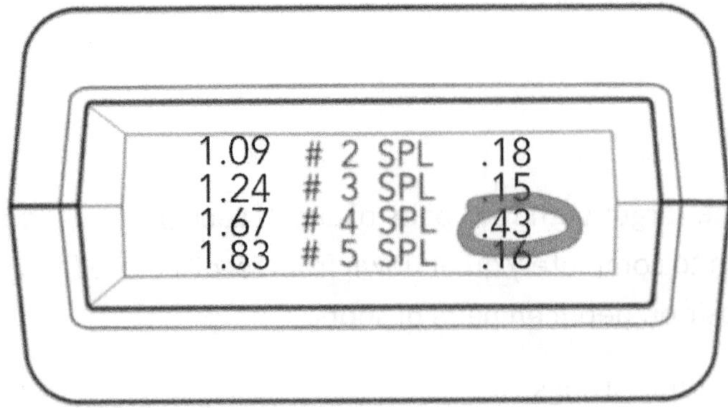

"Trigger Freeze" (the inability to reset the trigger for a second shot) is caused by an over tense firing hand in almost all cases.

Evolution:

As your control grows you can adjust the distance to the target and adjust your pace. This will give you a good idea of what sort of expectations are realistic in a match setting. As the range increases you will need to accept some points being dropped.

It is important you understand how the scoring system will affect aiming strategies. Be sure you are noting points down and assessing how you should handle different targets at different distances. You want to leverage your skills the best you can given the scoring system.

Tips:

It is important to think of this exercise as a grip exercise first and foremost. If you are gripping the gun correctly and consistently, you are going to get very good results. Pay attention to the feel of your hands as you are shooting. When you feel an errant shot happen because you pushed the gun sideways or some similar mistake then you will generally stop making that mistake so frequently. It is counterintuitive, but important, focus on your hands and do not worry so much about the way the sight picture looks.

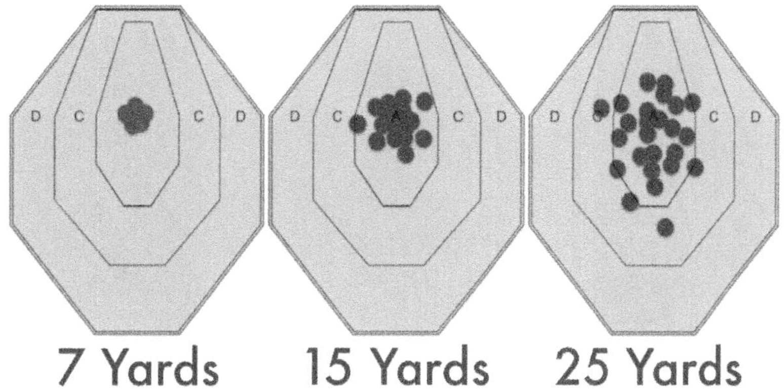

The goal is for your group to open concentrically as you increase the distance to the target. Flyers can, and will, still happen. Be looking at where the majority of the hits are going and for any patterns. Compare any patterns you see to how your hands feel as you are breaking the shot. Connecting the dots from a feeling you have to where the shots help towards eliminating marksmanship errors.

Drill Progress Tracker			
Date	Drill Time	Hit Factor	Notes

Notes:

Single-handed Shooting

Purpose/Goal:

Establish the ability to make shots using only one hand on the gun. Both dominant-hand only and non-dominant hand only need to be trained.

Shoot exactly at the pace of your sights (reactive shooting).

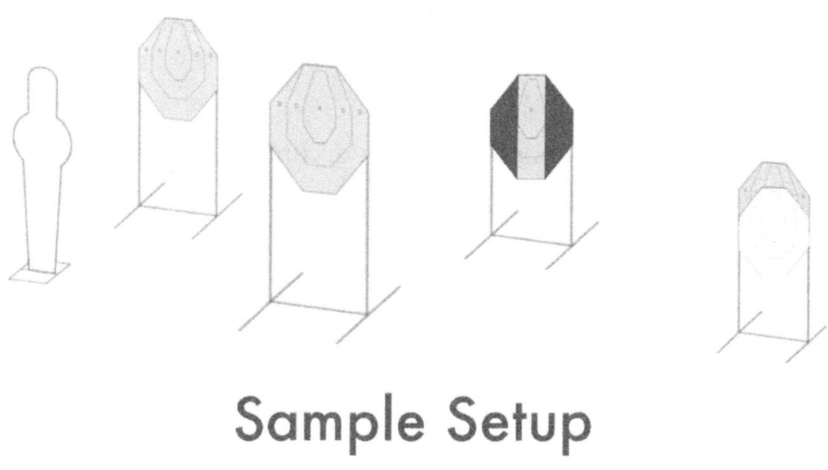

Sample Setup

Random Target Set

Setup notes:

Set up any target scenario you desire.

Instructions:

At the start, draw and engage the targets with a single hand. If you are using your non-dominant hand, draw the gun, transfer it to the correct hand, engage the targets.

Cues:

Pay attention to your firing hand. The most common issue you are going to run into is pushing down into the gun sympathetically as you press the trigger. Paying attention to your hand during the course of that drill is going to alleviate the issue.

Corrections:

Low/left shots when shooting right handed or low/right shots when shooting left handed are going to be very common, especially as you increase your speed. This issue is the primary one you should be focused on eliminating.

Evolution:

Try out a variety of start positions. "Gun on table" to start is fairly common when you come to a single-handed shooting stage in a match. You just want to make sure that you don't run into stuff that causes you to be nervous because the first time you have ever done it is in a match.

Feel free to do a bit of single-handed shooting on any training scenario you set up and work with. It isn't a bad idea to try a few runs of single-handed shooting on any drill you have set up. This will help ensure that your training is well rounded.

Tips:

It is critical that you do a lot of single-handed repetition dryfire. If you are using a dot sight this becomes even more important. You will need to develop a whole new index for your non-dominant hand to be able to bring the sight exactly to where it needs to be for you to be able to make hits. Do not neglect your dry training.

Experiment with technique. You may want to try "canting' the gun in. Right eye dominant shooters using their left hand may prefer to tilt the gun so the sight is still lined up with their right eye. This is ok, just be careful about the point of aim/point of impact discrepancy that can emerge if you are shooting at distance using this technique.

You may also want to try "blading" off towards the targets to get a better range of motion. An easy way to learn this is to step in with the gun side. This means if you are holding the gun in your right hand, step forward with your right foot.

Drill Progress Tracker			
Date	Drill Time	Hit Factor	Notes

Notes:

TRANSITION /VISION DRILLS

Target Transitions

Purpose/Goal:

Move the gun smoothly from one target to the next. Learn the optimal aiming schemes for the different target types and employ them.

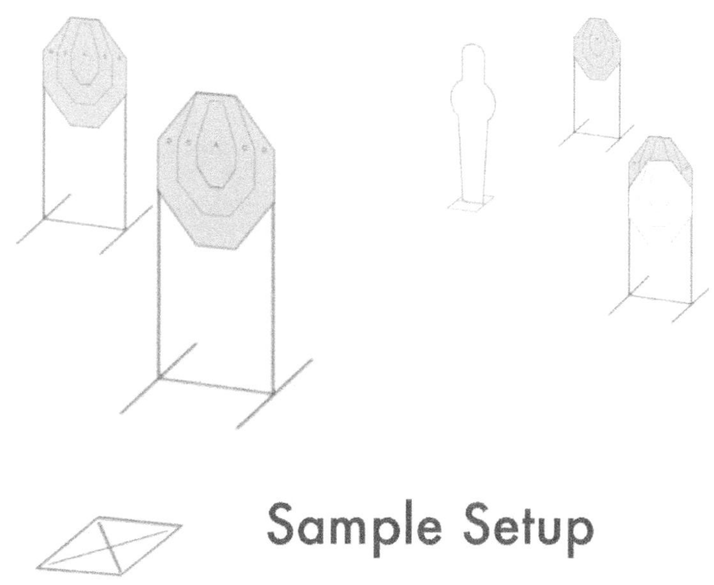

Set up:

Set up targets of mixed distance and shot difficulty. Mixing in steel plates or poppers are optional if you have them available. Try to create a very plain cross section of the targets you expect to encounter at matches.

Instructions:

At the start signal, engage each target. Keep the engagement order the same for a few repetitions. Shoot the drill at your practical match pace to begin and increase your speed as you feel comfortable doing so. Restore the targets after you assess them and change the engagement order if you wish for subsequent sets of repetitions on the exercise.

Cues:

Lead with your eyes. Look exactly where you wish to hit. You should not be looking at a big brown target, but picking an exact spot to move the gun to.

Do not muscle the gun around because it will cause the sights to stop imprecisely.

Make sure you understand where each shot is going and adjust aiming strategies as needed.

Corrections:

If the gun is not moving quickly or to your aim point, make sure you are leading with your eyes.

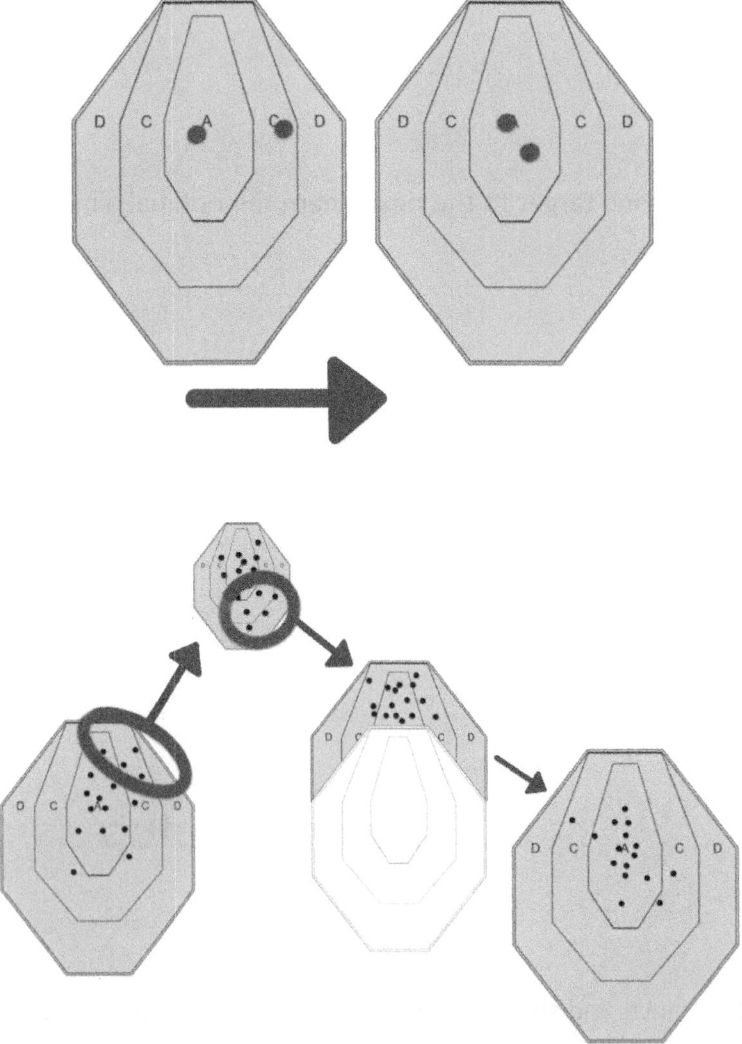

Moving your eyes off a target before you are done shooting it will drag the hits off the target. Drag off commonly happens on a target the shooter perceives to be lower difficulty. The shooter shifts their attention to the next task after firing the first shot on the target and the gun moves away from the target when the eyes do. Notice how your gun follows the path your eyes take. Train yourself to keep your eyes on the target as long as you are shooting it regardless of shot difficulty.

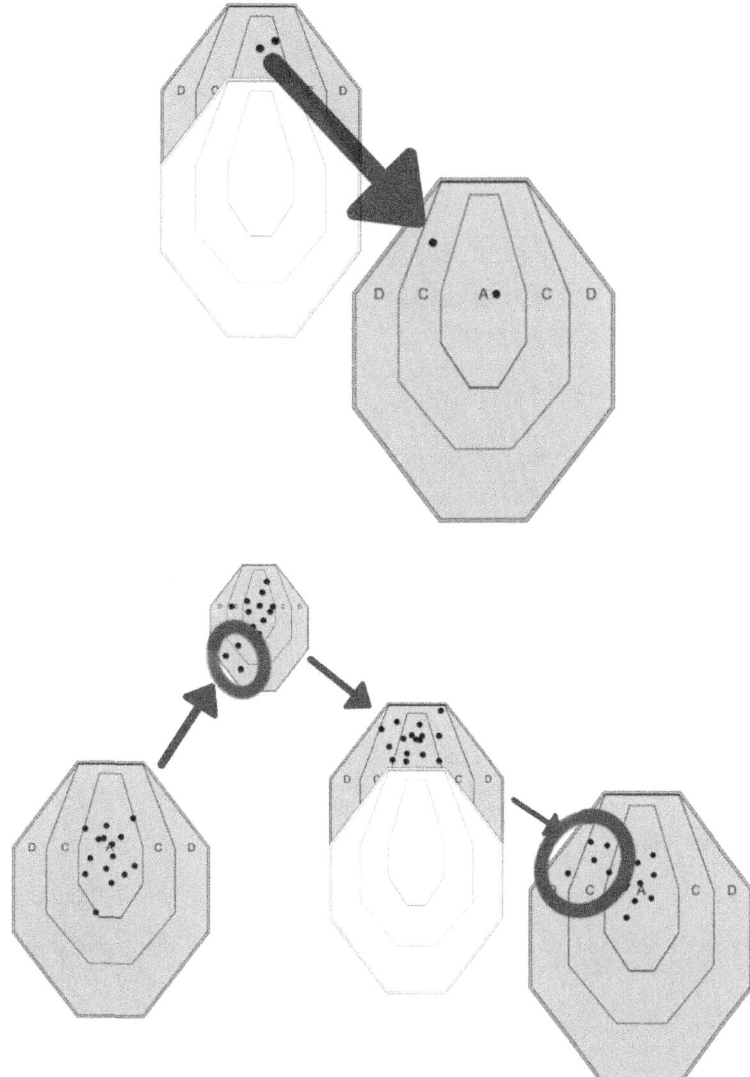

Pressing the trigger before the gun gets to the intended aimpoint will drag hits onto the target. The shot being drug into the target can vary from shooting a shot between targets, an edge D hit that barely scores, a C, or a hit on the A zone perforation. A common cause for this is trying to shoot a target very fast and attacking it. The correction is making sure you see your sights show up on the target you are transitioning to before firing.

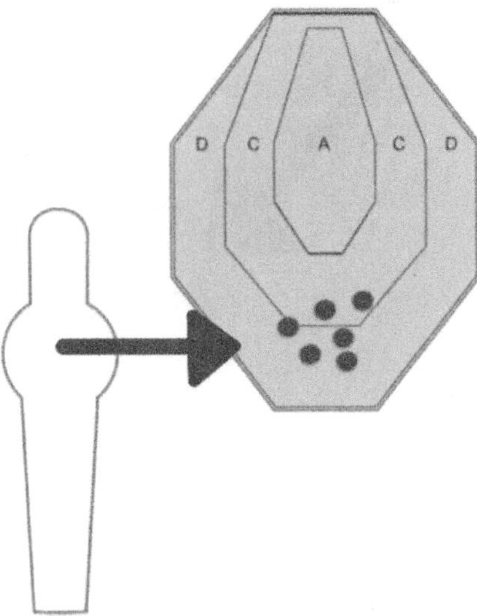

Be mindful of the vertical changes that occur in target arrays. Moving your gun straight left or right after shooting a target can cause high or low hits.

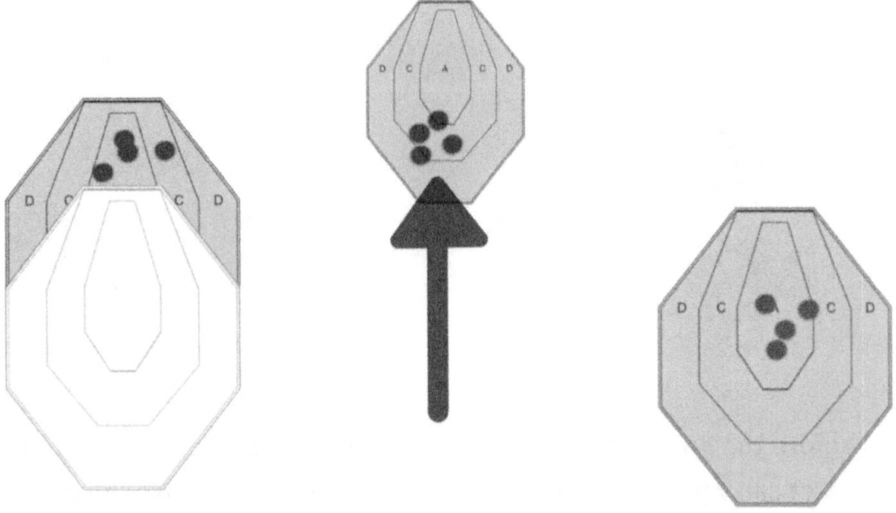

You are teaching yourself to have the sights show up where you look. Whether good or bad, the sights will go to the spot you are looking at. Make sure you are training your eyes to look at the exact spot you want to hit.

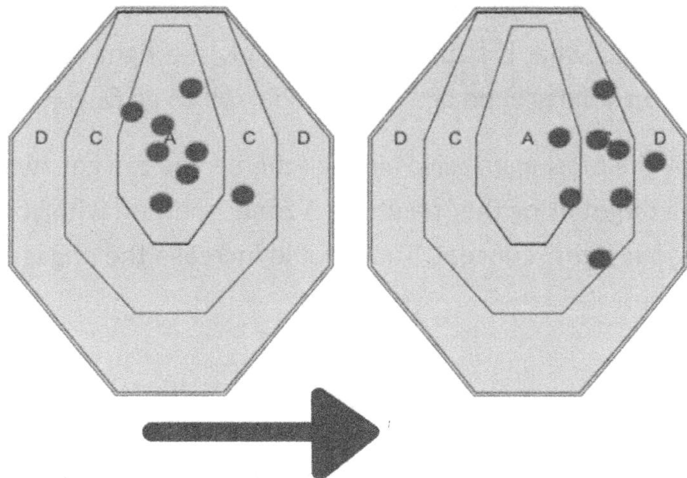

If you are overswinging/overdriving the gun, relax your shoulders. A telltale sign this is happening is if you feel very tense as you transition the gun. Your shoulders should not be any more raised or tense than if you were standing normally. Commonly, the hits will all trend on one side of the target.

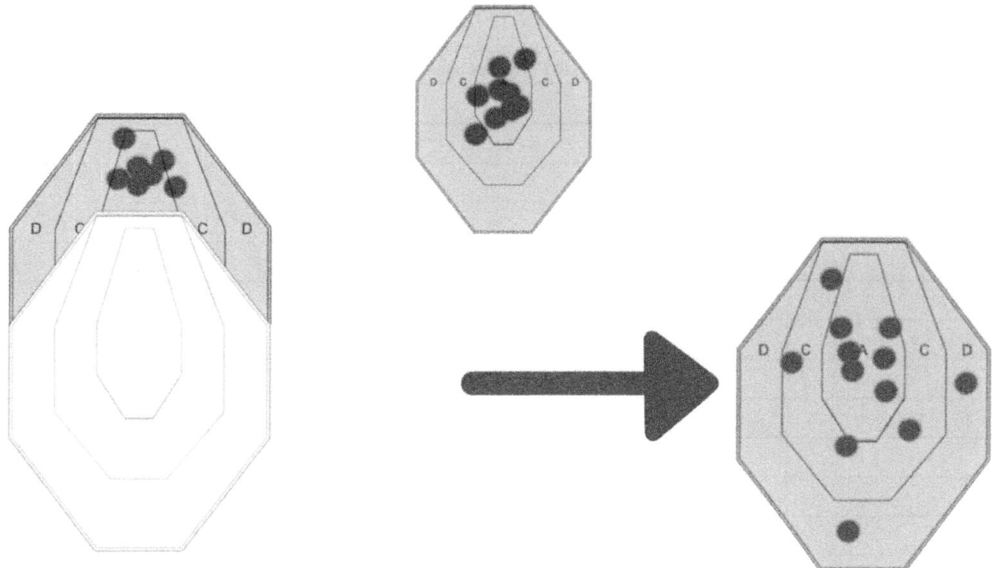

If the hits are widely scattered on a target with no real pattern, select a more precise aiming scheme.

Do not over aim/over confirm on close ranged open targets. Shoot immediately when you recognize the gun is on target. While training, be asking yourself the question, “Could I have been shooting sooner?”

Evolution:

Do dry aiming on each target at your full speed before doing live training. Move your vision from aimpoint to aimpoint on each target and learn to have the gun follow you. Make sure that you are not focusing on the sighting system as you move the gun from one target to the next, but instead your vision is out on the target. When you are consistently performing these skills dry then begin live training. After each set of runs on the drill then return to dryfire before the next set of runs.

If your shooting performance is going well, systematically push yourself to go faster. Understand that this will eventually induce you to make mistakes such as; shooting too early when coming onto the target, overrunning the intended target by pushing the gun too aggressively, or swinging the gun to the wrong spot on target. Pay attention to what is happening and apply the right corrections in order to improve. After you feel you are back on solid ground again, push yourself to go faster.

Make sure that you employ the most aggressive aiming scheme you can get away with. For example, if you are successfully engaging a target using the "paint the A zone" method with your dot then try to switch to the "react to the color of your sight" concept. That should increase the engagement speed and hopefully the accuracy will not degrade.

Tips:

Get in the habit of recalling what you just observed as you were shooting. As you learn to recall flashes of the sight pictures you were just seeing, the hits on targets will not be anywhere near as mysterious.

Watch out for technical errors throughout the drill. These errors include, but aren't limited to, following your sight in between targets, closing an eye, squinting and hunching down onto the gun. These things are common and will not in any way prevent you from being proficient as a shooter. As you develop your skills and attempt to go faster and faster, negative habits you have developed will become a problem.

Drill Progress Tracker			
Date	Drill Time	Hit Factor	Notes

Notes:

Wide Transitions

Purpose/Goal:

Learn proper wide transition technique.

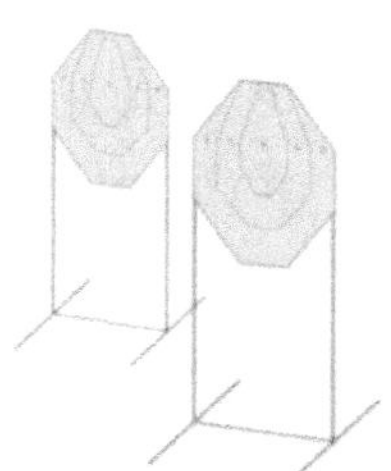

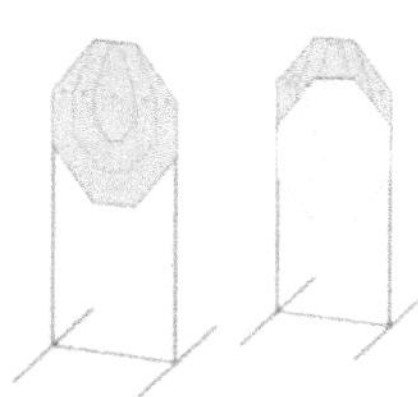

Sample Setup

Setup notes:

Create a scenario with two sets (arrays) of targets. Have a wide (90 degree or more) swing between the sets of targets.

Instructions:

Engage all the targets. Pay particular attention to the transition time between the two sets.

Cues:

Adopt a "fast then slow" or "attack and control" mindset. Aggressively drive the gun from one set to the other, slowing the gun down at the end of the transition. Ideally, you want the gun to stop perfectly stable and still correctly aimed.

Corrections:

Sample Setup

Hits patterning in the direction of the transition are often caused by "overdriving" the gun. There are two common corrections for this issue.

Firstly, make sure that you start applying the brakes during the wide transition before you get the gun to the target. Relaxing your shoulders can help remind you not to slam the gun into position.

Secondly, you may be tracking the sight the whole way through the wide transition. Again, this requires you to actively get your attention off the sight and into the center of the next target you intend to shoot.

Evolution:

You can get a lot of mileage out of this drill by simply altering the degrees of swing and the target difficulty. The goal here is to get comfortable with anything that may be required of you in a match. By getting used to transitioning the gun around quickly, you will be set up to do well on any sort of stage.

Drill Progress Tracker			
Date	Drill Time	Hit Factor	Notes

Notes:

Spot to Spot Transitions

Purpose/Goal:

Accurate and precise transitions.

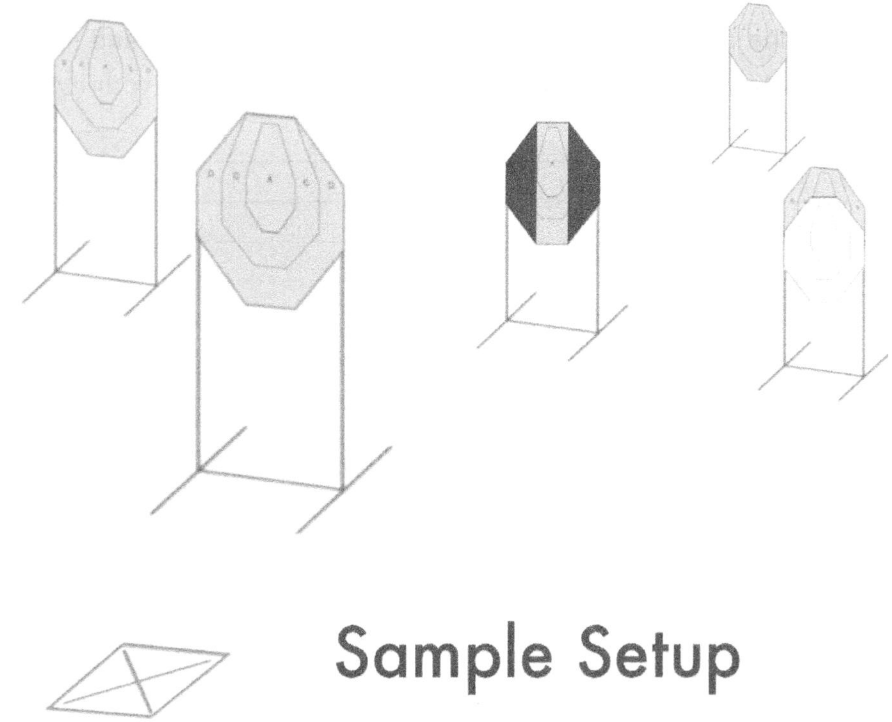

Random target setup

Setup notes:

This is a dry drill done during training. Do it on whatever target setup you are working on.

Instructions:

Practice moving your vision to exactly where you want the rounds to go on each target in sequence.

Cues:

Look at the exact spot where you want to hit.

Corrections:

There are two corrections that are normally needed.

Firstly, make sure you are finding a spot on the target, and not just looking at the color. Oftentimes people are satisfied by aiming at the brown blob and not finding a specific spot. Do not look for the shape or the color of the target, look exactly where you want to hit.

Secondly, do not "sweep" or "drag" your gaze through the target. Find a spot.

Evolution:

After you master the sequence, work in dry gun movement from spot to spot. Make sure you apply the correct aiming scheme.

Tips:

This drill should be done on a regular basis both on the training range and in matches. What you are essentially doing is practicing the transitions from spot to spot using just your eyes.

Drill Progress Tracker			
Date	Drill Time	Hit Factor	Notes

Notes:

Transition Exit/Entry

Purpose/Goal:

Break down the target transition technique into its most basic parts to understand it better.

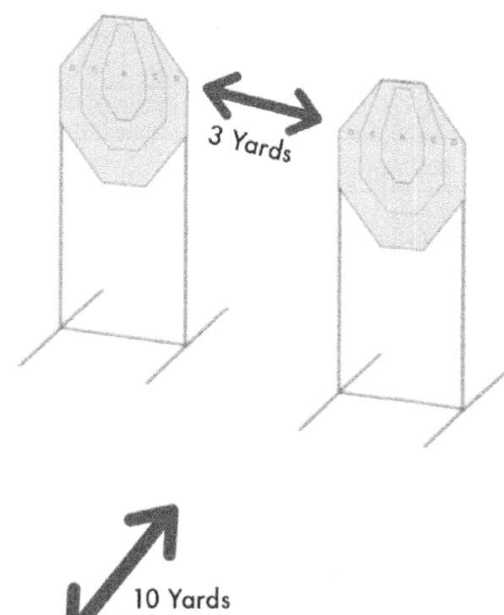

Setup notes:

2 targets. 3 yards apart. 10 yards distance.

Instructions:

Drill 1 (exit): Start with your pistol aimed at one of the targets. Your visual focus should be on the target you are aimed at. At the tone, engage the target with one round only then transition the gun to the other target. Get a good sight picture on that target but do not fire.

Drill 2(entry): Start with your pistol aimed at one of the targets. Your visual focus should be on the target you are aimed at. At the tone transition the gun to the other target. Get a good sight picture on that target and fire the shot.

Cues:

Your vision drives everything. Look exactly where you want the gun to go and allow it to go there smoothly.

Corrections:

Focus on the target while you transition, never the sight. If you have an excessively bright fiber or dot setup, this will be difficult. You need to get your vision out to the target.

Be aware of overswinging the gun or under swinging the gun. Look exactly where you want the gun to go and be extremely critical of any excess movement you see.

Drill Progress Tracker			
Date	Drill Time	Hit Factor	Notes

Notes:

Accelerator

Purpose/Goal:

Learn to employ different aiming schemes.

Par time 6 seconds

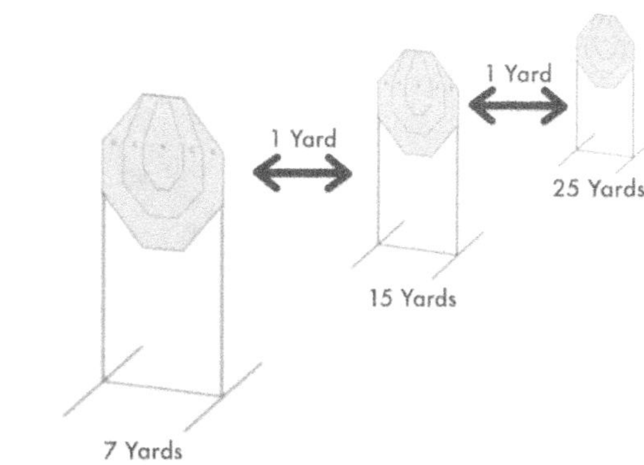

Setup notes:

Targets should be set so there is minimal transition laterally between the targets.

Instructions:

At the tone, engage each target with two rounds. Reload and re-engage each target with two more rounds.

Cues:

React immediately on the close target when your gun arrives in the center of it. Shoot right away without over aiming. React to seeing the color of fiber on your front sight or a blur of your dot on the target.

Allow the sight to settle on the far target for each shot. Press the trigger carefully and with discipline.

Make sure you stop your eyes on the center of the middle target. This is to avoid "dragging through" the target.

Corrections:

If you are struggling to hover near the par time for this drill you should look at draw and reload times. Drawing and reloading about 1 or 1.1 seconds on the close ranged target is fast enough to make the goal time. If you are lagging behind those times by a substantial amount you should look to dry training to improve those times.

If your draw/reload times are on point, but you are struggling to meet the par then ensure you are not delaying your movement off the target as soon as you finish shooting it. Oftentimes people have a fast pair of shots on the target, but they delay moving their eyes off the target as soon as they finish it. This will cause the gun to settle back down on a target that they should be transitioning away from. If you are seeing transition times between the targets longer that .4 seconds this is a likely cause.

The middle target is typically the one that people struggle with. You should be shooting a predictive pair, but it does not need to be your top speed split that you would be looking for on the close target. If you are not comfortable with a predictive pair on the middle target, look to specific training like Doubles drill.

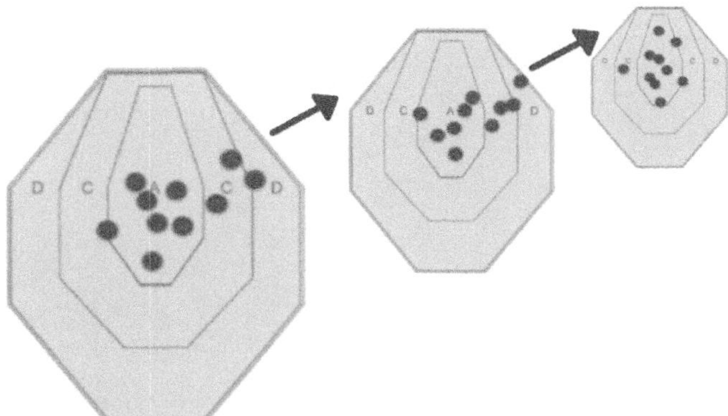

Make sure you are keeping your eyes on the target the entire time you are shooting it. Moving your vision away while you are still shooting a target will likely result in the shots dragging off the target. These can range from hits on the A/C line to D's, or completely missing the target.

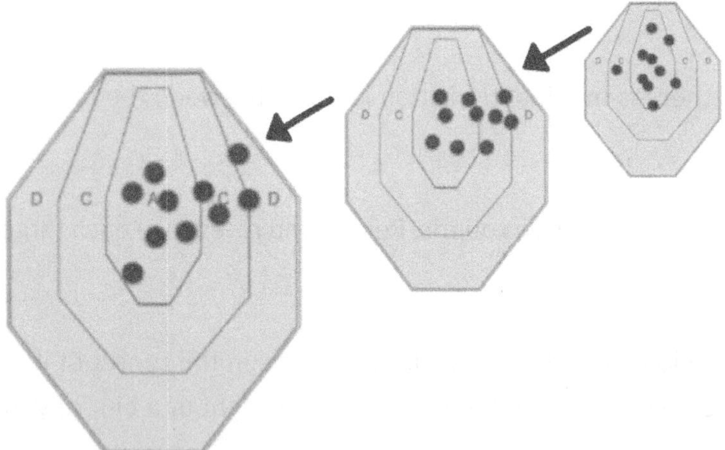

Drag on shots happen from shooting before the gun gets to the center of the target. A common theme for drag on issues is shooting as soon as you see the color of the target. The correction is looking at the center of the target and waiting for the sights to get to the spot you are looking at before firing.

Evolution:

Shoot this drill back to front and front to back. Make sure you are comfortable working either direction.

You should shoot a "goofy" order on this drill as well. A goofy order is one that makes no sense in a match setting. This would be starting or finishing on the middle target and forcing yourself to transition the gun around more.

Tips:

The most important advice to take on board for this drill is to shoot with your eyes, not your ears. This means that you should be shooting the drill where you address each target with the correct aiming scheme for you. The close ranged target should be shot using predictive shooting and a rapid-fire pair. The distant target should be shot in a disciplined manner. Make sure you see the sight return for the follow up shot. Less experienced shooters will try to "go fast" on the close stuff and "slow down" on the longer shooting. The recipe for success on this drill is to be process focused and not worried at all about how you think the drill is sounding.

Drill Progress Tracker			
Date	Drill Time	Hit Factor	Notes

Notes:

Distance Changeup

Purpose/Goal:

Get used to "changing gears" between different target types. 3.5 second par time.

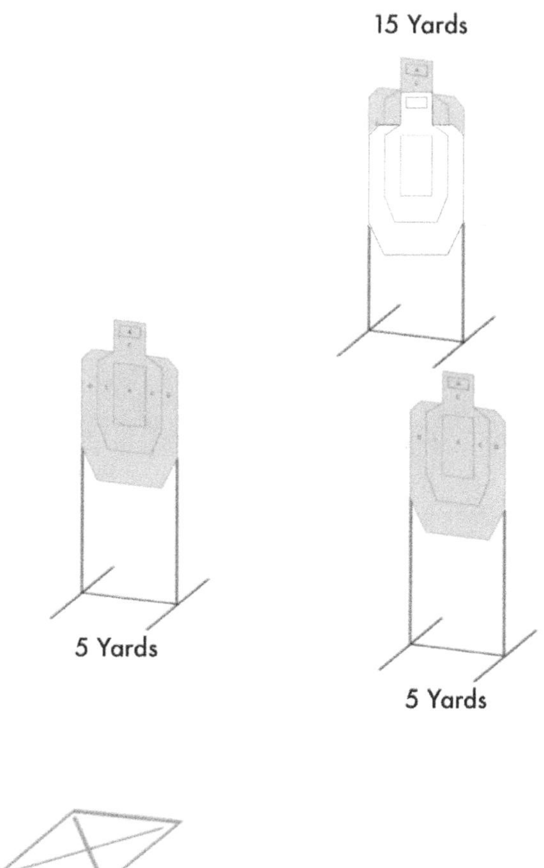

2 targets at 5 yards. A headbox or similar target should be set in between, 15 yards distant.

Setup notes:

Be sure you do not have a shoot through situation.

Instructions:

At the start, engage each target with two rounds.

Cues:

Aim! Make sure you confirm each shot. The tough shot in the back will require two distinct sight pictures. You may even need to switch your attention on to your firing hand to ensure you are not pushing the pistol off target.

The close-up targets generally induce a bit of dragging on/off the targets. You hit where you look, so make sure you keep your attention in the center of the close ranged targets to ensure you are actually done shooting them when you transition off.

Relax your firing hand/shoulders. Too much tension in these places can cause trigger freeze. It will also cause imprecise transitions in the form of overswinging.

Corrections:

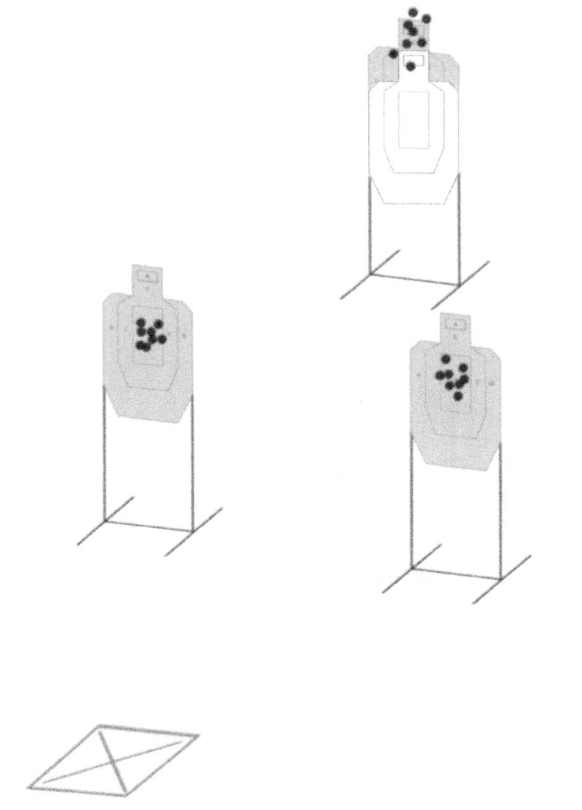

Watch your sights. The most common problem on this drill is inconsistent hits on the partial target. The main point of this exercise is for you to develop discipline on that target. You need to learn to "take your time in a hurry." Shoot quickly, but do not rush. Aim carefully, but do not waste time.

Get your eye off the front sight when you transition. Once you engage the partial you will catch yourself staring at the front sight during subsequent transitions. This needs to be actively mitigated by you paying attention to what your eyes are doing.

Evolution:

Change between different target orders. You can shoot left to right, right to left, near to far, or far to near. Each order will present the same sorts of challenges in slightly different ways. At the end of the day, this drill is about developing discipline.

Tips:

Make sure your sights are set up to work for you and not against you. Your dot or fiber front sight should not be so bright/overpowering that it is difficult for you to transition to the partial target. If you find your eye being sucked on to the dot or fiber, you should make an adjustment to the brightness level of your sight.

Drill Progress Tracker			
Date	Drill Time	Hit Factor	Notes

Notes:

MXAD

(Matt Xray Alpha Drill)

Purpose/Goal:

Get all A zone hits in under 2.75 seconds with some regularity.

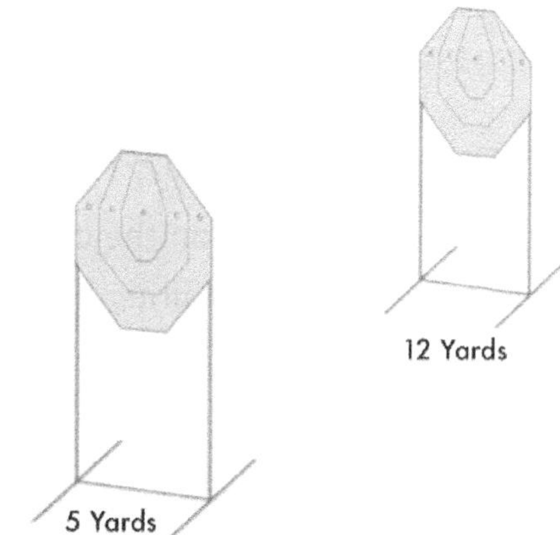

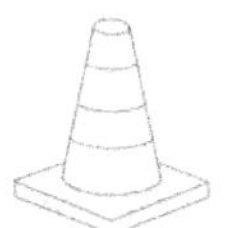

Target at 5 yards and target at 12 yards.

Setup notes:

This drill should be set up so that there is almost no swing of the gun from one target to the other. The transition is almost entirely in depth.

Instructions:

At the start signal, engage the close target with six rounds, engage the other target with two rounds.

Cues:

Relax. This is a close range, high speed drill that will induce tension in your shoulders. If your upper body gets overly tense, you will likely overswing the transition and get a poor result. Just hold the gun with your hands, do not try to fight it with your entire body. If you release that unnecessary tension, the drill only gets easier.

Look where you want to hit. It is critical you get your attention off of the sights and how they are bouncing. The motion in your sights will suck your eye in. This will then make the transition much more difficult. You need to learn to let the sights do their dance in your peripheral vision while you stay locked in to target focus.

Corrections:

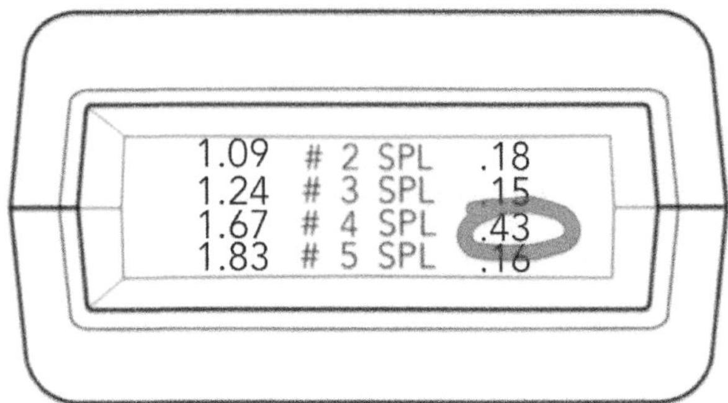

Relax your firing hand. If you are getting trigger freeze on the close target or having a hard time running the gun aggressively, the fix is likely to be relaxing your firing hand a bit. Death gripping the gun or over tension will induce the trigger freeze.

Evolution:

Shooting the far target first is an interesting evolution that I recommend. Shooting it this way often tempts people to start staring at their front sight or dot during the transition to the close target. This is counterproductive and you can start on the far target to work it out. If you shoot the far target first with six rounds, then the close target with two rounds, give yourself an extra half second on the goal time.

Tips:

You can learn a lot on this drill if you become hyper aware of what you are doing with your vision. Ideally, you want your vision to go from the center of one target to the center of the other target. Due to the close swing of the transition, it makes it difficult to keep from getting 'tunneled into" the sights while you are shooting the drill. Do your best to get your vision out to the targets where it needs to be.

Drill Progress Tracker			
Date	Drill Time	Hit Factor	Notes

Notes:

Designated Target

Purpose/Goal:

Another drill developed by Hwansik Kim, this drill will develop target transitions in a complex scenario.

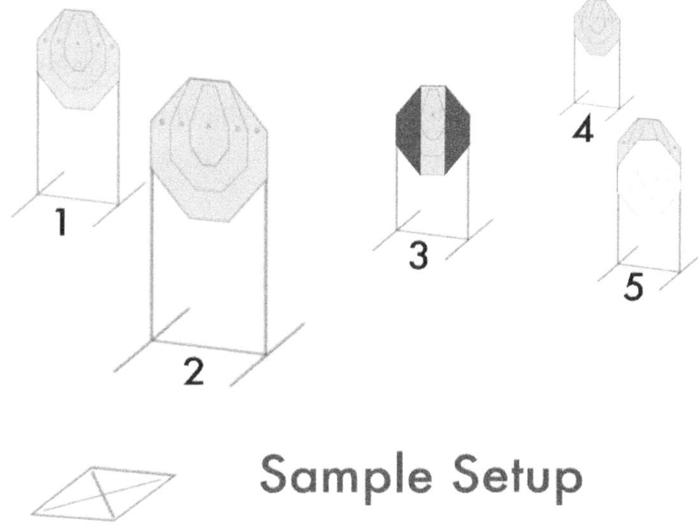

Setup notes:

Set up as many targets as you would like. The minimum number is three targets and the recommended number is five. If you go over five targets, the ammunition usage is excessive.

The targets should be of different distance and difficulty level to make the drill as interesting as possible.

Instructions:

For each set of runs, designate one target. Shoot the designated target, then another target. After engaging the second target, return to the designated target and re-engage it. After the second engagement on the designated target, engage a target you have not yet shot. Continue this pattern until all targets have been engaged. Finish the drill by engaging the designated target again. Reload as necessary throughout the drill.

Example of 5 target setup:

Target 3 is designated, and magazine capacity is 10. Engagement sequence: 3 1 3 2 3 RELOAD 4 3 5 3

Cues:

Relax your shoulders. This exercise will have you swinging your gun around all over the place. If you tense up your shoulders, it is likely you will be slow/inefficient due to overswinging the gun.

Make sure you do not "tunnel in" on the front sight or dot. This is a very common issue in this exercise because of the complexity. When people perceive the shooting as difficult, they tend to react by getting tunnel vision and nothing good will happen. Allow your head to come off the gun to find the next target.

Corrections:

This drill will bring out the worst in your transitions. You may have drag on/drag off issues. You might have difficulty locating the center of the target visually due to the visual confusion of crossing targets you are not engaging right away. You may have issues over confirming or under confirming sight pictures. Anything can happen.

Evolution:

The targets can be varied in any way imaginable. Feel free to do just that.

Drill Progress Tracker			
Date	Drill Time	Hit Factor	Notes

Notes:

Moving Targets

Purpose/Goal:

Learn to shoot and sequence moving targets.

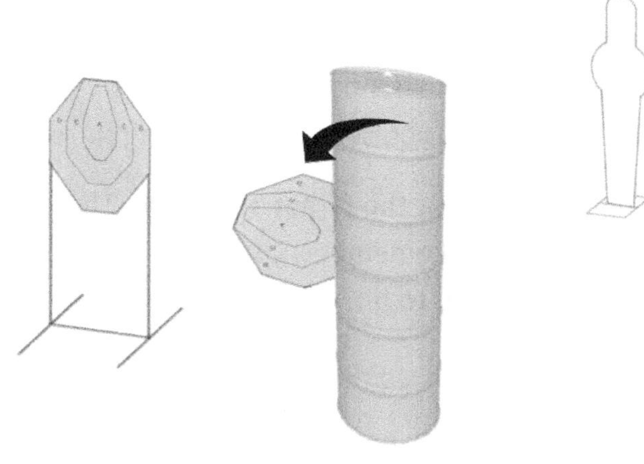

Setup notes:

Setup a simple scenario utilizing whatever props/targets you have at hand. If you wish to train on it, set it up. Utilize swingers, drop turners, max traps, windmills, or any other activated target type you want to use.

Instructions:

At the start, engage each target in your scenario.

Cues:

You should carefully create an engagement sequence. The idea here is to minimize waiting. This generally means that you will activate a moving target, shoot some other things, then engage the moving target. By varying the order of the targets you engage in your scenario you will better understand sequencing.

Track the target. The most important thing to remember when you are shooting a mover is your vision should be in the spot on the target that you wish to hit. Your gun will naturally track that spot if you keep your vision and attention focused there.

Corrections:

If you notice the activated target moving while engaging your sequence, it can sometimes pull your vision off the target you are engaging. Be on guard for this distraction as you work through your sequence. You need to get used to seeing things happen out of the corner of your eye while you shoot a target sequence, it will commonly happen in matches. Train yourself to stick to the order you visualized, and do not deviate from it regardless of what you see while shooting the sequence.

It is extremely common on swinging targets for the target be hit low. The low part of the swinger will attract your vision because it moves slower. Remember, you hit where you look. Make sure you lock your vision on the part of the target you want to hit.

Evolutions:

Make sure you set up and test yourself against any available activated target you have access to train on.

Drill Progress Tracker			
Date	Drill Time	Hit Factor	Notes

Notes:

Stage Skills/Movement

Bar Hop

Purpose/Goal:

Disconnect the shooting from your lower body/movement.

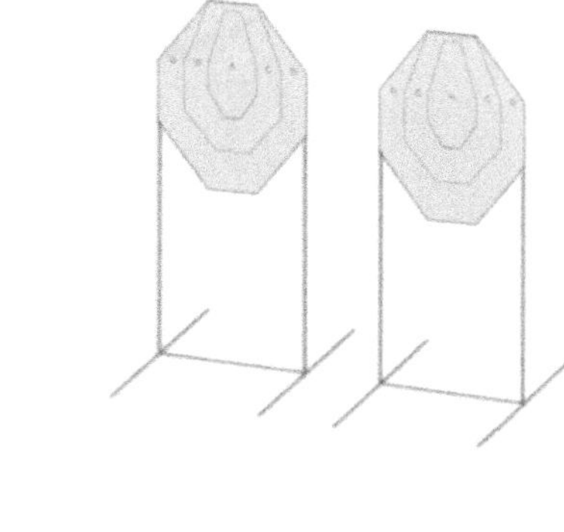

Setup notes:

For this drill you should lay a stick down on the ground to use to step over.

Instructions:

At the tone, engage each target with two rounds. Move to the opposite side of the stick and engage each target with an additional two rounds.

Make sure that you both start and finish the drill in a proper shooting stance. Do not accept an off balance or narrow stance, especially when you are finishing the drill.

Important note: The purpose of this drill is to "blend" the two shooting positions together using the stick as a contrivance to force you to move. The intent is not to view this like a competition fault line to assess penalties, but just to give you a mechanism to force you to move.

Cues:

If you are more robotic in style and not fluidly engaging targets on each side of the stick, start thinking in terms of shooting the targets continuously instead of a shoot-move-shoot mindset.

Get your stance wide so you do not have to drop step to move. You should have minimal extra or false steps.

Corrections:

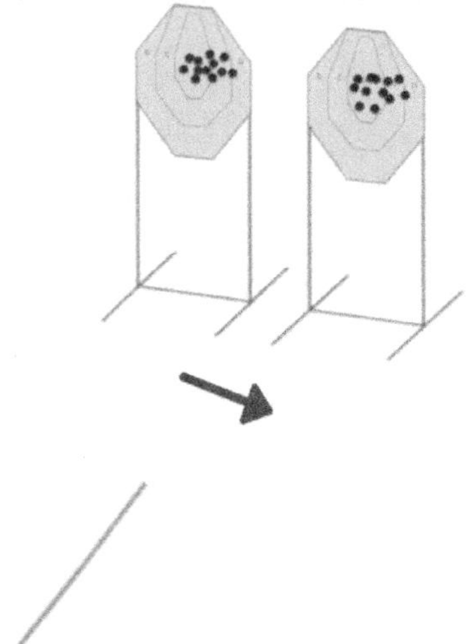

If your hits are trending in the direction of your movement, make sure you are shooting target focused and not sight focused. Look at the spot on the target exactly where you want to hit.

Ensure you are ready to move again when you finish a repetition of the drill. This does not show up on the timer when you are at the range. However, failure to learn the correct habit will hurt you in a competition setting.

Evolution:

In addition to varying target difficulty and direction of movement, you should feel free to adjust the distance of the actual movements from one engagement to the next. You need to be proficient in all sorts of circumstances. Make sure you are creating these circumstances in your training. Refer to the drills for mounted and unmounted movement if you are unclear on this idea.

Tips:

The hard part of this drill is fulfilling the requirements of shooting in the appropriate places (feet on the correct side of the stick) along with making your shooting style fluid. It will require training and repetitions to make this feel comfortable and smooth. The key thing to keep in mind is your gun should stay up and ready to go and you should always be looking to engage the next target.

This drill is a good one to use video on. The assessment of your movement style is virtually impossible to do without seeing it from a third person point of view. If you do not have a training partner watching you, be sure to check what is going on by using video.

Drill Progress Tracker			
Date	Drill Time	Hit Factor	Notes

Notes:

Unmounted Movement

Purpose/Goal:

Learn proper technique to move into and out of shooting positions. The movement distance should be long enough that it is sensible to dismount the gun completely and run aggressively.

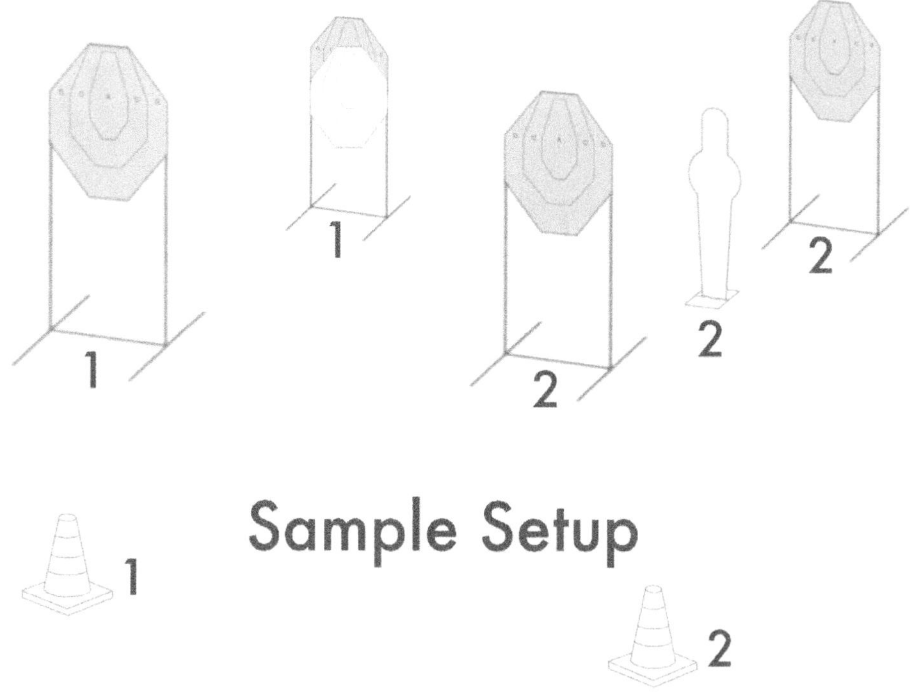

Setup notes:

Set a scenario that you have at least two shooting positions with a few targets to engage. Set these positions at least five steps apart.

Instructions:

Engage the targets in the first shooting position then move to the second position. From position two, engage the appropriate targets.

Cues:

Have your gun up ready to shoot as you enter a shooting position. You should see your sights in your field of view just before you mean to start shooting the first target in your second shooting location. It is not good enough just to have the gun up, you need to be actually seeing the sights. You save time by starting to shoot earlier and you need to see your sights to shoot.

After you finish a repetition of the exercise, you should consciously check to make sure you are standing properly. Remember: Knees bent, wide stance, 50/50 weight distribution, ready to MOVE.

Corrections:

When you move, move as athletically and aggressively as possible. After four or five repetitions, you should be out of breath. This ensures that you are training to maximize your physical potential. If you do training in slow motion expect to overrun positions in real matches when you are shooting "juiced up" from adrenaline.

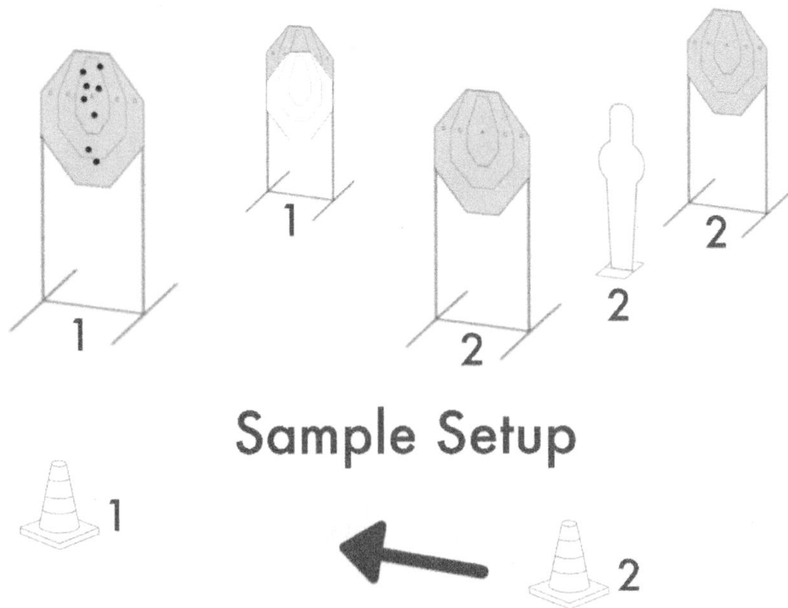

Slow down into the shooting position gently. Use soft steps to come to a clean stop so you can start engaging targets when your sights dictate. If you see your sights bouncing around an excessive amount when you are slowing to a stop, you need to fix the issue with your lower body mechanics.

Stop so you can move again immediately. You need to build the habit of stopping with your feet wide apart, square to the target, knees bent and 50/50 weight distribution.

Evolution:

It is important that you work on the whole spectrum of target difficulties and distances with this exercise. Close ranged targets require little in the way of aiming. They allow you to "cheat" the marksmanship rules in many respects. It is important to train close shooting so you see how early you can get moving from the first position and shooting in the second. You simply will not know what you can get away with unless you try some things in training.

If you are comfortable with this drill in two positions, try adding more. It can be as simple as shooting position one, position two, then back to position one. This will increase the difficulty by forcing you to set up properly in position two so you can aggressively get back to position one. Remember you are training to shoot multi position stages and you need to have correct technique in that circumstance. Testing this out in training is a wise idea.

Tips:

When practicing the proper movement technique, it is extremely helpful to have a competent training partner that can help spot problems. When it comes to movement training in particular, most people do not have awareness of what each part of their body is doing. The shooting mechanics layered on top of the movement and the time pressure is too much to keep track of. Your training partner can help cut through that and inform you about what your body is doing.

In the absence of a training partner, use your phone to video your runs. This can help eliminate any doubt in your mind as to what is actually happening.

Drill Progress Tracker			
Date	Drill Time	Hit Factor	Notes

Notes:

Mounted Movement

Purpose/Goal:

Perform short movements with the gun mounted and ready to fire. Shoot as the sights dictate.

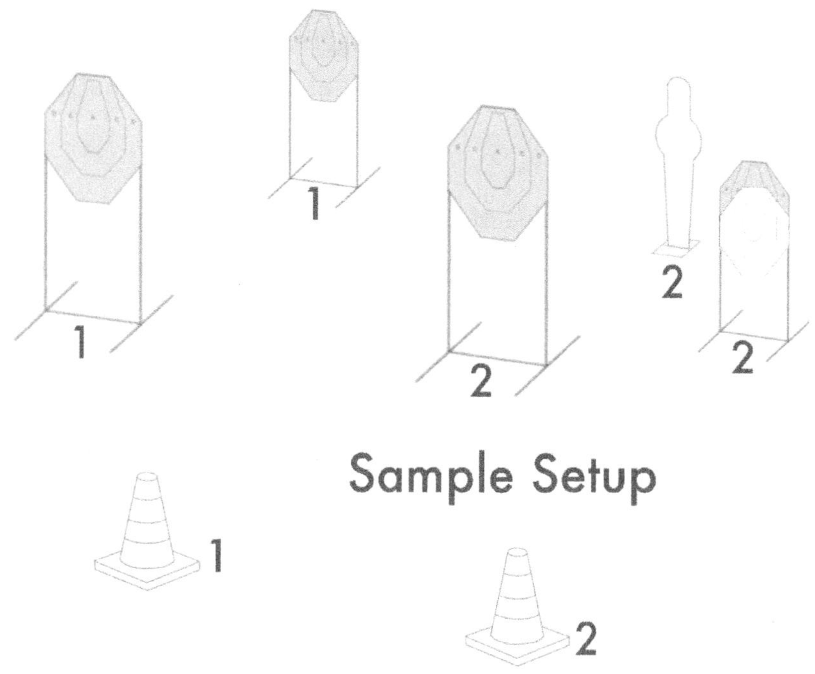

Setup notes:

Build a scenario that has targets shot from two positions. Set the positions between 1 and 4 steps apart.

Instructions:

Start in any desired position. Engage the targets from the appropriate shooting positions.

Cues:

Make sure you keep your gun up and ready to shoot. Always be looking to fire the next shot sooner.

Focus on blending the positions together rather than moving in between them quickly.

Make sure that you finish the exercise in a proper stance. You should be set up wide, low and 50/50 weight distribution if possible.

Corrections:

If the target or targets that you are engaging while your weight is off balance have poor hits, remember that your ability to shoot using predictive fire is going to be hampered. When you are off balance, moving, or the circumstances are in any way more challenging than normal, switch away from predictive shooting to reactive shooting. Make sure you are seeing your sights recover between shots. As you gain more and more stability (as your movement completes) you can switch to predictive shooting.

Evolution:

Run this exercise with movement in any direction. It is a quite common situation at matches where you will be keeping the gun in action and engaging targets while you move only a couple steps. It is important that you feel comfortable and secure in all possible scenarios.

Be sure to vary the target difficulty, especially on the targets you are engaging during the movement. Easier, low risk targets will lend themselves to more aggressive movement. Tougher targets will make movement during engagement more difficult. Work all these potential scenarios.

Tips:

It is important you do not conflate the idea of blending two positions together by shooting as you move between them with the idea of shooting faster. When learning these skills, many people early in their shooting career naturally want to shoot faster during this exercise. It is important that you DO NOT give in to this temptation. The movement serves the shooting and not the other way around.

Drill Progress Tracker			
Date	Drill Time	Hit Factor	Notes

Notes:

Hitting the Spot

Purpose/Goal:

Learn to navigate with precision through complicated target/positioning sequences.

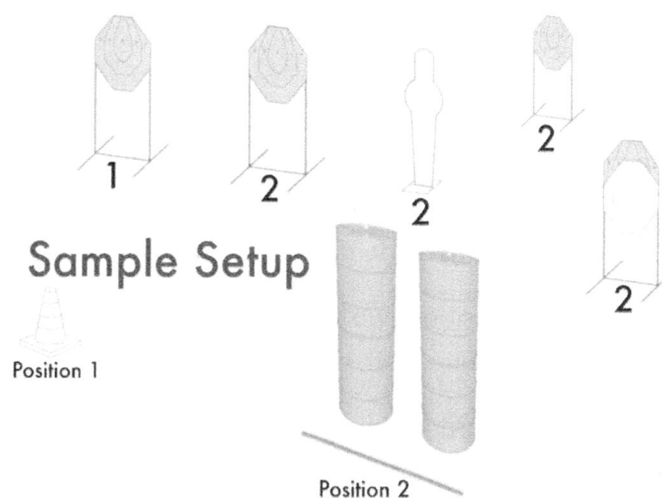

Setup notes:

This drill requires you to construct a narrow opening in between two vision barriers. Set the vision barriers close together to create an opening. When engaging the required targets from that shooting position, your shots all must pass through the opening. This is denoted as position two in the diagram.

You should use a fault line to force yourself to stay back from the opening in the vision barriers. When properly constructed, you will not be able to see all the targets in position two without shifting yourself around using your legs.

You will also need one conventional shooting position. There only needs to be one target associated with this position. This is denoted as position one in the diagram.

Instructions:

Start in position one. Shoot the appropriate targets from that spot. Move to position two and engage the appropriate targets. When you are finished in position two move back to position one and engage the appropriate target or targets from that location.

Cues:

When it comes to moving through this drill, the most important thing you can do is to get your stance nice and wide. If you set the drill up properly, you will need to make a few small position changes when working through position two of the drill. If you are standing tall with your feet close together, the difficulty of this will be magnified quickly. Get low, get wide and be ready to move.

When it comes to shooting, the best practice is to react to what you are seeing. You will be off balance or unstable as you work thorough position two. If your sights look good, start shooting. It is common on this drill for people to be far too conservative as it relates to what the sights need to look like.

Corrections:

If you find yourself excessively off balance or unstable, the likely cause is that you are making yourself lean a little bit to see a target as opposed to moving the extra half step so you can stand comfortably and engage it. This problem is common. I strongly recommend you move an extra little bit to make the shooting easier.

Evolution:

The main variable you can focus on to change things up is the opening in position two. By altering the width of the opening and the distance of that opening from the fault line you can make life for yourself extremely easy or very difficult. As you improve, do not be shy about making this drill very tough.

You should also alter your path through position two. You can work the position left to right or right to left and that will usually make things change quite a bit.

Do not be shy about stipulating a "goofy" order of target engagement. Goofy orders are orders that make no sense for a match. For example, shooting the center target in position two then the left and then finally the right target would add challenge. This makes for good training even if you would not do it in a match.

Tips:

The most important thing you need to bear in mind for this drill is, it requires you to have a plan. You need to take the drill seriously. Walk it through just like you would in a match. Find "markers" (spots on the vision barrier or the group) that help you find your shooting position. You must have a specific strategy to locate the exact, correct shooting locations when you move to position two. Do not neglect this step.

Drill Progress Tracker			
Date	Drill Time	Hit Factor	Notes

Notes:

Shooting on the Move

Purpose/Goal:

Ability to shoot accurately while you move from one location to another.

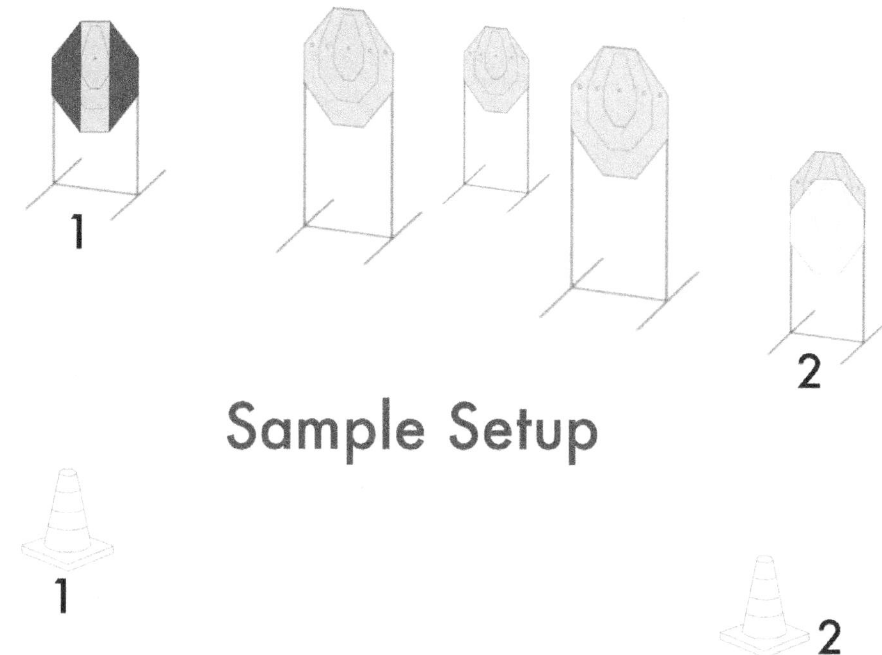

Setup notes:

Set up two shooting positions about 10 yards apart. Each position should be marked and have a single target set up to be challenging enough to encourage you to stop to shoot it. In between these two positions should be a "free fire zone" where you will be engaging the other targets you have set up while you move.

Instructions:

Engage the target in position one and then start moving to position two. Engage the targets in the "free fire zone" as effectively as possible while you move. Engage the target in position two from position two when you arrive.

Cues:

When there is movement involved, be it you are moving or the target moving, it is necessary to shoot with your vision focused on the target. This is the most missed element of shooting on the move and it cannot be repeated often enough. If you shoot focused on your front sight or dot, you will tend to "drag" hits in the same direction that you are moving. When you are focused on the sights, it becomes exceedingly difficult to "track" the target. When there is movement involved, you do need to continually adjust your aim. This adjustment happens nearly automatically when you focus on the target.

When you are shooting on the move, disregard what you think you know in terms of predictive shooting. Your ability to predict how the gun is going to track is greatly diminished when you add in the movement element. Switch to reactive shooting and you will see your results improve. Do NOT rush your shooting. You are saving time by shooting as you move so it is not necessary to shoot at maximum possible pace.

Bend your knees and get down nice and low. You are going to want to use your lower body to maintain stability. If you see your sights bouncing around an unacceptable amount, you will fix that with lower body mechanics.

Corrections:

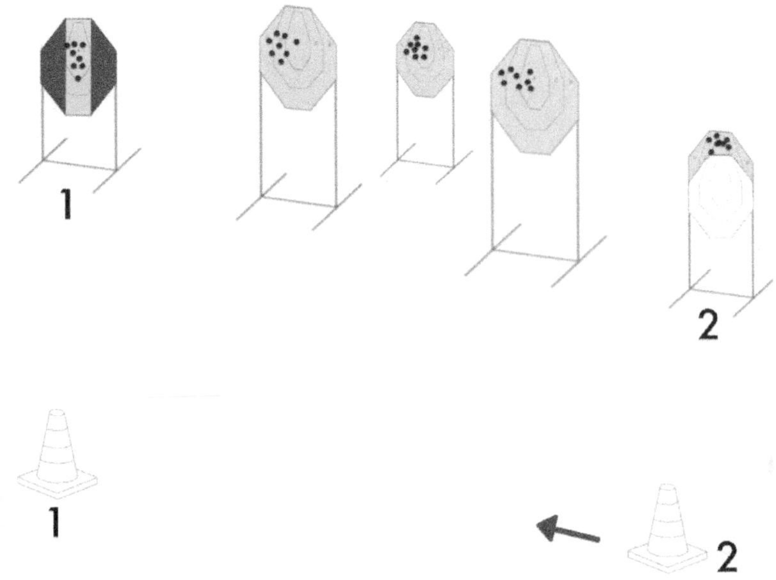

If you shoot focused on your sights, you will have hits trending in the direction you are travelling. It is imperative you shoot target focused.

Shoot reacting to your sights for each shot. Try to stay away from predictive shooting. If you are feeling rushed and shooting wildly, you will struggle. React to what you are seeing for each shot and the results will be excellent.

Evolution:

The main variable you should play around with on this exercise is the target difficulty/distance. Understanding what your abilities and limitations are is going to help you get an accurate "gut feeling" for what precisely you can get away with as it relates to shooting while you move. Don't be shy about putting no-shoots up to test yourself. Try setting the targets at very close range and see how aggressively you can move and still get acceptable hits. Experimentation is important.

Tips:

Moving through the drill while holding a half full water bottle upside-down at arm's length like you would hold your pistol can show you a lot about how your movement affects your sights. Notice how the water in the bottle moves as you experiment. Try setting your feet down more gently as you move and try taking shorter steps. Your sights are moving in the same way the water does.

Drill Progress Tracker			
Date	Drill Time	Hit Factor	Notes

Notes:

Track the A Zone

Purpose/Goal:

This drill was developed by Hwansik Kim in order to learn to "track" the A zone around and through vision barriers while you move and to ensure efficient movement.

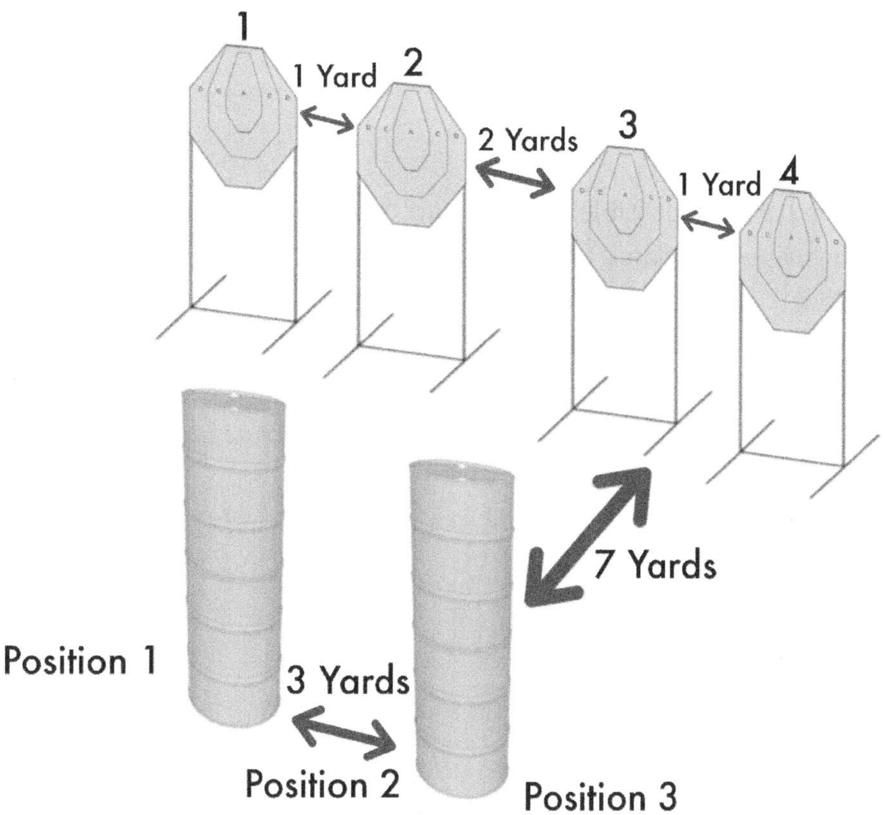

2 vision barriers and 4 targets

Setup notes:

Ensure you use an opaque vision barrier. Middle targets are 2 yards apart. Each outside target is 1 yard from the nearest middle target. Line of targets are 7 yards from the vision barrier.
Vision barriers should be 3 yards apart.

Instructions:

Engage all the targets in the sequence of your choosing. It could be any order. 1 2 3 4, 4 3 2 1, 2,1,3,4, etc. The only consideration is about where the targets are shot from. You always shoot target 1 from the left side of the vision barrier (position 1). You always shoot target 4 from the right side of the right vision barrier (position 3). Targets 2 and 3 are shot from the zone in between the vision barriers (position 2).

It is NOT a requirement of this drill that you be forced into any leaning. Do not place down fault lines.

Cues:

Be aware of the physical position of the vision barrier while you are shooting. It is common that bullets skim the vision barriers on this drill. You need to be comfortable quickly moving around and through stages and shooting scenarios similar to this exercise without shooting walls. Learning to cut it as close as you can on this drill will help.

Do a walkthrough of the drill with your arms at full extension. Use your gun for dry runs if the range permits it.

Corrections:

Look "through" the vision barrier if possible. The key part of this drill has you moving around as you are looking for A zones, while vision barriers get in the way. If you are noticing that your hits are sporadic, this is usually the problem.

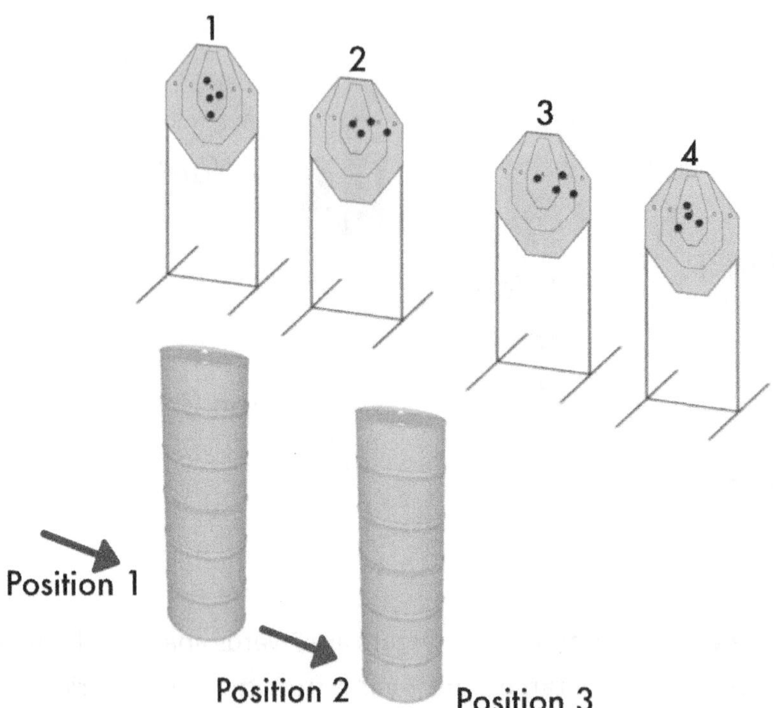

If you focus on your front sight or dot, instead of the target, expect to see hits dispersing in the same direction you are moving. Return to target focused shooting to correct this issue.

Evolutions:

A good test for this drill is to stand stationary in position 2 and engage each target. Do this until you get a good baseline for your performance. You can then take that baseline score and attempt to beat it shooting the drill in normal way, forcing yourself to use all 3 shooting positions.

Tips:

Walkthrough the exercise very carefully. Do it just like you would in a match. Make sure that you hold out your arms and practice tracking the A zone in 3-dimensional space.

Drill Progress Tracker			
Date	Drill Time	Hit Factor	Notes

Notes:

Go/Stop

Purpose/Goal:

This drill was developed by Hwansik Kim in order to ingrain the ability to stay low and ready to move.

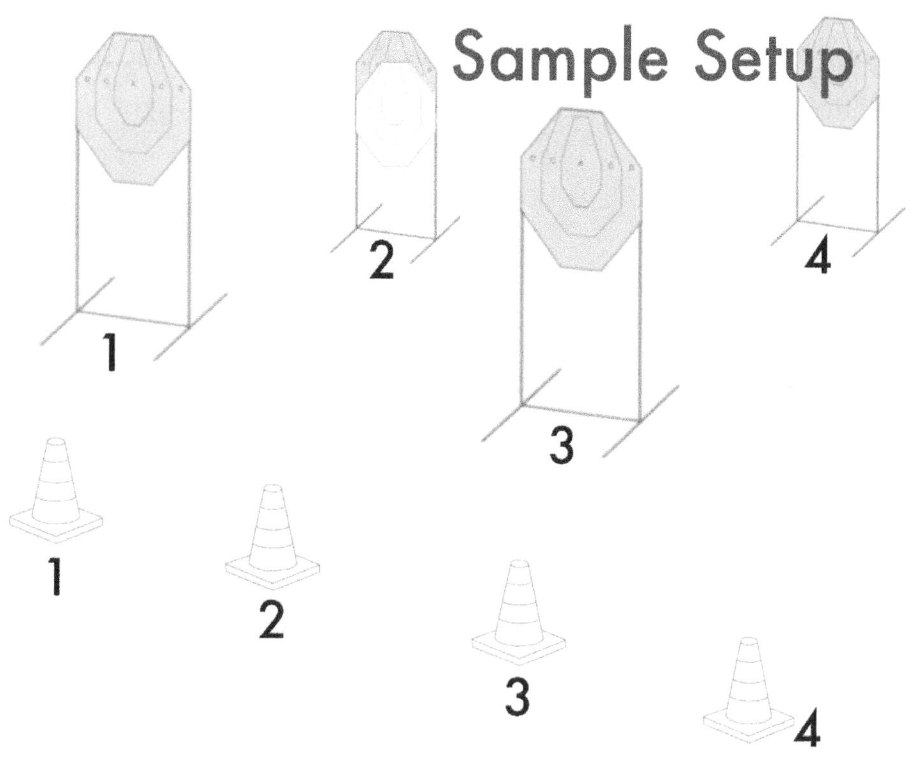

Setup notes:

Set up several shooting positions marked by cones. Each position needs to have a target associated with it.

Instructions:

Start at cone one. Engage the target associated with cone one, then move to cone two and engage the appropriate target. After cone two, move back to cone one and engage the associated target. Continue systematically working through the cones in this order, finishing after returning to cone 1. 1 2 1 3 1 4 1

Cues:

Move aggressively. This drill is physically demanding; we call it a "smoker." It is important that you leverage all your athletic ability to the greatest extent possible. This drill will not be an effective training tool without going at it aggressively to produce the errors you are attempting to fix.

Do your best to get your stance set up nice and wide. You want to have the ability to efficiently move to the next shooting position when you get done shooting.

Make sure you do not have extraneous steps or movement when you exit a shooting position. This means taking small steps to change your stance, coiling your body up like a spring, or drop stepping should not occur when you are trying to move. You should stop and stabilize in position already "pre-loaded" and ready to move.

Corrections:

If you feel like you are stopping rough into a shooting position, you want to take short steps as you approach the next position to help you decelerate. If you attempt to stop in the space of a single step, you will likely be unable to control your body and get it stopped properly.

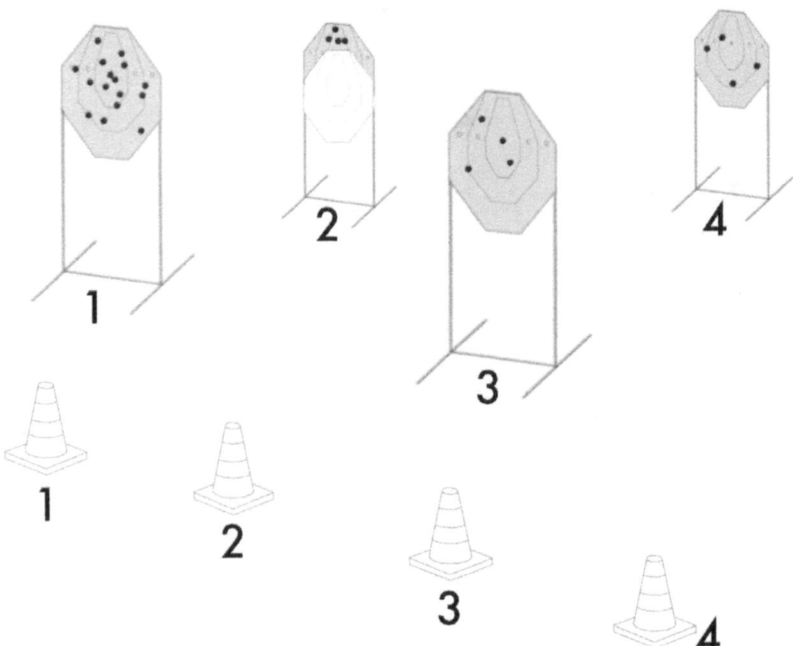

If you have widely scattered hits on the target you are engaging, make sure that you are waiting to get an appropriate sight picture on the targets.

Evolution:

Try this drill with targets of different difficulty and risk levels. Close ranged targets will place the emphasis for this drill on fast changes of direction. More difficult targets will punish you for not stopping correctly and getting to stability to shoot accurately. Work on the whole spectrum of possibilities.

Vary the direction of your movement. This drill can be run laterally, up range/downrange, or diagonally. As you improve, test out the less common movement directions to learn more.

Tips:

This drill is very physically demanding. If you are doing it properly, it will take substantial amounts of time to shoot the drill, physically recover and shoot the drill again. It is wise to set up a second drill alongside this one to avoid extended downtime and prolong the training session.

This drill is a good to use video on. The assessment of your movement style is virtually impossible to do without seeing it from a third person point of view. If you do not have a training partner watching you, be sure to check what is going on by using video.

Drill Progress Tracker			
Date	Drill Time	Hit Factor	Notes

Notes:

Mock Stage Training

Purpose/Goal:

Learn to smoothly execute a stage

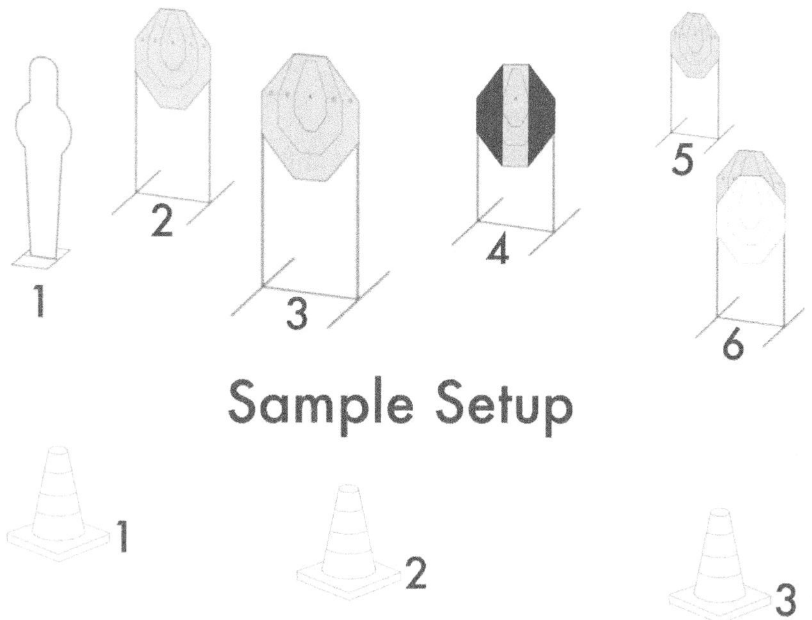

Setup notes:

Construct a multi position "stage." Using markers, such as cones, on the ground to denote shooting positions. Setting up non-falling steel and multiple paper targets is ideal to give target variety. Stipulate an order to engage the targets and what position to engage them from. Feel free to use the same target from more than one position.

Example: Engage Target 1-4 from position one. Engage Targets 3-6 from position two. Engage targets 2-3 from position three.

Instructions:

Shoot the stage to the best of your ability. Make sure that the stage is executed without needing to consciously think about what the next step is. Ensure that your shooting is accurate and disciplined.

After shooting your stage, change the position/target order for the next run.

Cues:

You should shoot your mock stage just like a match stage. Do not focus on training cues during your stage run.

Corrections:

Be on guard for undisciplined shooting. Apply the correct aiming scheme for each target. Do not over confirm or under confirm.

Evolution:

As your execution improves, start changing the stage. Eventually, you should be able to change the order of targets/positions every single run and be able to hold a good performance. Once you can pick an order, visualize it and then execute it without hesitation, you are in excellent shape.

You should alternate start positions and shooting style (one handed, kneeling, prone, etc.).

Tips:

The main reason to do full stage training is to observe your abilities. You should take this as an opportunity to test your shooting under a variety of circumstances. You want to make sure that you spot weak points in technique or mindset so you can do additional training on those areas.

Consider the "training philosophy" section at the front of this book. The way you shoot, your style, your inclinations and your habits are what you are assessing when doing this exercise. You are not trying to accomplish anything specific by doing this training. The larger goal here is to see what happens and spot the 'big picture" trends.

Ask yourself the following:

- What mistakes am I making repeatedly?
- What specific exercises should I do to mitigate these mistakes?
- Am I confident that I can perform to an acceptable level on a random set of competition stages?

The above questions are just examples of the type of questions you should be interested in. The way to summarize the best mindset for this type of training is, you spot the patterns in your shooting that are holding you back as a shooter.

Drill Progress Tracker			
Date	Drill Time	Hit Factor	Notes

Notes:

SPECIAL DRILLS

Confirmation Drill

Purpose/Goal:

Build an understanding of how different methods of confirmation/aiming scheme affect the outcome on the target.

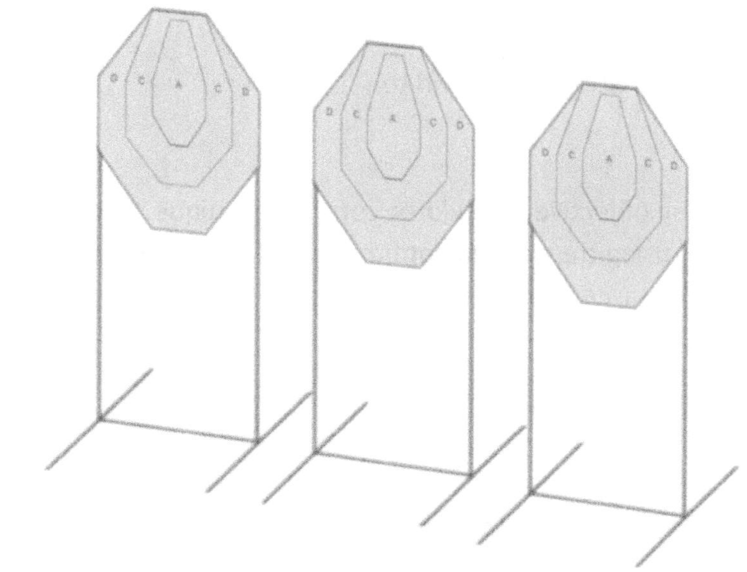

Setup notes:

Set up targets for comparison at 5 yards distance.

Instructions:

This drill will consist of many repetitions for each aiming scheme you are testing.

The start position for the drill is a two-handed grip on the gun, aimed at the bottom of the target stand of the target you are shooting.

At the tone, engage the very center of the A zone using the aiming scheme you are testing on that target. Fire one round only. Note the time.

Do the correct number of repetitions on each target. For example: Engage target 1 using confirmation 1 for 10 repetitions. Engage target two with confirmation 2 for 10 reps. Engage target 3 with confirmation 3 for 10 reps.

At the end of this test you should have a good sample of data that gives you an idea of the time and accuracy difference between different levels of confirmation. Check out the "tips" section of this drill if this is unclear to you.

Cues:

Make sure you use the confirmation you intend to.

Corrections:

This drill does not have any objective to build or correct technique. Your only job is to ensure that you actually execute each shot using the desired confirmation. This means that you need to create good data for yourself, not necessarily a good result on the target. Make sure you rigidly enforce your desired confirmation level.

Make sure you use the confirmation you intend to.

Evolution:

Feel free to attempt any confirmation/aiming scheme on any target type. This will give you more data and a good sense for what outcome you can expect given the particular aiming strategy.

This drill was developed using the following scheme:

Confirmation 1:

Kinesthetic alignment only. You "feel" your arms are pointed in the correct place and then you shoot. NO VISUAL CONFIRMATION

Confirmation 2:

You react to the color of your sight crossing your intended aiming area. With an optic you shoot as soon as you see the optical color. With a fiber optic iron sight setup, you shoot when you see the color of your front sight.

Confirmation 3:

Your dot is stopped and stable in your intended aiming area. Your dot should appear as a dot and not as a streak. With iron sights you see the front sight stopped through the rear notch.

This is a near perfect sight picture sort of setup.

As you move up in confirmation it will take more time, but the result on the targets will be much cleaner.

Shooting iron sights you might find it useful to distinguish between a perfectly aligned sight picture and seeing the front sight through the rear notch, but perhaps a bit misaligned. You might think of the sights slightly misaligned as confirmation 2.5.

There is no limit to what you can experiment with on this drill. Just remember, your goal with the drill is to put in a specific aiming scheme and then assess your outcome. You are not trying to get a "good" or "bad" outcome. You just want to see how it all works. Once you get a sense of this, it should be easy to apply these concepts to your other training.

Tips:

This drill was developed by Hwansik Kim in order to isolate the effect of the aiming strategy, confirmation level and aiming scheme on the target.

The component of target acquisition and engagement where you have a lot of control over speed is how you aim the gun at the target. More specifically, it is the reference you are using to confirm the gun is aimed. Traditionally, the expectation is that every sight picture looks the same on every target. People are generally trained in non-practical shooting context to get a "perfect" sight picture for each and every shot. As soon as you move beyond level 1 in this text that is no longer the advice or expectation.

Learning how much "perfect" sight picture you can trade away in order to go faster is one of the most important things that a practical shooter can do. As soon as you understand what sort of sight picture will produce what sort of outcome all you need to do is train yourself to address each target with the optimal strategy and your results will be excellent.

This exercise exists to strip away every other layer and show you the effect of the aiming strategy on the target outcome.

Drill Progress Tracker			
Date	Drill Time	Hit Factor	Notes

Notes:

Measurement Drill

Purpose/Goal:

Build an understanding of how much energy it requires to return your pistol to point of aim after firing a shot.

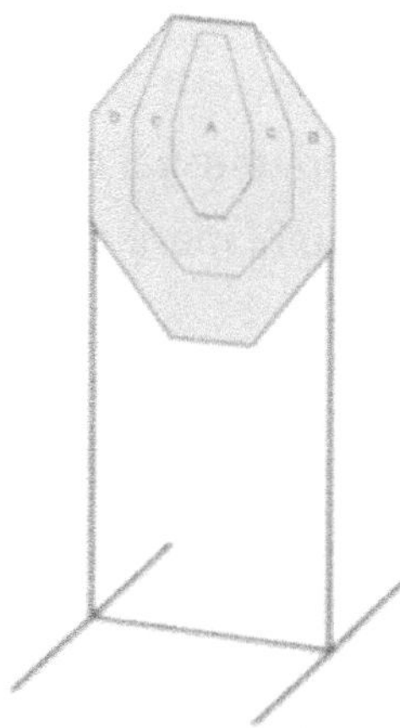

Setup notes:

This drill requires only one target. 5 yards is a good distance to use.

Instructions:

Grip your pistol properly. Engage the very center of the A zone of your target with one carefully fired shot. DO NOT PUSH THE GUN BACK DOWN AFTER FIRING THE SHOT. Fire a second shot at the point the gun recoiled to without re-aiming to your aimpoint. The distance between the two shots is the information you are looking for. This will measure how much the muzzle rises and thus how much it should be returned. Repeat this until you have a good sense of the distance the muzzle rises.

After you understand the distance of muzzle rise, start returning the muzzle back down to the original point of aim between the first and second shots. Start going slowly (1 or 2 seconds between shots). As you continue to train and understand, increase your speed until you are shooting as fast as you can pull the trigger.

Cues:

This drill does not have any objective to build or correct technique. Your only job is to learn how much energy it requires to return your pistol to point of aim after firing a shot.

Corrections:

This drill does not have any objective to build or correct technique.

Evolution:

Feel free to attempt this drill in unusual circumstances. Consider trying leans, awkward positions, or one-handed shooting in order to build more understanding.

Tips:

The point of this drill is to measure how much the muzzle rises when you fire a shot. This might seem like a strange thing to do but with a little more context it will make sense.

This drill was developed by Hwansik Kim to work on the concept of recoil control. Most people have an incorrect concept of recoil control. They believe that it will take a lot of muscle mass, force and effort to control the recoil of their pistol. The point of this drill is to facilitate you demonstrating to yourself that none of this is true. You do not need to work all that hard in order to bring your pistol down out of recoil. The muzzle of your pistol should only marginally rise when you fire a shot. The main issue you will have as you learn to shoot faster and faster is battling your tendency to overcorrect or overcontrol that recoil. Once you internalize how little force is required to return the gun it should improve your concept of recoil control.

Drill Progress Tracker			
Date	Drill Time	Hit Factor	Notes

Notes:

Sight Tracking

Purpose/Goal:

Learn to watch your sights. Test the cause and affect relationships related to your grip.

No targets needed

Setup notes:

Do not use a target. Fire the rounds in a safe direction into the backstop. Do not even aim at a particular spot on the backdrop.

Instructions:

Aim your gun in a safe direction. Watch the sights closely as you fire your gun. Assess how the sights move.

Cues:

Pay attention to your hands. Notice how the sights track differently as you adjust your hand pressure.

Corrections:

Keep your eyes open. If you are not sure what you just saw, you did not see enough. The gun is telling you a story as it moves in recoil, you need to keep your eyes open to be aware of the story.

Drill Progress Tracker			
Date	Drill Time	Hit Factor	Notes

Notes:

Classifier Training

Purpose/Goal:

Train on and experiment with USPSA classifier stages in order to expand your knowledge and skillset.

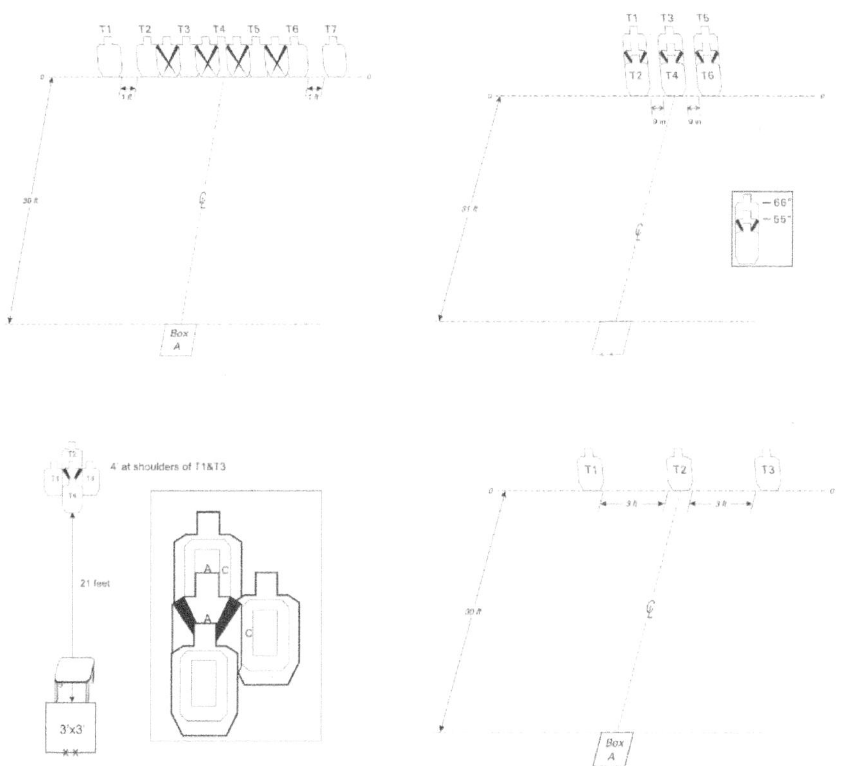

ANY DESIRED CLASSIFIER

Setup notes:

Setup any desired USPSA Classifier.

Instructions:

Set up any desired USPSA Classifier.

Shoot the classifier stage the desired number of times. Note time, points and hit factor. Your goal is to competently execute the skills required. You should be able to consistently execute the classifier without incurring penalties. Your goal is to consistently shoot over 85% of the national high hit factor.

Drill Progress Tracker			
Date	Drill Time	Hit Factor	Notes

Notes:

Rhythm Drill

Purpose/Goal:

"Flip the script" on target transition technique to better understand the technique.

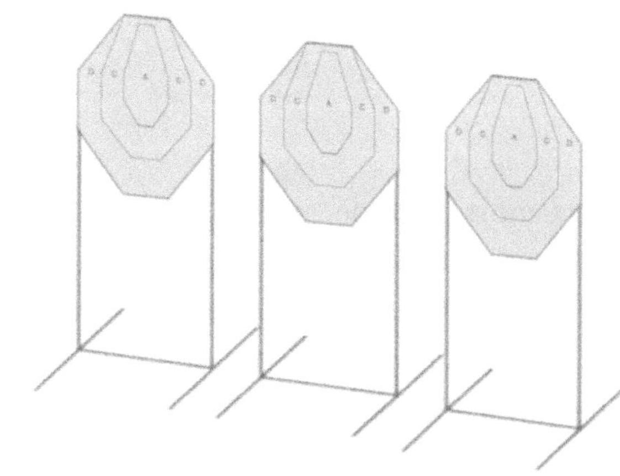

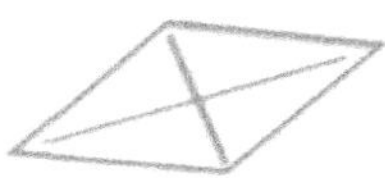

Setup notes:

Set up an "El Prez" array. Make sure the spacing is close (1 yard apart) and the distance is near (7 yards maximum).

Instructions:

WARNING: DO NOT DO THIS IN A MATCH. THIS IS A TRAINING EXERCISE ONLY.

Establish a "rhythm" in your mind you are going to shoot. Each shot must be evenly spaced. This means you will shoot every split and transition in the same time. For example: You will shoot all .50 splits/transitions. You can pick any pace you desire, but I recommend you start slowly to understand the drill. As you go along, start speeding up the rhythm.

You are REQUIRED to shoot the selected rhythm irrespective of anything else. As you speed up, you will eventually be pulling the trigger without any visual confirmation. This is a normal part of the drill.

The idea is by keeping to a rhythm, your job will become getting your eyes exactly where they need to be and bringing the gun to the next target precisely.

Keep speeding up the rhythm until you find your breaking point. Eventually you will be unable to hold things together at the rhythm you are shooting. Back off just a little bit from that point and you will have found a good 'training zone" to stick in.

Cues:

Relax. As you speed up, there will be excess tension coming into your firing hand, your shoulders and your arms. If you can let go of that tension, you might be shocked how quickly and effectively you can transition the gun.

Look exactly where you want to hit. The gun will go to where you are looking as if on autopilot as long as you stay loose and relaxed in your upper body.

Corrections:

Drag on/drag off transitions are the most common issue on this drill. Especially as you speed up to a .18 to .20 pace of splits (or beyond) it is very difficult to keep your vision under control. It is a very natural mistake to mentally leave a target before you are done shooting it, or to be too slow getting the gun to the next target. Remember, on this drill you are FORCED to shoot your predetermined cadence. Waiting for visual confirmation on a target is not allowed because it would undermine the rhythm aspect of the drill.

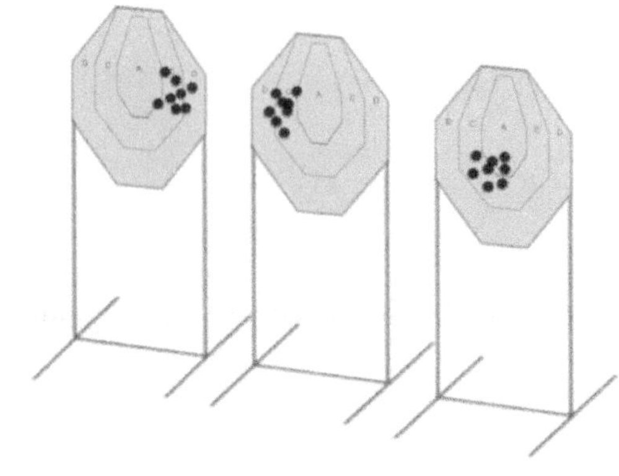

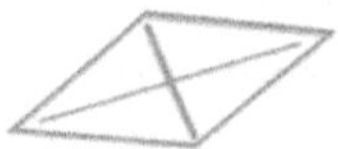

Hits clustered outside of the A-zone is indicative of looking at the wrong spot on the target. You need to get your vision to the center of the target to drive the gun there. If you aren't finding the center of the target with your eyes, hits will cluster in strange places.

Evolution:

If you are shooting at your maximum pace and still unable to break your technique, you can simply widen out the setup of the targets. This will push you to the edge.

Feel fry to apply the "rhythm" concept to any other drill or scenario. Establish a rhythm that makes sense and work within it.

Tips:

Assessing your draw speed is not a part of this drill. As you speed up your shooting, you will likely be tempted to speed up the draw along with it. This is unnecessary and counterproductive. The only piece you should be worried about is the actual shooting. Let your draw be what it naturally is so you are doing the exercise with a good grip.

Drill Progress Tracker			
Date	Drill Time	Hit Factor	Notes

Notes:

Special Challenges

Purpose/Goal:

Become comfortable with non-standard scenarios that may present themselves in matches. Things such as off body start positions, shooting in awkward positions, or shooting one handed.

Make sure that you can aggressively execute shooting accurately in a variety of positions and circumstances.

If you are getting erratic results, make sure you are not doing predictive shooting. It is not productive to get a marginal time advantage, but have spotty results. Predictive shooting is best done when the circumstances are more normal.

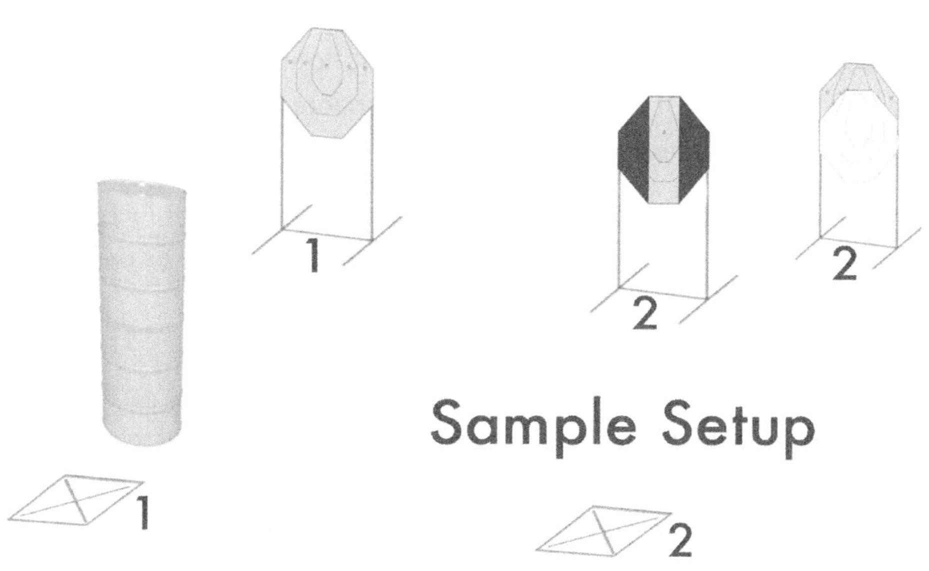

Setup notes:

Construct challenges that you expect to see in future matches. Keep the scenarios small, simple and focused.

Things like leans, crouches, one handed, prone and other types of shooting positions and circumstances should be trained to the point that you can aggressively navigate them with speed in a match.

Instructions:

At the tone, engage the targets in your setup while observing the special conditions you have set for yourself. Example: Engaging the targets while kneeling would be the procedure if you are working on kneeling shooting.

Cues:

When the shooting is awkward or difficult, remember shooting fundamentals. Confirm sight alignment and carefully stack pressure onto the trigger for each demanding shot and you will get the best chance at a good score you could possibly have that day.

Constantly evaluate the aiming scheme you are using for each target. Are you over/under confirming for the given target? Look for opportunities to increase your speed or optimize your points scored.

Corrections:

Pay close attention to the sight pictures you are seeing. As the shooting gets more awkward or difficult, your gun will not behave the same as when you are standing comfortably in your preferred stance. If you sense the gun is not properly aimed where it needs to be, have the discipline to hold off on shooting until it is.

If the gun is not returning to your point of aim as quickly as it normally does, you will need to resist the temptation to force that to happen. It is quite common for shooters to aggressively over return the gun back to the target and induce even more errors.

It is common for people to use wildly incorrect aiming schemes when negotiating special challenges. Some aggressive shooters barely look at their sights, and some people go entirely the other direction and over confirm. Be sure you are carefully assessing yourself as you go.

Evolution:

As you get comfortable with whatever challenge you are working on, increase the difficulty of the challenge. Move the targets further away, add partials, make the position more demanding, or do whatever else makes sense to increase the difficulty for the given challenge.

If you are working on shooting from an awkward position and you are successful, you can modify the exercise. An example is to require you to start outside your shooting position, shoot, and then get back out of that position. This will make the training similar to what you should expect to see in a match setting. Example: Start at position A and engage a target. Move to position B and negotiate the targets from your special challenge. Move back to position A and re-engage that target. This will require you to get in and out of your position at speed.

Tips:

The best piece of advice to remember for special challenges is that you do not need to be the best at everything. You need to be able to hit the targets under pressure. Shooting from an awkward position is a challenge for everyone and no one is going to be comfortable doing it. Suppress the feelings you have about being too slow and simply execute the shots.

Drill Progress Tracker			
Date	Drill Time	Hit Factor	Notes

Notes:

LEVEL 4

Goal: Achieve Competitive Excellence

If you are basically training every day and have already ranked up inside your shooting sport, you likely are looking to train at level 4. This level is appropriate for those who are chasing important titles at big matches. This is for the top guys who are not afraid of any challenge. If you are able to accomplish (after a bit of practice) pretty much any skill with a handgun that you see on Instagram and want to do very well at big matches, this level is for you. This level emphasizes consistency of performance and building a deep understanding of how to blend different techniques together to marginally improve scores.

It is certainly a difficult thing to master shooting technique to the point that you have a high rank and are even able to go after titles. You did the work to get to this point, but you should accept that to get some big wins under your belt it will take more training, dedication, sacrifice and some luck. The fact is, there are no guarantees at this level. Even if you do your part perfectly, someone else can do their part as well. You will need to be dedicated to break through these situations.

This section will force you to understand technique at a different level. You will blend predictive shooting with different aiming schemes in complicated scenarios to find the little details in your technique that are not quite right. You will spend weeks fixing those little pieces and testing them again from a different angle to find more cracks.

This section will ask you to be smart. You need to understand scoring on deep level. You should not need a calculator most of the time to understand what is good and what is bad. You should be able to memorize complex target orders and execute them correctly the first time. If this sort of thing does not sound good to you, then you will have a hard time doing high level training.

This section should cultivate that competitive spark inside of you. I have experience chasing and catching big titles. I did not get any of them by being more talented than anyone else. I did get them by outthinking conventional training wisdom and (quite literally) rewriting the book on how to train for practical shooting. I hope this section ignites the same passion in you and the whole discipline is elevated by contributions you and people like you will eventually make.

Above all else, high level training requires you to be accountable to yourself. This is not a hollow platitude that you should read and ignore. It also is not meant in a negative way. You are accountable to you for all the good you accomplish and the bad that befalls you. By taking the time to do your part in your training and preparation, you give yourself the best odds in competition.

Level 4 Training Standards

The Destination:

This training level is designed to get you a lottery ticket for a big title. This means that if you have the right training, mindset and talent this section will show you how to best leverage what you have. If you do the work properly you will get a ticket for a chance to win a big match. If you keep doing the work and keep buying tickets the hope is that eventually you will start to win.

The ticket will not be cheap, but I will show you how to attain it.

Input:

This level will require that you do dryfire training on a daily, or near daily basis. It will also necessitate frequent trips to the range for live training. Expect to train with about 50k rounds per year.

What Comes Next:

Using the drills in this section you should be able to tune your shooting to the maximum possible level. You should hunt down and mitigate weak spots in your game. You should learn to dominate at a high level.

Specific Standards:

Level 4 training requires the following:

Fast/Competent gun handing. Using a .8 second draw time and 1 second reload time you should be able to get fast and confident with gun manipulation in dryfire.

With live ammunition learn to control the gun when shooting as fast as you can pull the trigger (about .2 splits). You should be able to hold the A zone at 10 yards. You should be confident shooting fast predictive pairs at 15 yards or more.

The target time for El Prezidente is 5 seconds.

If you are using an optic you should expect to have to shoot even faster.

Knowledge/mindset:

This level requires you to leverage your good training habits over a longer period of time.

Sometimes shooters with age on their side and/or a high level of talent, can rank up very quickly. It can happen in a matter of a few short months in many cases.

Like it says above, this section will show you how to spend your time, energy, money and ammunition to get a ticket. The ticket is good for a shot at a title you want. Having a long-term focused mindset like this will help keep you motivated through the issues you will undoubtedly have as you move through your shooting career.

Standard Practice Setup

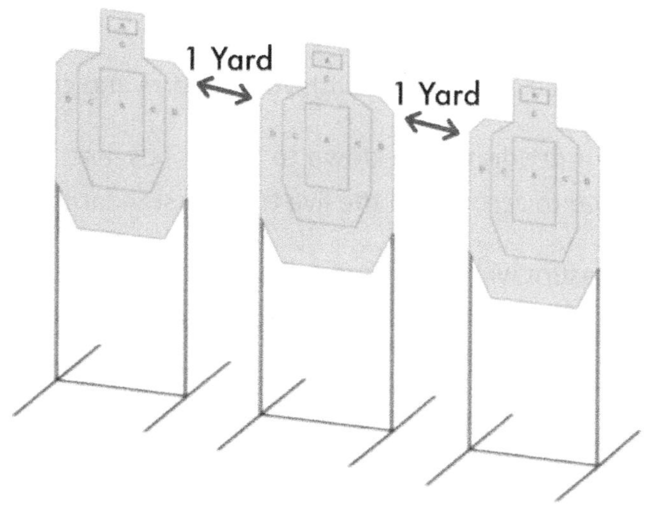

Livefire Level 4

Drill Name	Procedure	goal draw/reload times	3 yards	7 yards	10 yards	15 yards	25 yards	add time for: surrender	facing uprange	unloaded start
One Per Target	Engage each target with 1 round	0.9/na	1.3	1.4	1.6	1.9	2.3	0.1	0.1	1
Pairs on One Target	Engage one target with 2 rounds	0.9/na	0.9	1.1	1.2	1.3	1.5	0.1	0.1	1
4 Aces	Engage 1 target with 2 rounds, reload, reengage w/ 2 rounds.	0.9/1.1	1.9	2	2.5	2.8	3.2	0.1	0.1	1
Bill Drill	Engage one target with 6 rounds	0.9/na	1.7	1.8	2	2.2	3	0.1	0.1	1
Bill/Reload/Bill	Engage one, 6 rounds, reload, 6 more	0.9/1.1	3.5	4	4.5	5	6	0.1	0.1	1
Blake Drill	Engage each target with 2 rounds	0.9/na	1.8	2	2.3	2.9	3.3	0.1	0.1	1
El Prez	Turn, draw, engage each target w/2, reload, reengage each w/2	1.1/1.1	4	4.5	5	6	8	0.1	0.1	1
Criss Cross	Engage each of the 6 A zones in a criss cross pattern	0.9 (1.3 head)/ 1.2 (1.5 head)	4.5	4.8	5.3	6.3	n/a	0.1	0.1	1
Stong Hand Only	Engage each target w/ 2 rounds Strong hand only	1.2/na	2.5	2.8	3.3	4.5	n/a	0.1	0.1	1
Weak Hand Only	Engage each target w/ 2 rounds weak hand only	1.5 w/transfer/na	2.8	3.1	3.6	4.8	n/a	0.1	0.1	1

This is a set of standards designed to give a rough idea about general ability. The par times are set so you should be able to do a proper repetition 9/10 times to demonstrate proficiency. A single attempt does not mean much; you are looking for consistency. If you are using a red dot sight, subtract 5% from the times as you simulate distances of 15 yards or greater. If you are scoring major, subtract another 5% from the times at 15 yards or greater. These two conditions "stack," so open guns subtract 10% in total.

Dryfire Training 4

This is a brief primer on how to do the dry training component of your preparation.

Training Focal Points

Your focus should be to build speed and comfort with your firearm and gun handling skills.

Make sure you are getting your dry draw time down to .7 seconds, and your dry reloads are less than 1 second. You will need this speed to accomplish the live training standard times.

The most difficult thing to measure will be gun movement when you transition or move. Be sensitive to how the gun arrives on target and when you move it onto a new target.

Training Schedule

To facilitate developing the required skills, you will need regular training. Commonly, someone will train five days a week for a period of years to compete at a high level.

Level 4 Drills

The drills you should train on, in addition to the standard dry drills with par times listed below are dryfire versions of all the other level 4 drills. Construct the drill to scale as described in the dryfire training section in the general information section of this book.

Standards

This level requires you to leverage your good training habits over a longer period.

Dryfire Level 4

								add time for:		
Drill Name	**Procedure**	**goal draw/reload times**	**3 yards**	**7 yards**	**10 yards**	**15 yards**	**25 yards**	**surrender**	**facing uprange**	**unloaded start**
One Per Target	Engage each target with 1 round	0.9/na	1.3	1.4	1.6	1.9	2.3	0.1	0.1	1
Pairs on One Target	Engage one target with 2 rounds	0.9/na	0.9	1	1.1	1.1	1.3	0.1	0.1	1
4 Aces	Engage 1 target with 2 rounds, reload, reengage w/ 2 rounds.	0.9/1.1	1.8	1.9	2.4	2.6	3.1	0.1	0.1	1
Bill Drill	Engage one target with 6 rounds	0.9/na	1.5	1.7	1.9	2.1	2.9	0.1	0.1	1
Bill/Reload/Bill	Engage one, 6 rounds, reload, 6 more	0.9/1.1	3.2	3.4	3.8	4.1	4.8	0.1	0.1	1
Blake Drill	Engage each target with 2 rounds	0.9/na	1.6	1.8	2.1	2.7	3.1	0.1	0.1	1
El Prez	Turn, draw, engage each target w/2, reload, reengage each w/2	1.1/1.1	3.8	4.3	4.8	5.8	7.8	0.1	0.1	1
Criss Cross	Engage each of the 6 A zones in a criss cross pattern	0.9 (1.3 head)/ 1.2 (1.5 head)	4.3	4.6	5.1	7.8	n/a	0.1	0.1	1
Stong Hand Only	Engage each target w/ 2 rounds Strong hand only	1.2/na	2	3	3.5	4.5	n/a	0.1	0.1	1
Weak Hand Only	Engage each target w/ 2 rounds weak hand only	1.5 w/transfer/na	2.6	2.9	3.4	4.6	n/a	0.1	0.1	1

This is a set of standards designed to give a rough idea about general ability. The par times are set so you should be able to do a proper repetition 9/10 times to demonstrate proficiency. A single attempt does not mean much; you are looking for consistency. If you are using a red dot sight, subtract 10% from the times as you simulate distances of 15 yards or greater.

MARKSMANSHIP FUNDAMENTALS

Group Shooting

Purpose/Goal:

Ability to shoot A zone hits without any time pressure. Shooting all A's at 25 yards is a good goal. Shooting 100% hits on a reduced target surface (like a USPSA headbox) is also important. Occasional groups shooting work out to 50 yards is important. Shoot the gun as well as it will mechanically shoot.

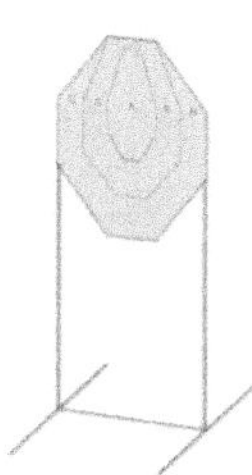

Instructions:

With no time limit, engage the target with as many rounds as desired. Shooting at least a five shot group is a good test of consistency.

Cues:

The most important cue to pay attention to is the tactile feel of your firing hand. It is counterintuitive in many respects to pay attention to the feel of your hands instead of the visual component of sight alignment. In most cases you will get better results by focusing on the feel inside your hands.

Corrections:

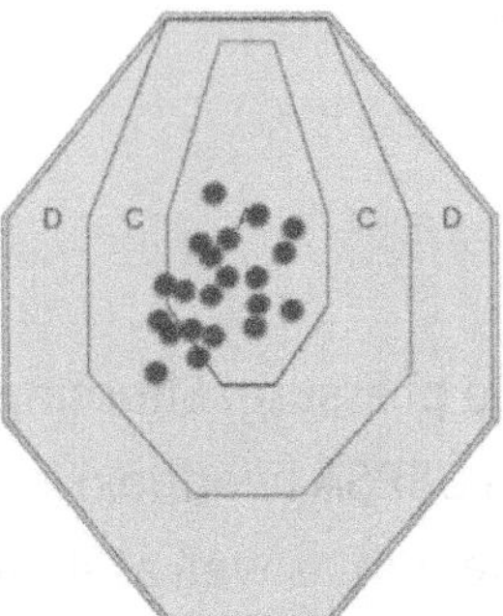

Hitting low/left is the classic sign of pushing down into the anticipated recoil. Focus on holding your firing hand still while you press the trigger straight.

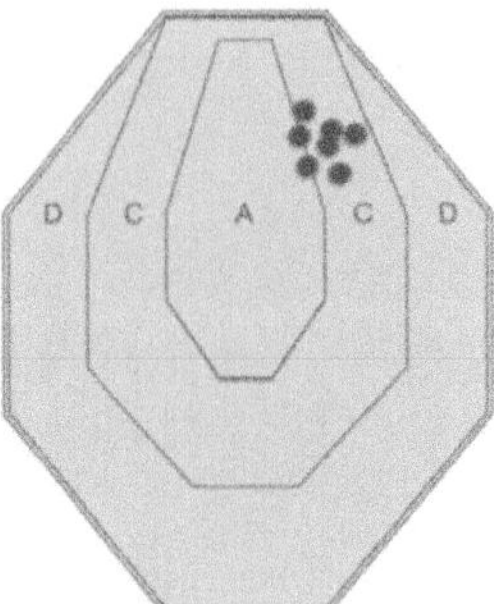

If you are forming a small group but in the wrong spot of the target, consider adjusting your sights. You may also not be focused on the center of the target.

Evolution:

Be sure to vary the target configuration. Try using no-shoots or hardcovers to block off part of the target. Forcing yourself to work around the obstruction will help you learn what your sights should look like when engaging a target that is partially obstructed.

Tips:

Shooting tight groups is an important skill to develop for any practical shooter. This skill will allow you to make sure that your pistol is mechanically accurate and able to hit any reasonable target at any reasonable distance.

The best results during group shooting are typically going to be had when you are focused on the feel of your hands rather than the visual component of aiming. The most common error that we observe during group shooting training is when the shooter sees a desirable sight picture, they immediately want to press the trigger. Typically, this is accompanied by pushing down into the anticipated recoil. If this shooter accepts a little bit of "wobble" in the sight picture and focuses on smoothly and cleanly releasing that shot, they will get a much better result.

Drill Progress Tracker			
Date	Drill Time	Hit Factor	Notes

Notes:

Trigger Control at Speed

Purpose/Goal:

Learn to press the trigger straight.

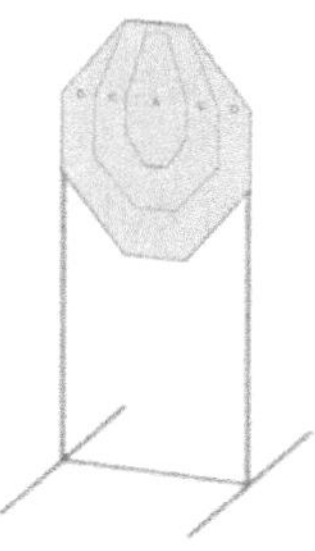

Single target

Setup notes:

Use a single target at any desired distance.

Instructions:

Start with the gun mounted and a perfect sight picture on your target. Your finger should be just out of contact with the trigger. At the tone, fire a shot. The shot should come in under .25 seconds or it is a "fail" for the drill.

Cues:

Your hand tension is going to tell you a lot. If your firing hand tenses up, or you have sympathetic movement in your fingers, the shot will not hit precisely on your intended impact point. Pay attention to your hands and you will learn quickly.

Corrections:

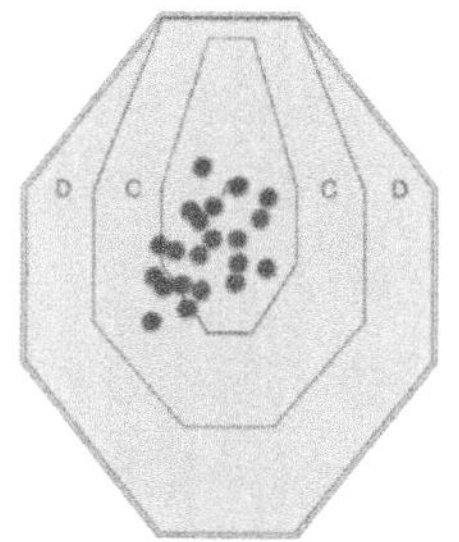

Most commonly shots will be pressed down and left for a right-handed shooter. Hold your hand still. Isolate your trigger finger. Putting more attention on the sights will not help.

Evolution:

This is an excellent drill to try single-handed as well. You can master dominant hand only shooting. You can work on weak hand trigger control as well.

You can also start the drill with your finger out of the trigger guard and try to match the same time it took to get the shot off with your finger in the trigger guard. By doing this you stress pressing the trigger straight on back.

Drill Progress Tracker			
Date	Drill Time	Hit Factor	Notes

Notes:

Practical Accuracy

Purpose/Goal:

Shoot the gun with acceptable accuracy at practical pace. Learn to grip your gun properly. Shooting all A's at 25 yards in under 3 seconds consistently is a reasonable goal.

Mastering risky partial target presentations is important.

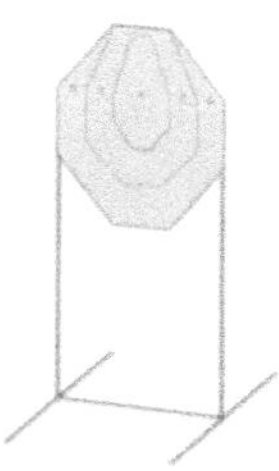

Instructions:

At the start signal, draw and engage the center of the A zone with six rounds. Fire a follow on shot as soon as your sights recover. There isn't a specific time limit, but the idea for the exercise is to shoot as soon as the sights recover.

Six strings at a time is recommended.

Cues:

Pay close attention to the feel of your gun in your hands. Once you feel yourself making some sort of mistake with your grip or trigger control you are going to be able to correct it much more easily.

Look to the spot on the target you want to hit. Do not look for the target's outline or at the color of the target.

Corrections:

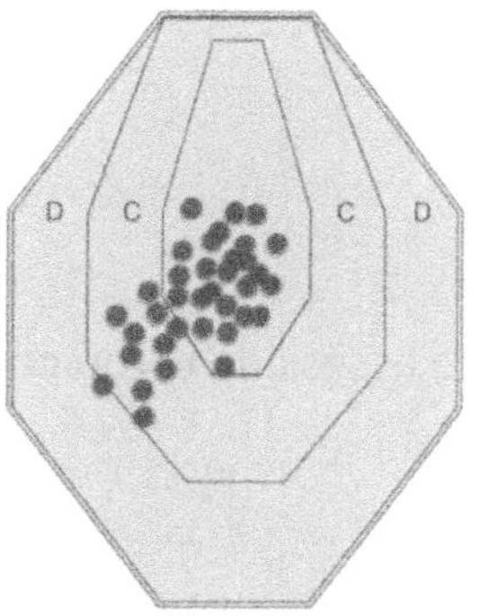

Low/left hits are almost always caused by moving the gun with the firing hand while shooting.

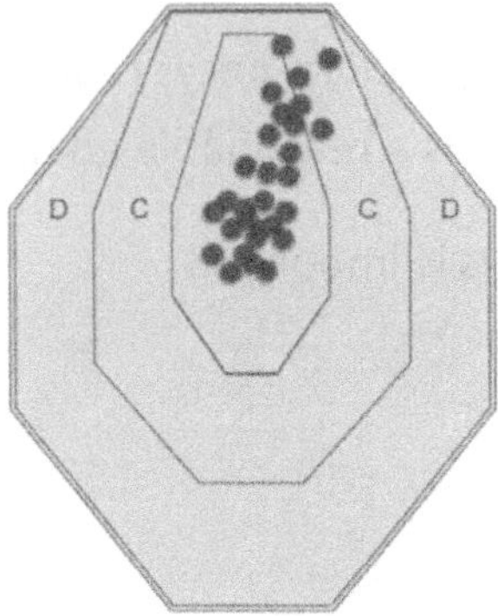

High hits generally come from insufficient support hand pressure or from shifting your vision onto the sights themselves instead of the target.

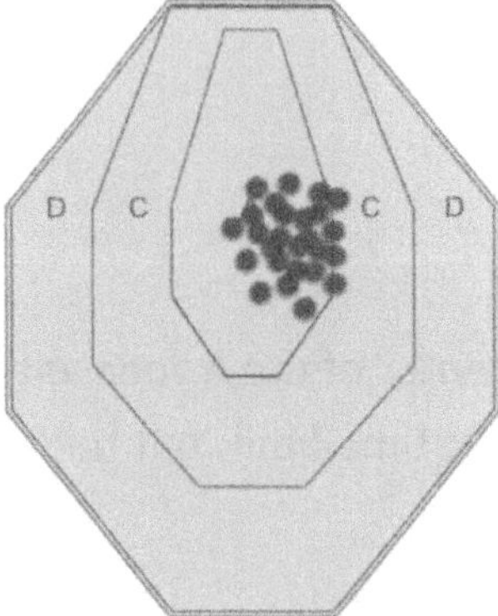

Hits trending in a small way to one direction or another can often be mitigated by small adjustments to grip pressure and trigger finger placement. Experiment to find what works best.

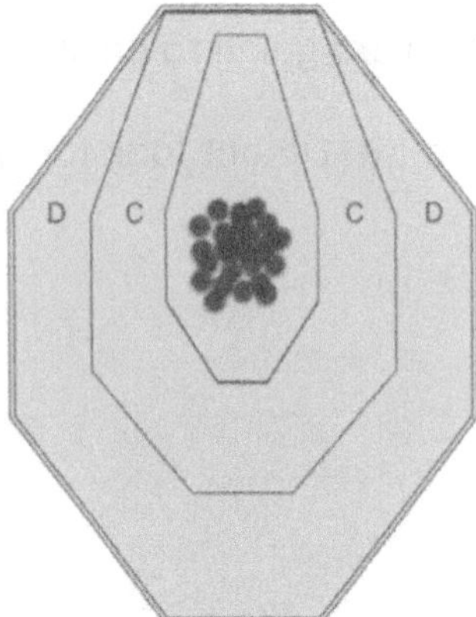

Even if your target looks great, constantly be assessing if you could have shot sooner or more aggressively.

Evolution:

Try to draw and shoot Alpha's from any desired distance or on any target configuration.

Use partial targets such as hardcovers on each side of the A zone in order to get comfortable with sight pictures on partial targets.

Try this exercise one handed.

Tips:

It is important to think of this exercise as a grip exercise first and foremost. If you are gripping the gun correctly and consistently then you are going to get very good results. Pay attention to the feel of your hands as you are shooting. When you feel an errant shot happen because you pushed the gun sideways or some similar mistake then you will generally stop making that mistake so frequently. It is counterintuitive but important, focus on your hands and don't worry so much about the way the sight picture looks.

Make sure you are in control of the pace of your shooting. You want to develop the ability to shoot reacting to a sight picture for each individual shot. This means follow up shots should be in the range of.3 to .6 seconds between shots. If follow up shots get to be much faster than .3 seconds it is quite likely that you did not see the sight return and consciously make a choice to fire. You are likely shooting to a rhythm. If your follow up shots start to get long, .6 seconds or more then it is likely you are over confirming your sight picture. When the sights come back you need to shoot. Sitting on that sight picture will not help you.

Keep looking at a particular spot on the target while you are shooting. The spot you look at should be the size of a coin. Just staring at that spot is going to make you much more accurate and likely to hit near that small spot. Be mindful of where your vision is focused. If you start to focus on your front sight or dot, your shots will tend to climb up higher on the target because you will not be precisely resetting the sight back down onto the aimpoint. If your vision stays on the aimpoint your sight will tend to come back to that point.

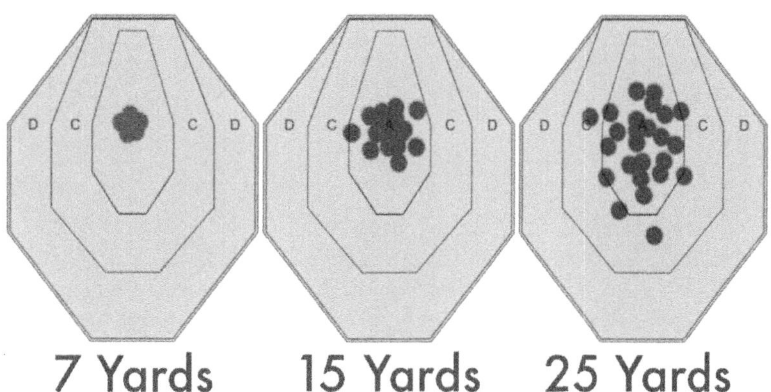

The goal is for your group to open concentrically as you increase the distance to the target. Flyers can, and will, still happen. Be looking at where the majority of the hits are going and be looking for any patterns. Compare any patterns you see to how your hands feel as you are breaking the shot. Connecting the dots from a feeling you have to where the shots are going will go a long way towards being able to eliminate marksmanship errors.

Drill Progress Tracker

Date	Drill Time	Hit Factor	Notes

Notes:

Doubles

Purpose/Goal:

Refine grip and marksmanship

Refine predictive shooting ability to cover a vast array of circumstances.

Hold the A zone at 7 yards while firing as fast as you can pull the trigger.

Shoot A's and close C's at 20 yards at predictive pace with consistency.

Blend predictive shooting into awkward body positions.

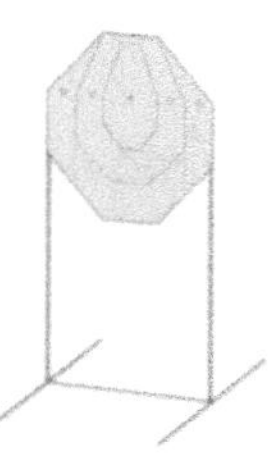

Instructions:

At the start signal, engage the target with four pairs of shots. Each pair should be fired as fast as you can pull the trigger. Allow the gun to completely quiet down from recoil before firing the next pair. Return your trigger finger to a relaxed position between pairs of shots.

Repeat this procedure for multiple strings.

Cues:

Pay close attention to the feel of your gun in your hands. Once you feel yourself making some sort of mistake with your grip or trigger control you are going to be able to correct it much more easily. Isolate the trigger finger. Make sure your firing hand fingers are not curling due to an over tense firing hand.

Observe the movement of the sights in recoil. This will provide clues for how to improve your technique moving forward.

Corrections:

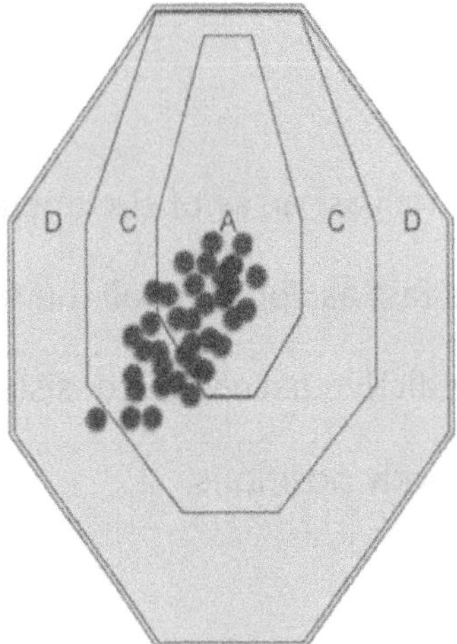

Low/left hits are almost always caused by moving the gun with the firing hand while shooting.

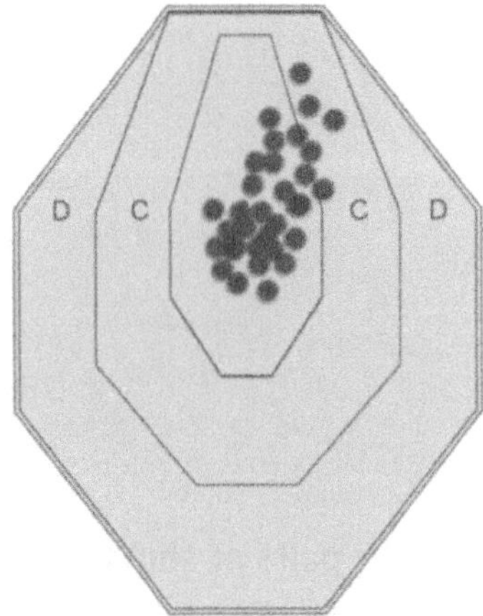

High hits generally come from insufficient support hand pressure.

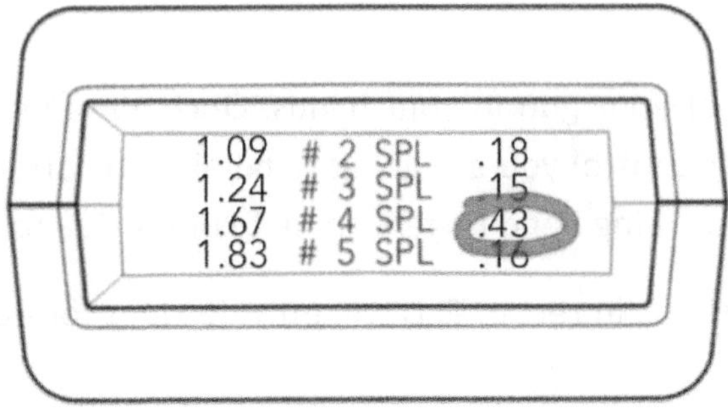

"Trigger Freeze" (the inability to reset the trigger for a second shot) is caused by an over tense firing hand in almost all cases.

Evolution:

As your control grows you can adjust the distance to the target and adjust your pace. This will give you a good idea of what sort of expectations are realistic in a match setting. As the range increases you will need to accept some points being dropped.

It is important that you understand how the scoring system will affect aiming strategies. Be sure you are noting points down and assessing how you should handle different targets at different distances. You want to leverage your skills the best you can given the scoring system.

You should try doing Doubles drill while leaning, kneeling, crouching, etc. As you play around with the effects of different body positions and target configurations your understanding will grow and you will be able to optimize your shooting pace for the largest possible variety of circumstances.

Tips:

It is important to think of this exercise as a grip exercise first and foremost. If you are gripping the gun correctly and consistently then you are going to get very good results. Pay attention to the feel of your hands as you are shooting. When you feel an errant shot happen because you pushed the gun sideways or some similar mistake then you will generally stop making that mistake so frequently. It is counterintuitive, but important. Focus on your hands and do not worry so much about the way the sight picture looks.

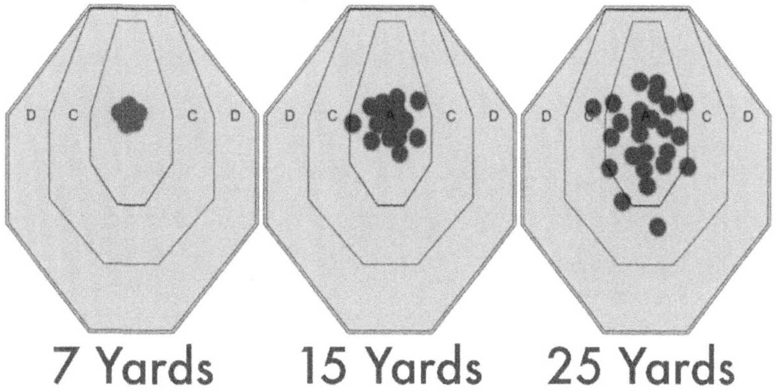

The goal is for your group to open concentrically as you increase the distance to the target. Flyers can, and will, still happen. Be looking at where the majority of the hits are going and be looking for any patterns. Compare any patterns you see to how your hands feel as you are breaking the shot. Connecting the dots from a feeling you have to where the shots are going will go a long way towards being able to eliminate marksmanship errors.

Drill Progress Tracker			
Date	Drill Time	Hit Factor	Notes

Notes:

Single-handed Shooting

Purpose/Goal:

Ability to make shots using only one hand on the gun. Both dominant-hand only and non-dominant hand only need to be trained.

Shoot exactly at the pace of your sights (reactive shooting)

Experiment with predictive shooting

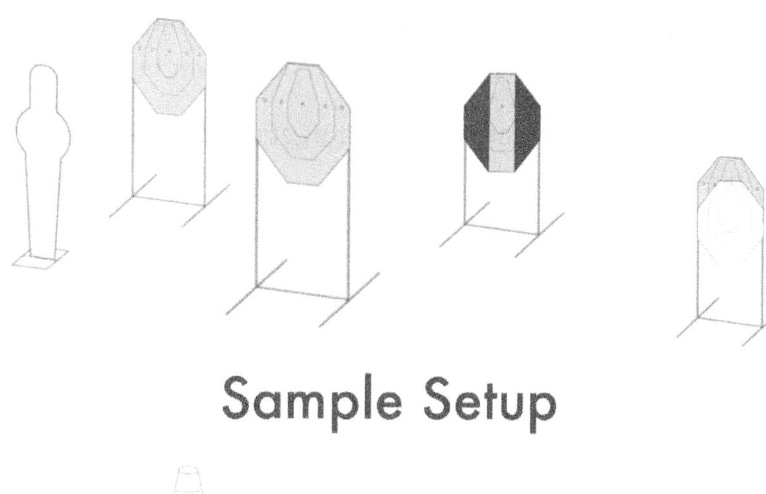

Random Target Set

Setup notes:

Set up any target scenario you desire.

Instructions:

At the start, draw and engage the targets with a single hand. If you are using your non-dominant hand, draw the gun, transfer it to the correct hand, engage the targets.

Cues:

Pay attention to your firing hand. The most common issue you are going to run into is pushing down into the gun sympathetically as you press the trigger. Paying attention to your hand during the course of that drill is going to mitigate that issue.

Corrections:

Low/left shots when shooting right handed or low/right shots when shooting left handed are going to be very common, especially as you increase your speed. This issue is the primary one you should be focused on mitigating.

High hits can be caused by shooting so fast you don't return the gun in time. Ensure this is not the case. Consider experimenting with single-handed doubles to learn more about this.

Evolution:

Try out a variety of start positions. "Gun on table" to start is fairly common when you come to a single-handed shooting stage in a match. You just want to make sure that you don't run into stuff that causes you to be nervous because the first time you have ever done it is in a match.

Feel fry to do a bit of single-handed shooting on any training scenario you set up and work with. It isn't a bad idea to try a few runs of single-handed shooting on any drill you have set up. This will help ensure that your training is well rounded. Also, getting good with one hand never hurts the two-handed shooting.

Leverage predictive shooting where you can. On close targets (7 yards and in) you should be able to get away with a little bit of predictive shooting.

Tips:

If you are aiming, you will feel slow. A big part of most people's training is developing the discipline to aim and press the trigger properly no matter how long it *feels like* it is taking.

It is critical that you do lots of single-handed repetition dryfire. If you are using a dot sight this becomes even more important. You will need to develop a whole new index for your non-dominant hand to be able to bring the sight exactly to where it needs to be for you to be able to make hits. Do not neglect your dry training.

Experiment with technique. Firstly, you may want to try "canting' the gun in. Right eye dominant shooters using their left hand may prefer to tilt the gun so the sight is still lined up with their right eye. This is ok, just be careful about the point of aim/point of impact discrepancy that can emerge if you are shooting at distance using this technique.

You may also want to try "blading" off towards the targets to get a better range of motion. An easy way to learn this is to step in with the gun side. This means if you are holding the gun in your right hand, step forward with your right foot.

Drill Progress Tracker			
Date	Drill Time	Hit Factor	Notes

Notes:

Transition/Vision Drills

Target Transitions

Purpose/Goal:

Move the gun smoothly and precisely from one target to the next. Learn the optimal aiming schemes for the different target types and employ them.

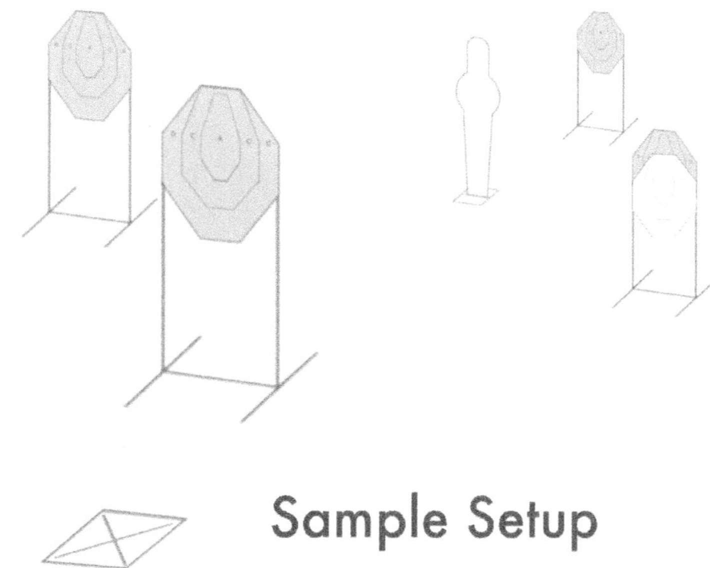

Instructions:

Set up targets of mixed distance and shot difficulty. Mixing in steel plates or poppers are optional if you have them available. Try to create a very plain cross section of the targets you expect to encounter at matches. At the start signal, engage each target. Keep the engagement order the same for a few repetitions. Shoot the drill at your practical match pace to begin and increase your speed as you feel comfortable doing so. Restore the targets after you assess them and change the engagement order if you wish for subsequent sets of repetitions on the exercise.

Cues:

Lead with your eyes. Look exactly where you wish to hit. You should not be looking at a big brown target, but picking a precise spot to move the gun to.

Do not muscle the gun around because it will cause the sights to stop imprecisely.

Make sure you understand where each shot is going and adjust aiming strategies as needed.

Be comfortable shooting any target order. Practice the engagement orders you like the least.

Corrections:

If the gun is not moving quickly or to your aim point, make sure you are leading with your eyes.

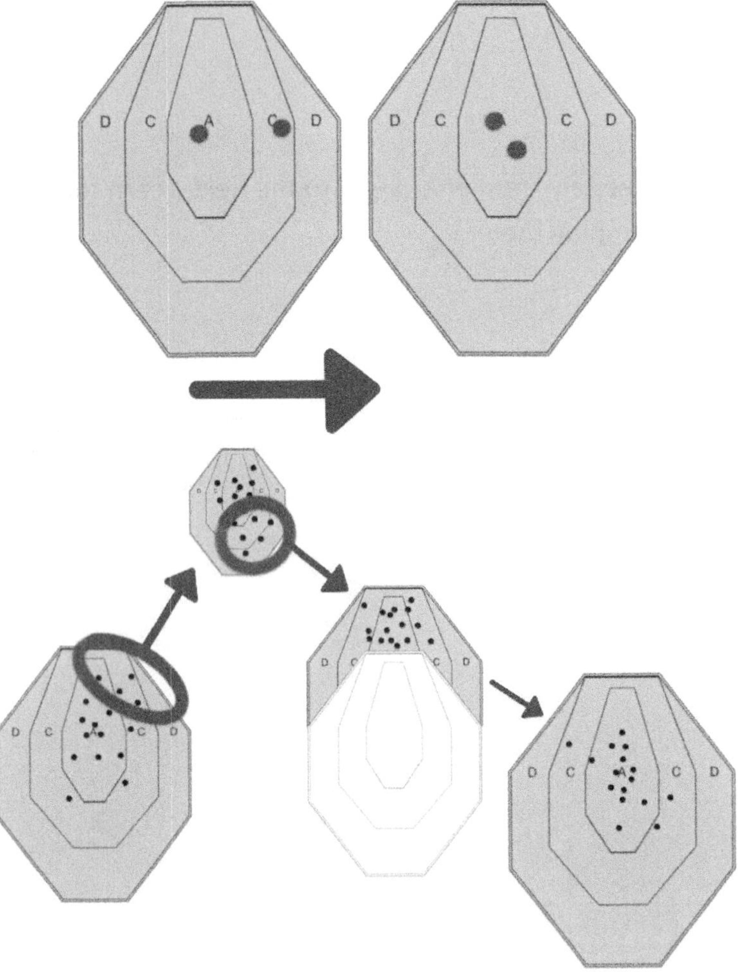

Moving your eyes off a target before you are done shooting it will drag the hits off the target. Drag off commonly happens on a target the shooter perceives to be lower difficulty. The shooter shifts their attention to the next task after firing the first shot on the target and the gun moves away from the target when the eyes do. Notice how your gun follows the path your eyes take. Train yourself to keep your eyes on the target as long as you are shooting it regardless of shot difficulty.

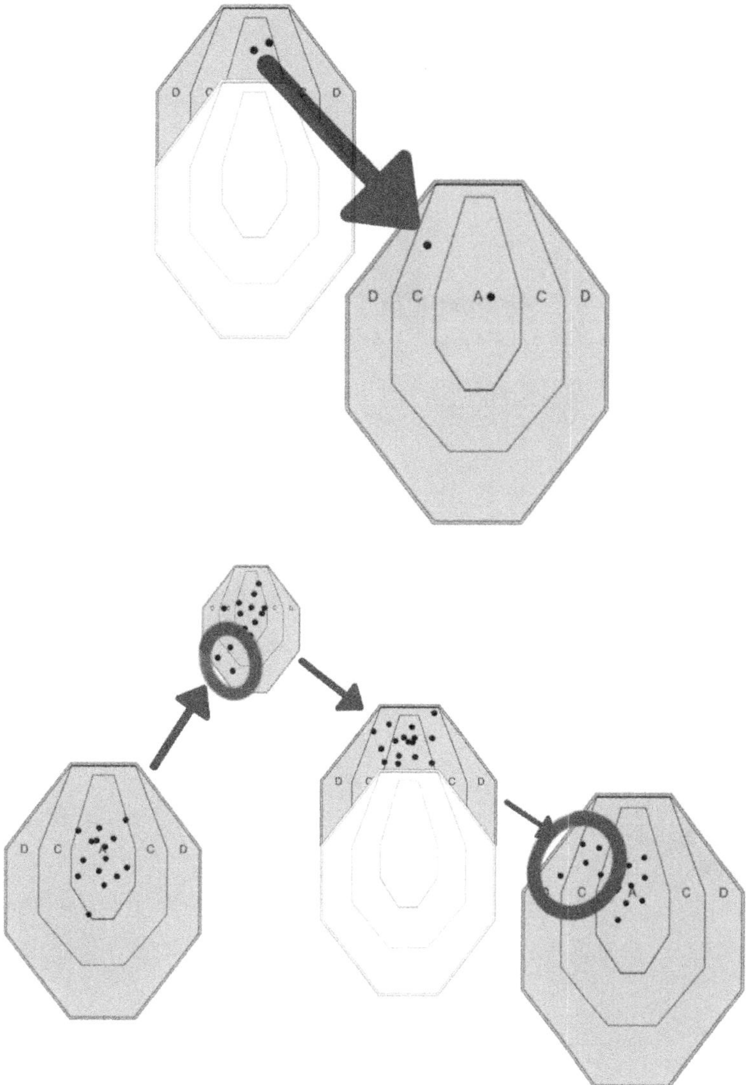

Pressing the trigger before the gun gets to the intended aimpoint will drag hits onto the target. The shot being drug into the target can vary from shooting a shot between targets, an edge Delta hit that barely scores, a Charlie, or a hit on the Alpha zone perforation. A common cause for this is trying to shoot a target very fast and attacking it. The correction is making sure you see your sights show up on the target you are transitioning to before firing.

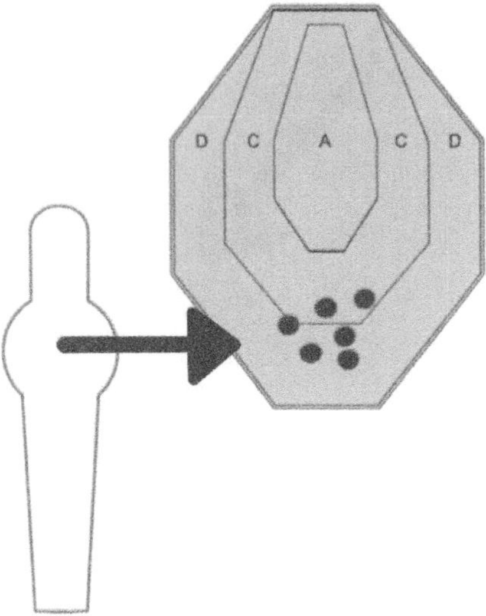

Be mindful of the vertical changes that occur in target arrays. Moving your gun straight left or right after shooting a target can cause high or low hits.

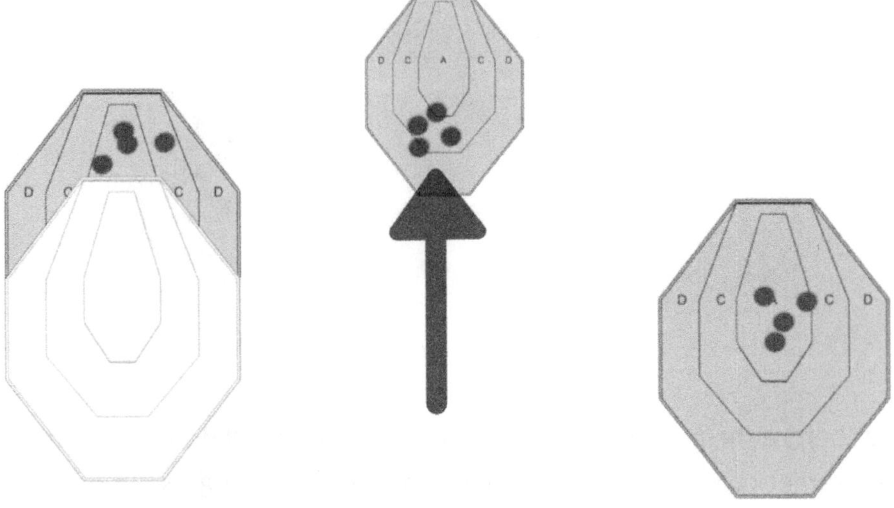

You are teaching yourself to have the sights show up where you look. Whether it is good or bad, the sights will go to the spot you are looking at. Make sure you are training your eyes to look at the exact spot you want to hit.

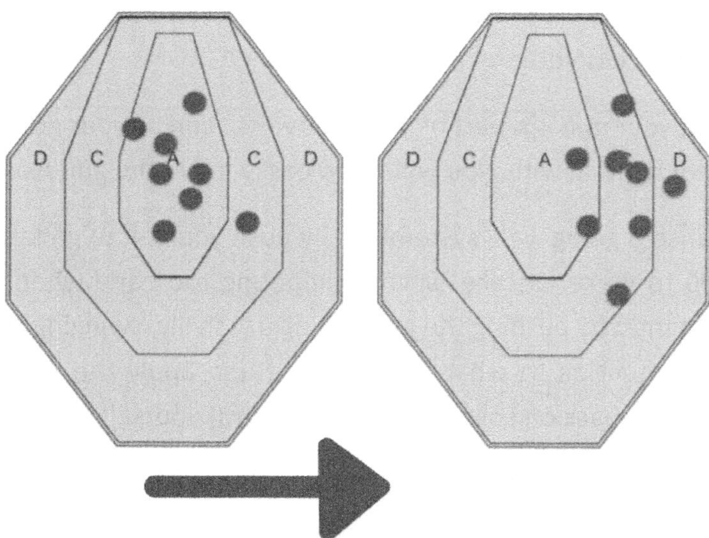

If you are overswinging/overdriving the gun, relax your shoulders. A telltale sign this is happening is if you feel very tense as you transition the gun. Your shoulders should not be any more raised or tense than if you were standing normally. Commonly, the hits will all trend on one side of the target.

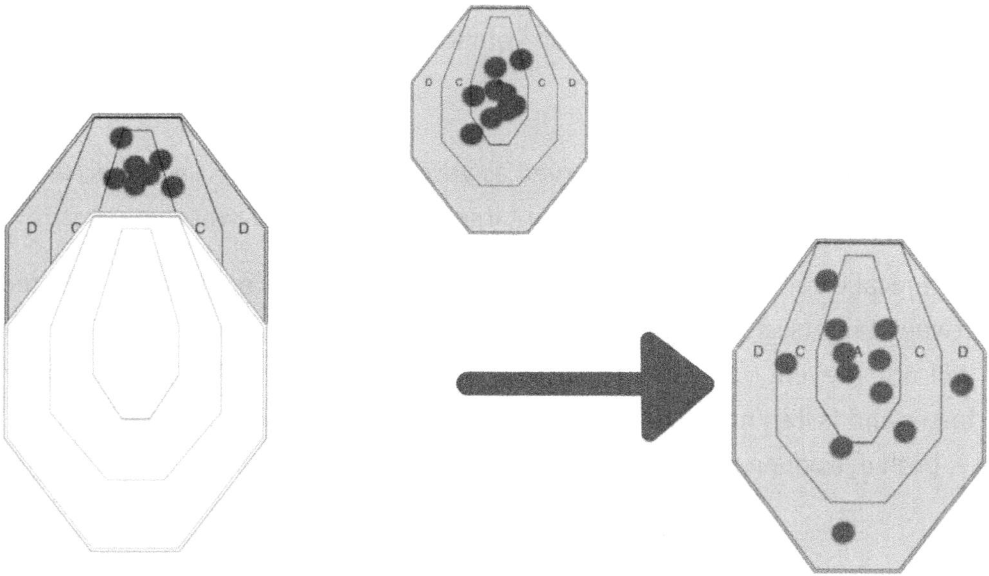

If the hits are widely scattered on a target with no real pattern, select a more exact aiming scheme.

Do not over aim/over confirm on close ranged open targets. Shoot immediately when you recognize the gun is on target. While training, be asking yourself the question, "Could I have been shooting sooner?"

Evolution:

Do dry aiming on each target at your full speed before doing live training. Move your vision from aimpoint to aimpoint on each target and learn to have the gun follow you. Make sure that you are not focusing on the sighting system as you move the gun from one target to the next but instead your vision is out on the target. When you are consistently performing these skills dry then begin live training. After each set of runs on the drill return to dryfire before the next set of runs.

Try to develop a sense that your gun is a part of your body. As soon as your gun feels like an extension of your hands that you are not fighting with, you will more easily move the gun from target to target.

If your shooting performance is going well, systematically push yourself to go faster. Understand that this will eventually induce you to make mistakes such as shooting too early when coming onto the target, overrunning the intended target by pushing the gun too aggressively, swinging the gun to the wrong spot on target, and so on. Pay attention to what is happening and apply the right corrections in order to improve. After you feel you are back on solid ground again, push yourself to go faster.

Make sure that you employ the most aggressive aiming scheme you can get away with. For example, if you are successfully engaging a target using the "paint the A zone" method with your dot then try to switch to the "react to the color of your sight" concept. That should increase the engagement speed and hopefully the accuracy will not degrade.

It is important that you do not have a strong preference for engagement order. Be comfortable shooting front to back, back to front, left to right, right to left, etc. If you strongly prefer one style to another then you will be in a weaker position when it comes to stage strategies in competition. You need to be comfortable doing any order and you should train yourself that way on the practice range.

Tips:

Get in the habit of recalling what you just observed as you were shooting. As you learn to recall flashes of the sight pictures you were just seeing, the hits on targets will not be anywhere near as mysterious.

Watch out for technical errors throughout the drill. These errors include, but aren't limited to, following your sight in between targets, closing an eye, squinting and hunching down onto the gun. These things are common and will not prevent you from being proficient as a shooter. As you develop your skills and attempt to go faster and faster, negative habits you have developed will become a problem. The best way to do business is both eyes open and be target focused.

Drill Progress Tracker			
Date	Drill Time	Hit Factor	Notes

Notes:

Wide Transitions

Purpose/Goal:

Proper wide transition technique.

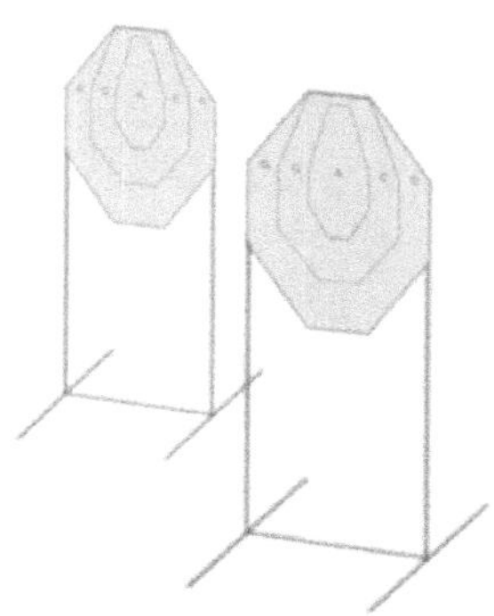

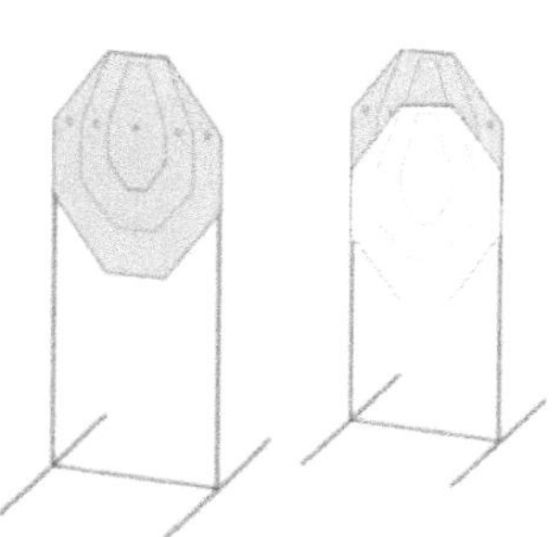

Sample Setup

Setup notes:

Create a scenario with two sets (arrays) of targets. Have a wide (90 degree or more) swing between the sets of targets.

Instructions:

Engage all the targets. Pay particular attention to the transition time between the two sets.

Cues:

Adopt a "fast then slow" or "attack and control" mindset. Aggressively drive the gun from one set to the other, slowing the gun down at the end of the transition. Ideally, you want the gun to stop perfectly stable and still correctly aimed.

Corrections:

Sample Setup

Hits patterning in the direction of the transition are often caused by "overdriving" the gun. There are two common corrections for this issue.

Firstly, make sure that you start applying the brakes during the wide transition before you get the gun to the target. Relaxing your shoulders can help remind you not to slam the gun into position.

Secondly, you may be tracking the sight the whole way through the wide transition. Again, this requires you to actively get your attention off the sight and into the center of the next target you intend to shoot.

Evolution:

You can get a lot of mileage out of this drill by simply altering the degrees of swing and the target difficulty. The goal here is to get comfortable with anything that may be required of you in a match. By getting used to transitioning the gun around quickly, you will be set up to do well on any sort of stage.

Drill Progress Tracker			
Date	Drill Time	Hit Factor	Notes

Notes:

Spot to Spot Transitions

Purpose/Goal:

Accurate and precise transitions

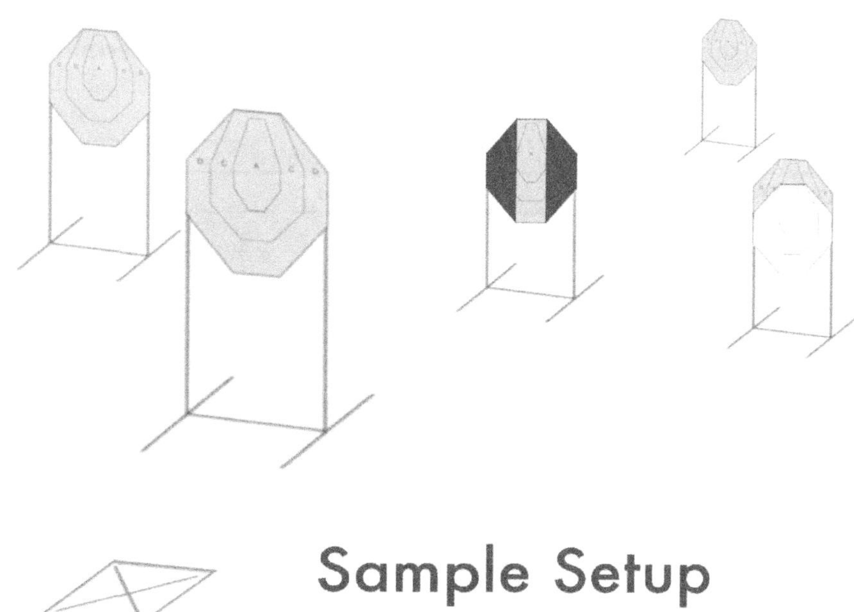

Random target setup

Setup notes:

This is a dry drill done during training. Do it on whatever target setup you are working on.

Instructions:

Practice moving your vision to exactly where you want the rounds to go on each target in sequence.

Cues:

Look at the exact spot where you want to hit

Corrections:

There are two corrections that are normally needed.

Firstly, make sure you are finding a spot on the target, and not just looking at the color. Oftentimes people are satisfied by aiming at the brown blob and not finding a specific spot. Do not look for the shape or the color of the target, look exactly where you want to hit.

Secondly, do not “sweep” or “drag” your gaze through the target. Find a spot.

Evolution:

After you master the sequence, work in dry gun movement from spot to spot. Make sure you apply the correct aiming scheme.

Tips:

This drill should be done on a regular basis both on the training range and in matches. Practice the transitions from spot to spot using just your eyes. This will help you determine the specific focal points that you need to be paying attention to.

Drill Progress Tracker			
Date	Drill Time	Hit Factor	Notes

Notes:

Transition Exit/Entry

Purpose/Goal:

Break down the target transition technique into its most basic parts to understand it better.

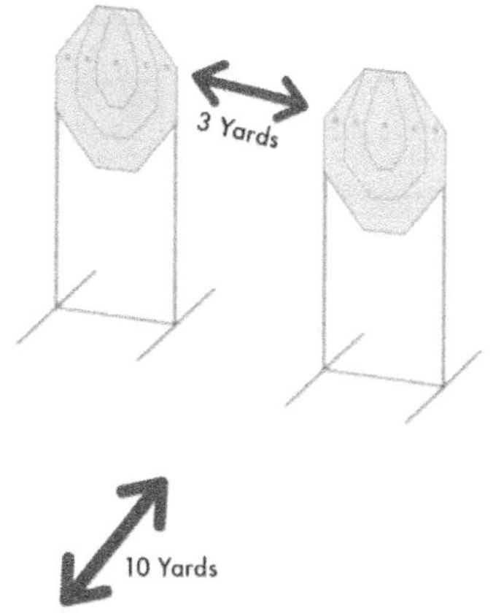

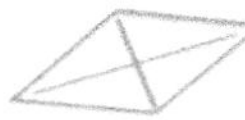

Setup notes:

2 targets 3 yards apart. 10 yards distance.

Instructions:

Drill 1 (exit): Start with your pistol aimed at one of the targets. Your visual focus should be on the target you are aimed at. At the tone, engage the target with one round, only then transition the gun to the other target. Get a good sight picture on that target, but do not fire.

Drill 2(entry): Start with your pistol aimed at one of the targets. Your visual focus should be on the target you are aimed at. At the tone transition the gun to the other target. Get a good sight picture on that target and fire the shot.

Cues:

Your vision drives everything. Look exactly where you want the gun to go and allow it to go there smoothly and precisely.

Corrections:

Focus on the target while you transition, never the sight. If you have an excessively bright fiber or dot setup, this will be difficult. You need to get your vision out to the target. Look exactly where you want the gun to go and be extremely critical of any excess movement you see.

Drill Progress Tracker			
Date	Drill Time	Hit Factor	Notes

Notes:

Accelerator

Purpose/Goal:

Learn to employ different aiming schemes.

Par time 5 seconds

Hit factor 10 or higher

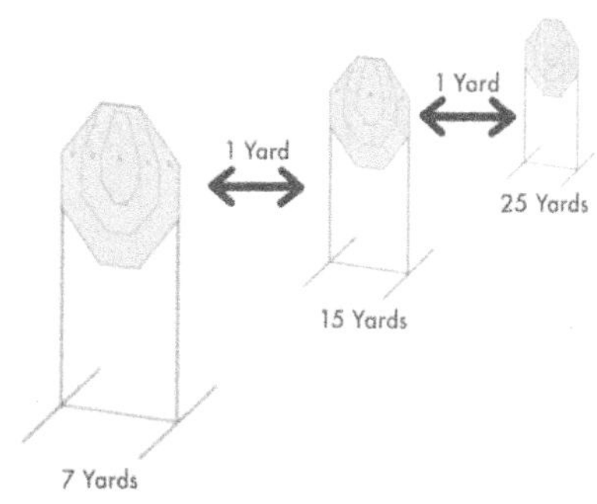

Setup notes:

Targets should be set so there is minimal transition laterally between the targets.

Instructions:

At the tone, engage each target with two rounds. Reload and re-engage each target with two more rounds.

Cues:

React immediately on the close target when your gun arrives in the center of it. Shoot right away without over aiming. React to seeing the color of your front sight or a blur of your dot on the target.

Allow the sight to settle on the long target for each shot. Press the trigger carefully and with discipline.

Make sure you stop your eyes on the center of the middle target. This is to avoid "dragging through" the target.

Corrections:

If you are struggling to hover near the par time for this drill you should look at draw and reload times. Drawing and reloading 1 second or less on the close ranged target is fast enough to make the goal time. If you are lagging behind those times by a substantial amount you should look to dry training to improve those times.

If your draw/reload times are on point, but you are struggling to meet the par then ensure you are not delaying your movement off the target you are shooting as soon as you finish shooting it. Oftentimes people have a fast pair of shots on the target, but they delay moving their eyes off the target as soon as they finish it. This will cause the gun to settle back down on a target that they should be transitioning away from. If you are seeing transition times between the targets longer that .3 seconds this is a likely cause.

The middle target is typically the one that people struggle with. You should be shooting a predictive pair, but it does not need to be your top speed split that you would be looking for on the close target. If you are not comfortable with a predictive pair on the middle target, then look to specific training like Doubles drill.

If you judge your shooting on the back target as too slow to hover around the par time, then consider shooting a predictive pair on it. This is a viable strategy for competition as the hit factor on this drill is quite high and you will not need to shoot all Alpha's for a good score.

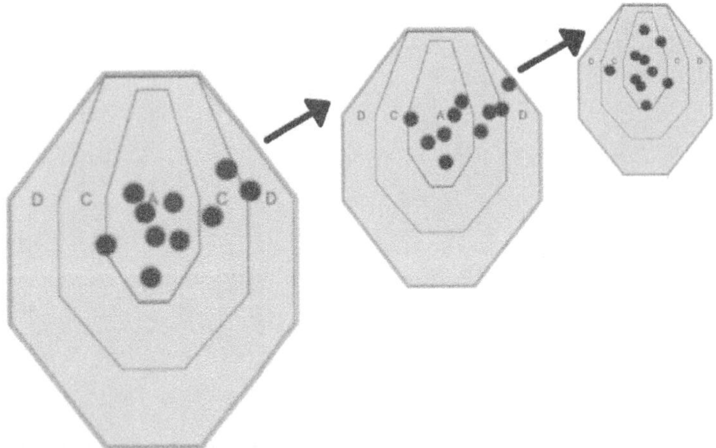

Make sure you are keeping your eyes on the target the entire time you are shooting it. Moving your vision away while you are still shooting a target will likely result in the shots dragging off the target. These can range from hits on the A/C line to Delta's, or even completely missing the target.

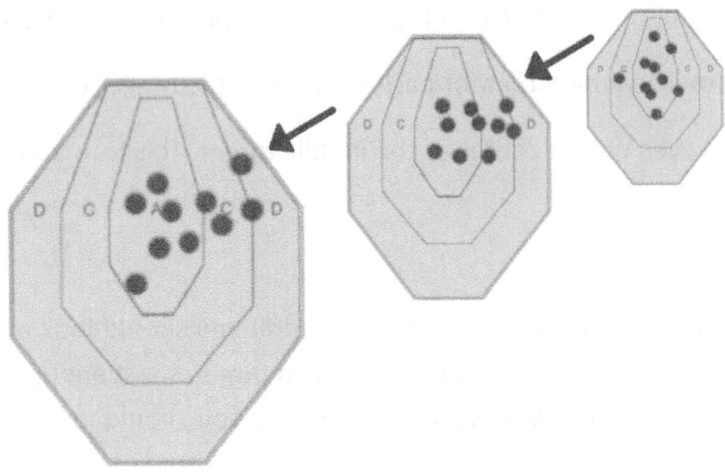

Drag on shots happen from shooting before the gun gets to the center of the target. A common theme for drag on issues is shooting as soon as you see the color brown of the target. The correction is looking at the center of the target and waiting for the sights to get to the spot you are looking at before firing.

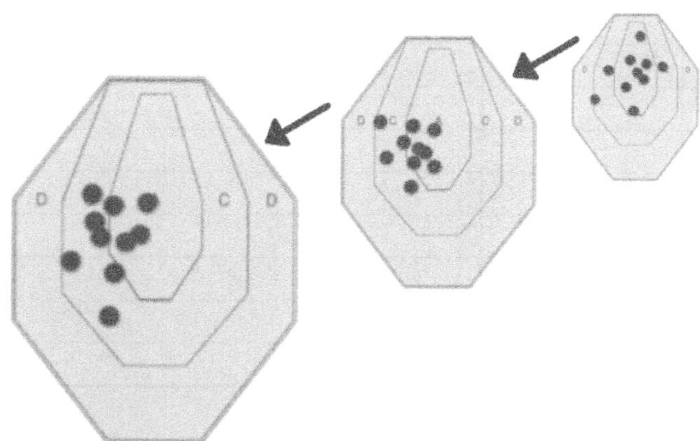

Be conscious of what your shoulders are doing and make sure you are not pushing the gun too hard. Patterns on the left or right side of the targets can be caused by using your shoulders to throw the gun causing imprecise transitions.

Evolution:

Shoot this drill back to front and front to back. Make sure you are comfortable working either direction.

You should feel free to shoot a "goofy" order on this drill as well. A goofy order is one that makes no sense in a match setting. This would be starting or finishing on the middle target and forcing yourself to transition the gun around more.

Try shooting predictive pairs on the back target.

Tips:

The most important advice to take on board for this drill is to shoot with your eyes, not your ears. This means that you should be shooting the drill where you address each target with the correct aiming scheme for you. The close ranged target should be shot using predictive shooting and a rapid-fire pair. The distant target should be shot in a disciplined manner. Make sure you see the sight return for the follow up shot. It is frequently the case that less experienced shooters will try to "go fast" on the close stuff and "slow down" on the longer shooting. The recipe for success on this drill is to be process focused and not worried at all about how you think the drill is sounding.

Drill Progress Tracker			
Date	Drill Time	Hit Factor	Notes

Notes:

Distance Changeup

Purpose/Goal: Get used to "changing gears" between different target types. 3 second par time, 2.75 if using a dot sight.

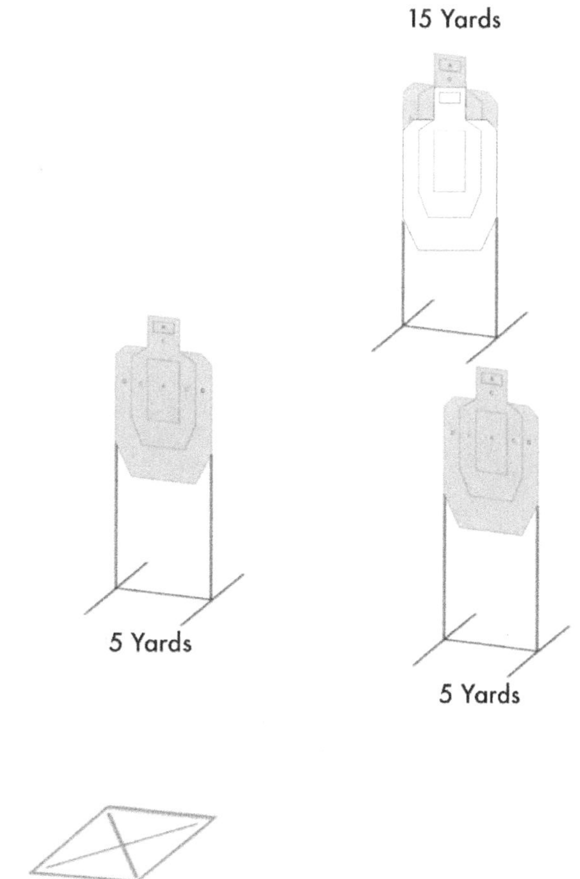

2 targets at 5 yards. A headbox or similar target should be set in between, 15 yards distant.

Setup notes:

Be sure you do not have a shoot through situation.

Instructions:

At the start, engage each target with two rounds.

Cues:

Aim. Make sure you confirm each shot. The tough shot in the back will require two distinct sight pictures. You may even need to switch your attention on to your firing hand to ensure you aren't pushing the pistol off target.

The close-up targets generally induce a bit of dragging on/off the targets. You hit where you look so make sure you keep your attention in the center of the close ranged targets to ensure you are actually done shooting them when you transition off.

Relax your firing hand/shoulders. Too much tension in these places is likely to cause trigger freeze. It will also cause imprecise transitions in the form of overswinging.

Corrections:

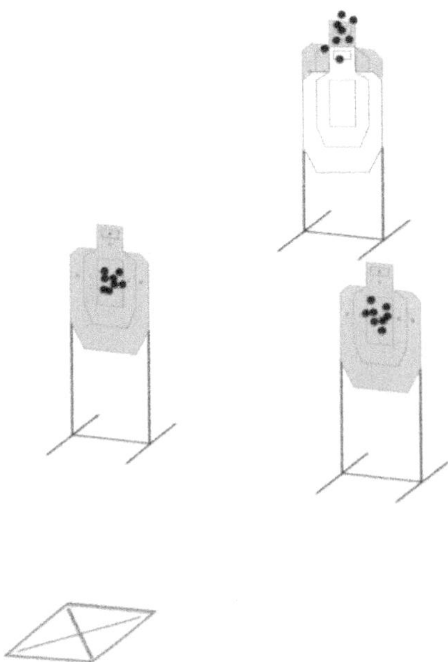

Watch your sights. The most common problem on this drill is inconsistent hits on the partial target. The main point of this exercise is for you to develop discipline on that target. You need to learn to "take your time in a hurry." Shoot quickly, but do not rush. Aim carefully, but do not waste time. It is not an easy thing to learn.

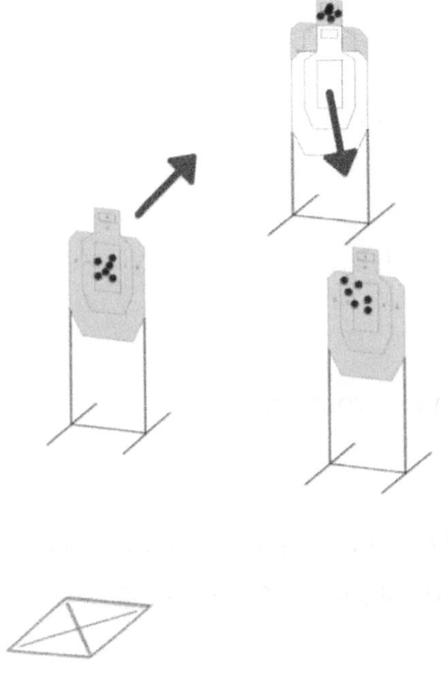

Get your eye off the front sight when you transition! Once you engage the partial you will catch yourself staring at the front sight during subsequent transitions. This needs to be actively mitigated by you paying attention to what your eyes are actually doing.

Evolution:

Change between different target orders. You can shoot left to right, right to left, near to far, or far to near. Each order will present the same sorts of challenges in slightly different ways. At the end of the day, this drill is about developing discipline.

Tips:

Make sure your sights are set up to work for you and not against you. Your dot or fiber front sight should not be so bright/overpowering that it is difficult for you to transition to the partial target. If you find your eye being sucked on to the dot or fiber, you should make an adjustment to the brightness level of your sight.

Drill Progress Tracker			
Date	Drill Time	Hit Factor	Notes

Notes:

MXAD

(Matt Xray Alpha Drill)

Purpose/Goal:

Get all A zone hits in under 2.3 seconds with some regularity.

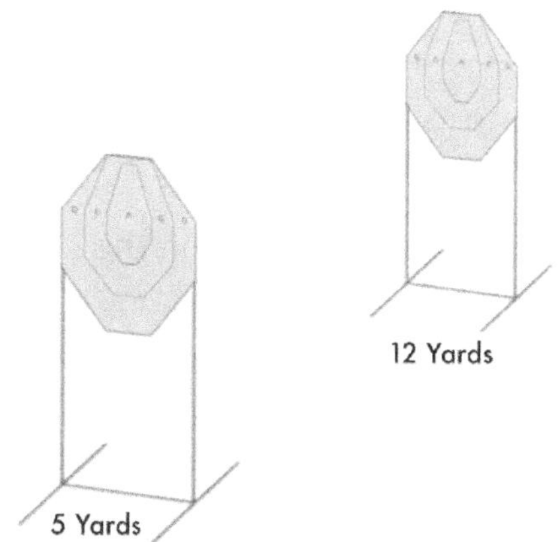

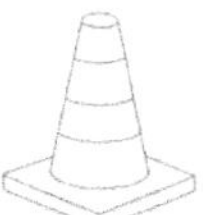

Target at 5 yards and target at 12 yards

Setup notes:

This drill should be set up so that there is almost no swing of the gun from one target to the other. The transition is almost entirely in depth.

Instructions:

At the start signal, engage the close target with six rounds, then engage the other target with two rounds.

Cues:

Relax. This is a close range, high speed drill that will induce tension in your shoulders. If your upper body gets overly tense, you will likely overswing the transition and get a poor result. Just hold the gun with your hands, do not try to fight it with your entire body. If you release that unnecessary tension, the drill only gets easier.

Look where you want to hit. It is critical you get your attention off of the sights and how they are bouncing. The motion in your sights will suck your eye in. This will make the transition much more difficult. You need to learn to let the sights do their dance in your peripheral vision while you stay locked in to target focus.

Corrections:

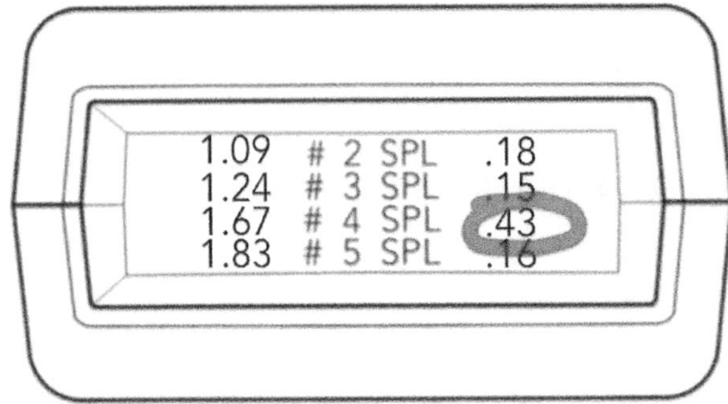

Relax your firing hand. If you are getting trigger freeze on the close target or having a hard time running the gun aggressively, the fix is likely to be relaxing your firing hand a bit. Death gripping the gun or over tension will induce the trigger freeze.

Evolution:

Shooting the far target first is an interesting evolution that I recommend you try. Shooting the far target first often tempts people to start staring at their front sight or dot during the transition to the close target. This is counterproductive, and you can start on the far target to work it out. If you shoot the far target first with six rounds, then the close target with two rounds, give yourself an extra 1/4 second on the goal time.

Tips:

You can learn a lot on this drill if you become hyper aware of what you are doing with your vision. Ideally, you want your vision to go from the center of one target to the center of the other target. Due to the close swing of the transition, it makes it difficult to keep from getting 'tunneled into" the sights while you are shooting the drill. Do your best to get your vision out to the targets where it needs to be.

Drill Progress Tracker			
Date	Drill Time	Hit Factor	Notes

Notes:

Designated Target

Purpose/Goal:

Another drill developed by Hwansik Kim, this drill will develop target transitions in a complex scenario.

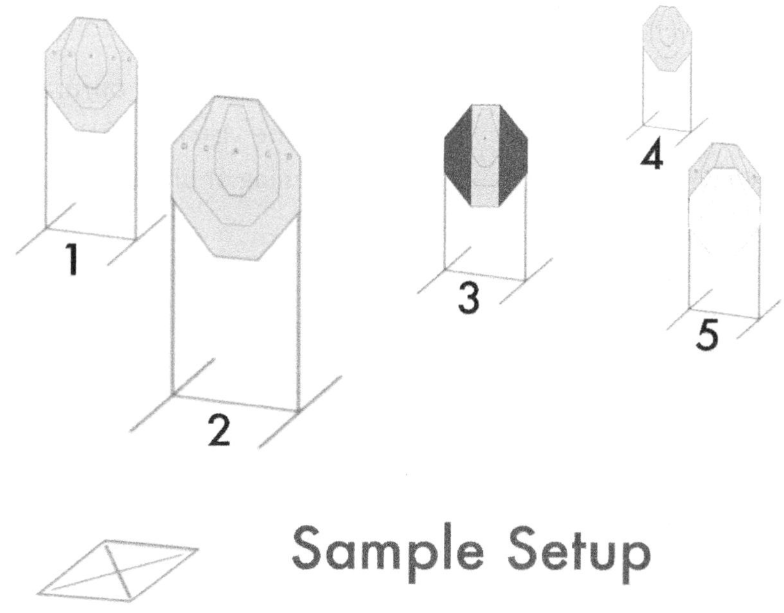

Setup notes:

Set up some targets, use as many as you like. The minimum number is three targets, and the recommended number is five. As you go over five targets, the ammunition usage is excessive.

The targets should be of different distance and difficulty level in order to make the drill as interesting as possible.

Instructions:

For each set of runs, designate one target. Shoot the designated target, then another target. After engaging the second target, return to the designated target and re-engage it. After the second engagement on the designated target, engage a target you have not yet shot. Continue this pattern until all targets have been engaged. Finish the drill by engaging the designated target again. Reload as necessary throughout the drill.

Example of five target setup:

Target three is designated and magazine capacity is 10. Engagement sequence: 3 1 3 2 3 RELOAD 4 3 5 3

Cues:

Relax your shoulders. This exercise will have you swinging your gun around all over the place. If you tense up your shoulders, it is likely you will be slow/inefficient due to overswinging the gun.

Make sure you do not "tunnel in" on the front sight or dot. This is a very common issue in this exercise because of the complexity. When people perceive the shooting as difficult, they tend to react by getting that tunnel vision. Allow your head to come off the gun to find the next target.

Corrections:

This drill will bring out the worst in your transitions. You may have drag on/drag off issues. You might have difficulty locating the center of the target visually due to the visual confusion of crossing targets you are not engaging right away. You may have issues over confirming or under confirming sight pictures.

Evolution:

The targets can be varied in any way imaginable.

Tips:

Go through the timer in a detailed fashion. Compare your actual transition times to similar transition times on other exercises. You will likely find you are a bit slower transition for transition on a designated target. This is due to the complexity of the drill. Challenge yourself to match your "ideal" transition times from other drills while doing designated targets. It is not easy to do.

Drill Progress Tracker			
Date	Drill Time	Hit Factor	Notes

Notes:

Moving Targets

Purpose/Goal:

Learn to shoot and sequence complex sets of moving targets.

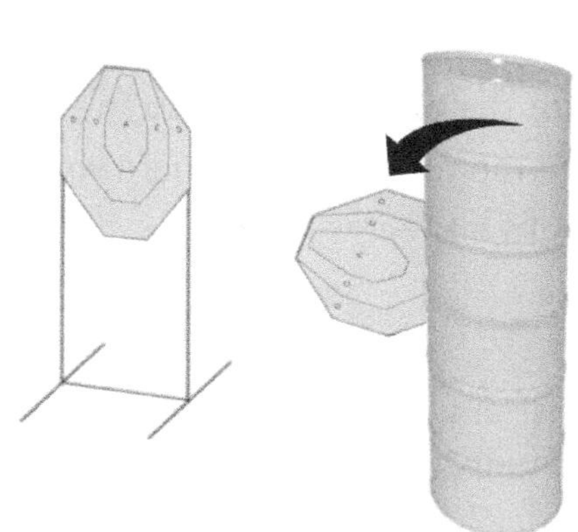

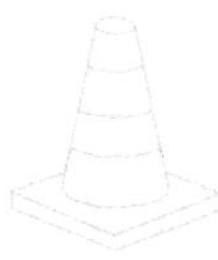

Setup notes:

Setup a simple scenario utilizing whatever props/targets you have at hand. If you wish to train on it, set it up. Utilize swingers, drop turners, max traps, windmills, or any other activated target type you want to use.

Instructions:

At the start, engage each target in your scenario.

Cues:

You should carefully create an engagement sequence. The idea here is to minimize waiting. This generally means that you will activate a moving target, shoot some other things, then engage the moving target. By varying the order of the targets you engage in your scenario you will better understand sequencing.

Track the target. The most important thing to remember when you are shooting a mover is your vision should be in the spot on the target that you wish to hit. Your gun will naturally track that spot if you keep your vision and attention focused there.

Corrections:

If you notice the activated target moving while engaging your sequence, it can sometimes pull your vision off the target you are engaging. Be on guard for this distraction as you work through your sequence. You need to get used to seeing things happen out of the corner of your eye while you shoot a target sequence, it will commonly happen in matches. Train yourself to stick to the order you visualized, and do not deviate from it regardless of what you see while shooting the sequence.

It is extremely common on swinging targets for the target be hit low. The low part of the swinger will attract your vision because it moves slower. Remember, you hit where you look. Make sure you lock your vision on the part of the target you want to hit.

Evolutions:

Make sure you set up and test yourself against any type of moving target you can find. Your goal at this level is to make sure there is nothing you run into in a match that you are not prepared for. Scour the internet for footage of matches. Find interesting/challenging bits of moving targets online and set it up and test it.

Drill Progress Tracker			
Date	Drill Time	Hit Factor	Notes

Notes:

STAGE SKILLS/MOVEMENT

Bar Hop

Purpose/Goal:

Disconnect the shooting from your lower body/movement.

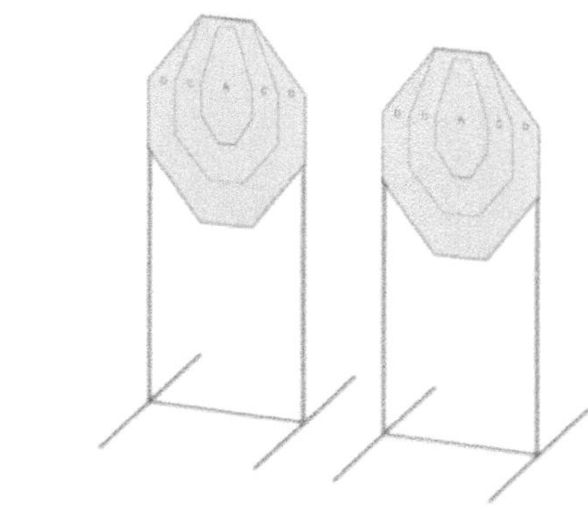

Setup notes:

For this drill you should lay a stick down on the ground to use to step over.

Instructions:

At the tone, engage each target with two rounds. Move to the opposite side of the stick and engage each target with an additional two rounds.

Make sure that you both start and finish the drill in a proper shooting stance. Do not accept an off balance or narrow stance, especially when you are finishing the drill.

Important note: The purpose of this drill is to "blend" the two shooting positions together using the stick as a contrivance to force you to move. The intent is not to view this like a competition fault line to assess penalties, but just to give you a mechanism to force you to move.

Cues:

If you are more robotic in style and not fluidly engaging targets on each side of the stick, start thinking in terms of shooting the targets continuously instead of a shoot-move-shoot mindset.

Get your stance wide so you do not have to drop step to move. You should have minimal extra or false steps.

When the targets are close (10 yards or less), you might find it helpful to force yourself to continuously be shooting. Your string of fire should *sound* like four targets being shot. From the sound alone there should be no indication that there is a stick you are stepping over. Use this cue with care and make sure you do not induce marksmanship issues by forcing yourself to shoot more aggressively.

Corrections:

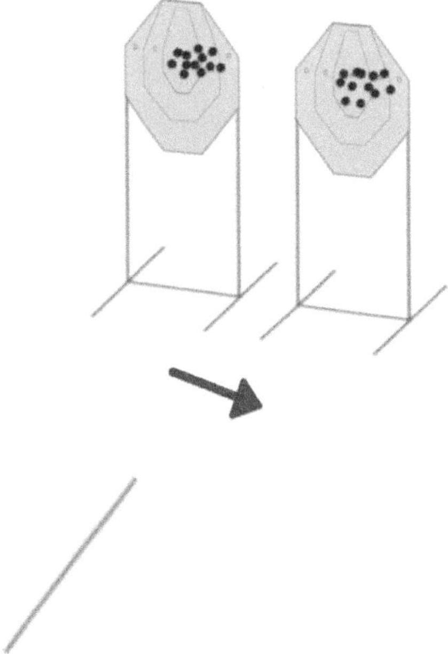

If your hits are trending in the direction of your movement, make sure you are shooting target focused, and not sight focused. Look at the spot on the target exactly where you want to hit.

Ensure you are ready to move again when you finish a repetition of the drill. This does not show up on the timer when you are at the range. However, failure to develop the correct habit will hurt you in a competition setting.

Evolution:

In addition to varying target difficulty and direction of movement, you should feel free to adjust the distance of the actual movements from one engagement to the next. You need to be proficient in all sorts of circumstances. Make sure you are creating these circumstances in your training. Refer to the drills for mounted and unmounted movement if you are unclear on this idea.

Tips:

Experiment with different footwork styles. You may "cross step" or "long step" depending on the circumstances. Cross stepping does a good job of facilitating close ranged shooting while you move. Stepping long and getting stabilized lends itself to shooting this drill at more distance. Experiment for yourself and understand what works for you.

The hard part of this drill is fulfilling the requirements of shooting in the appropriate places (feet on the correct side of the stick) along with making your shooting style fluid. It will require training and repetitions to make this feel comfortable and smooth. The key thing to keep in mind is your gun should stay up and ready to go and you should always be looking to engage the next target.

This drill is a good one to use video on. The assessment of your movement style is virtually impossible to do without seeing it from a third person point of view. If you do not have a training partner watching you, be sure to check what is going on by using video.

Drill Progress Tracker			
Date	Drill Time	Hit Factor	Notes

Notes:

Unmounted Movement

Purpose/Goal:

Proper technique to move into and out of shooting positions. The movement distance should be long enough that it is sensible to dismount the gun completely and run aggressively.

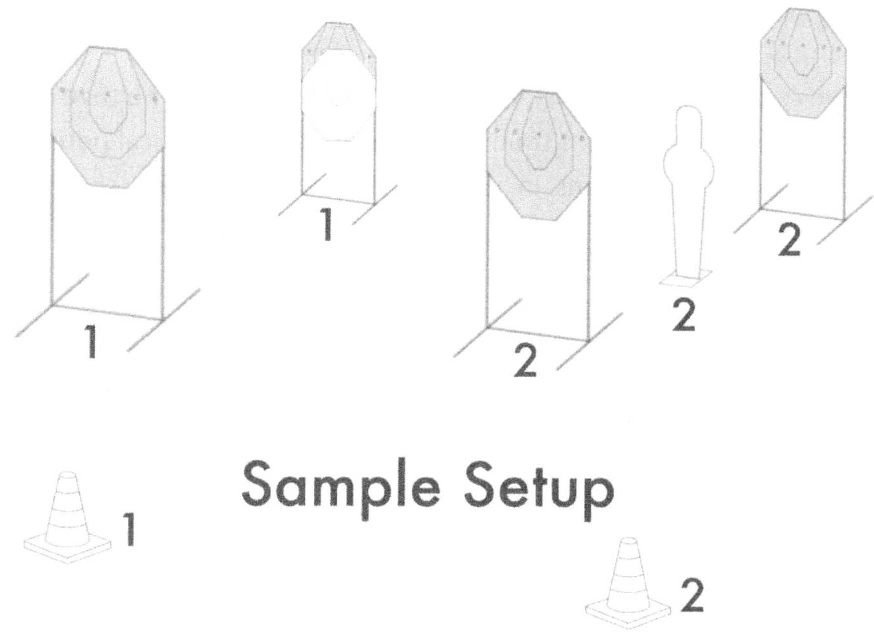

Setup notes:

Set a scenario such that you have at least two shooting positions with a few targets to engage. Set these positions at least five steps apart.

Instructions:

Engage the targets in the first shooting position then move to the second position. From position two, engage the appropriate targets.

Cues:

Have your gun up ready to shoot as you enter a shooting position. You should see your sights in your field of view just before you mean to start shooting the first target in your second shooting location. It is not good enough just to have the gun up, you need to be actually seeing the sights. You save time by starting to shoot earlier and you need to see your sights to shoot.

After you finish a repetition of the exercise, you should consciously check to make sure you are standing properly. Remember: Knees bent, wide stance, 50/50 weight distribution, ready to MOVE.

If you are suffering from a "false step" or inadvertent "drop step", start thinking about throwing your shoulders in the direction you intend to move. This will mitigate stepping backwards a half step before you step forward.

Look to where you are headed. This will line your body up in the direction you intend to travel. Do not look downrange towards the targets if you are not actively looking to engage them. This tends to slow down your movement.

Corrections:

When you move, move as athletically and aggressively as possible. After four or five repetitions, you should be out of breath. This ensures that you are training to maximize your physical potential. If you do train in slow motion expect to overrun positions in real matches when you are shooting "juiced up" from adrenaline.

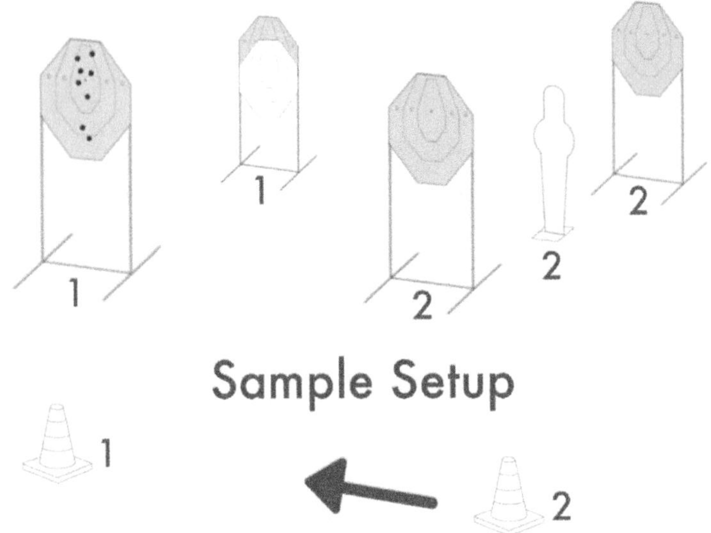

Slow down into the shooting position gently. Use soft steps to come to a clean stop so you can start engaging targets when your sights dictate. If you see your sights bouncing around an excessive amount when you are slowing to a stop, you need to fix the issue with your lower body mechanics.

Stop so you can move again immediately. You need to build the habit of stopping with your feet wide apart, square to the target, knees bent, and 50/50 weight distribution.

As you exit a shooting position, make sure that you are not making a "false step" where you load up your weight and then take off. The "drop step" technique is only needed when you are getting out of a leaning position.

Evolution:

It is important that you work on the whole spectrum of target difficulties and distances with this exercise. Close ranged targets require little in the way of aiming. They allow you to "cheat" the marksmanship rules in many respects. It is important to train close shooting so you see how early you can get moving from the first position and shooting in the second. You will not know what you can get away with unless you try some things in training.

If you are comfortable with this drill in two positions, try adding more. It can be as simple as shooting position one, position two, then back to position one. This will increase the difficulty by forcing you to set up properly in position two so you can aggressively get back to position one. Remember you are training to shoot multi position stages, and you need to be able to have correct technique in that circumstance. Testing this out in training is a wise idea.

Tips:

When working towards proper movement technique, it is extremely helpful to have a competent training partner that can help spot problems. When it comes to movement training in particular, most people simply do not have awareness of what each part of their body is doing. The shooting mechanics layered on top of the movement and the time pressure is too much to keep track of. Your training partner can help cut through that and inform you about what your body is doing.

In the absence of a training partner, use your phone to video your runs. This can help eliminate any doubt in your mind as to what is actually happening.

Drill Progress Tracker			
Date	Drill Time	Hit Factor	Notes

Notes:

Mounted Movement

Purpose/Goal:

Perform short movements with the gun mounted and ready to fire. Shoot as the sights dictate.

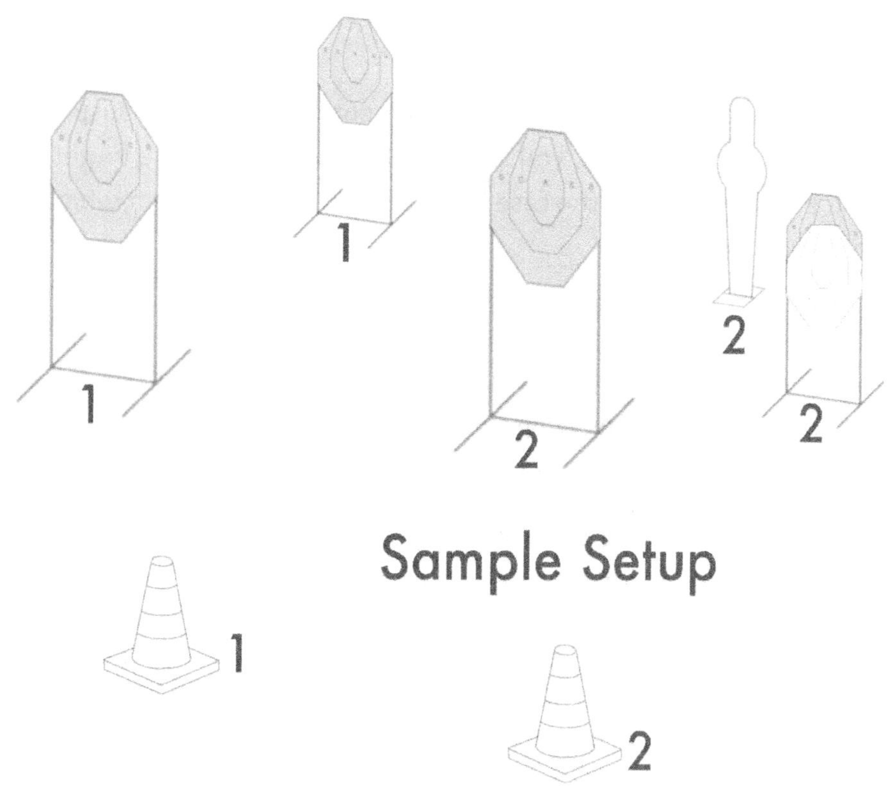

Setup notes:

Build a scenario that has targets shot from two positions. Set the positions between 1 and 4 steps apart.

Instructions:

Start in any desired position. Engage the targets from the appropriate shooting positions.

Cues:

Make sure you keep your gun up and ready to shoot. Always be looking to fire the next shot sooner.

Focus on blending the positions together rather than moving in between them quickly.

Make sure that you finish the exercise in a proper stance. You should be set up wide, low and 50/50 weight distribution if possible.

Make sure you remain target focused during the movement.

Corrections:

If the target or targets that you are engaging while your weight is off balance have poor hits, remember that your ability to shoot using predictive fire is going to be seriously hampered. When you are off balance, moving, or the circumstances are in any way more challenging than normal, switch away from predictive shooting and do reactive shooting. Make sure you are seeing your sights recover between shots. As you gain more and more stability (as your movement completes) you can switch to predictive shooting.

If you have shots trending in the direction of your movement, you should be suspicious that you are not shooting target focused. When you move, you will tend to drag shots off the target if you stare at the front sight or the dot. Ensure this is not the case by frequently thinking about what your vision is doing while you assess your repetitions.

Evolution:

Run this exercise with movement in any direction. It is a quite common situation at matches where you will be keeping the gun in action and engaging targets while you move only a couple steps. It is important that you feel comfortable and secure in all possible scenarios.

Be sure to vary the target difficulty, especially on the targets you are engaging during the movement. Easier/low risk targets will lend themselves to more aggressive movement. Tougher targets will make movement during engagement more difficult. Work all these potential scenarios.

You should occasionally set up the targets to be more difficult than you find reasonable. This will allow you to assess your limits and perhaps realize that you have expanded them somewhat.

Tips:

It is important you do not conflate the idea of blending two positions together by shooting as you move between them with the idea of shooting faster. Many people, when learning these skills early on in their shooting career naturally want to shoot faster during this exercise. It is important that you DO NOT give in to this temptation. The movement serves the shooting and not the other way around.

Drill Progress Tracker			
Date	Drill Time	Hit Factor	Notes

Notes:

Hitting the Spot

Purpose/Goal:

Learn to navigate with precision through complicated target/positioning sequences.

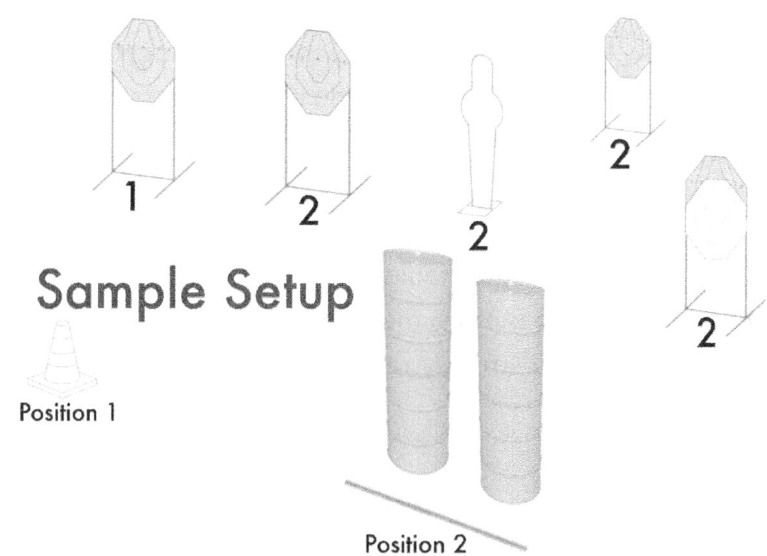

Setup notes:

This drill requires you to construct a narrow opening in between two vision barriers. Set the vision barriers close together to create an opening. When engaging the required targets from that shooting position, your shots all must pass through the opening. This is denoted as position two in the diagram.

You should use a fault line to force yourself to stay back from the opening in the vision barriers. When properly constructed you will not be able to see all the targets in position two without shifting yourself around using your legs.

You will also need one conventional shooting position. There only needs to be one target associated with this position. This is denoted as position one in the diagram.

Instructions:

Start in position one. Shoot the appropriate targets from that spot. Move to position two and engage the appropriate targets. When you are finished in position two move back to position one and engage the appropriate target or targets from that location.

Cues:

When it comes to moving through this drill, the most important thing you can do is to get your stance out nice and wide. If you set the drill up properly, you will need to make a few small position changes when working through position two of the drill. If you are standing tall with your feet close together, the difficulty of this will be magnified. Get low, get wide and be ready to move.

When it comes to shooting, the best practice is to react to what you are seeing. You will be off balance or unstable as you work thorough position two. If your sights look good, start shooting. It is common on this drill for people to be far too conservative as it relates to what the sights need to look like.

Assess position two very carefully. If there is a viable way to "blend" together the targets where you can in any way maintain motion through the position, try to do it. The little tricks like this are the time savers at matches that make the difference in major championship matches.

Corrections:

If you find yourself excessively off balance or unstable, the likely cause is that you are making yourself lean a little bit to see a target as opposed to moving the extra half step so you can stand comfortably and engage it. This problem is common and I strongly recommend you move an extra little bit to make the shooting easier.

Evolution:

The main variable you can focus on to change things up is the opening in position two. By altering the width of the opening and the distance of that opening from the fault line you can make life for yourself extremely easy or very difficult. As you improve, do not be shy about making this drill very tough.

You should also alter your path through position two. You can work the position left to right or right to left and that will usually make things change quite a bit.

Try stipulating a "goofy" order of target engagement. Goofy orders are orders that make no sense for a match. For example, shooting the center target in position two then the left and then finally the right target would add challenge. This makes for good training even if you would not do it in a match.

Tips:

The most important thing you need to bear in mind for this drill is, it requires you to have a plan. You need to take the drill seriously. Walk it through just like you would in a match. Find "markers" (spots on the vision barrier or the group) that help you find your exact shooting position. You must have a specific strategy to locate the correct shooting locations when you move to position two. Do not neglect this step.

Drill Progress Tracker			
Date	Drill Time	Hit Factor	Notes

Notes:

Shooting on the Move

Purpose/Goal:

Ability to shoot accurately while you move from one location to another.

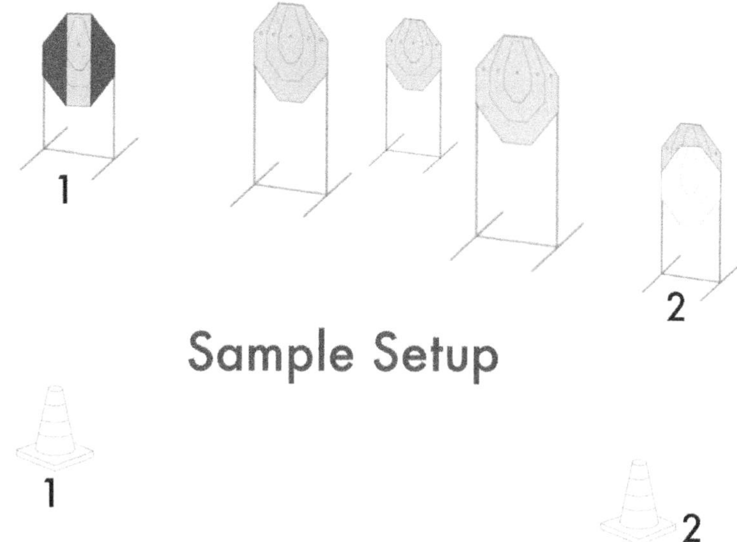

Setup notes:

Set up two shooting positions about 10 yards apart. Each position should be marked and should have a single target set up to be challenging enough to encourage you to stop to shoot it. In between these two positions should be a "free fire zone" where you will be engaging the other targets you have set up while you move.

Instructions:

Engage the target in position one and then start moving to position two. Engage the targets in the "free fire zone" as effectively as possible while you move. Engage the target in position two from position two when you arrive.

Cues:

When there is movement involved, be it you are moving or the target moving, it is necessary to shoot with your vision focused on the target. This is the most missed element of shooting on the move and it cannot be repeated often enough. If you shoot focused on your front sight or dot, you will tend to "drag" hits in the same direction that you are moving. When you are focused on the sights, it becomes exceedingly difficult to "track" the target. When there is movement involved, you do need to continually adjust your aim. This adjustment happens nearly automatically when you focus on the target.

When you are shooting on the move, disregard what you think you know in terms of predictive shooting. Your ability to predict how the gun is going to track is greatly diminished when you add in the movement element. Switch to reactive shooting and you will see your results improve. Do NOT rush your shooting. You are saving time by shooting as you move so it is not necessary to shoot at maximum possible pace.

Bend your knees and get down nice and low. You are going to want to use your lower body to maintain stability. If you see your sights bouncing around an unacceptable amount, you will fix that with lower body mechanics.

Corrections:

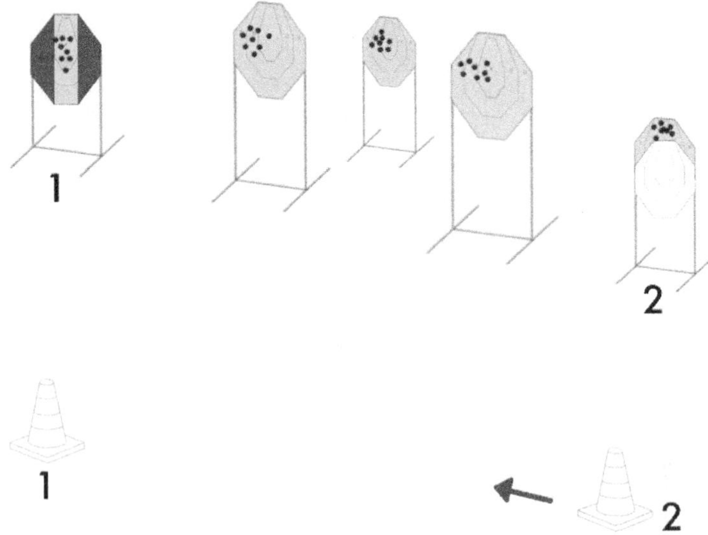

If you shoot focused on your sights, you will have hits trending in the direction you are travelling. It is imperative you shoot target focused.

Shoot reacting to your sights for each shot. Try to stay away from predictive shooting. If you are feeling rushed and shooting wildly, you will struggle. React to what you are seeing for each shot and the results will be excellent.

Evolution:

The main variable you should play around with on this exercise is the target difficulty/distance. Understanding what your abilities and limitations are is going to help you get an accurate "gut feeling" for what precisely you can get away with as it relates to shooting while you move. Do not be shy about putting no-shoots up to test yourself. Try setting the targets at very close range and see how aggressively you can move and still get acceptable hits. Experimentation is important.

Modulate your movement speed as you do more repetitions. This will help you get a sense for how quickly you can move and still get acceptable hits. To get an accurate assessment of this, you can calculate hit factors over a number of runs using a number of different strategies.

Tips:

Moving through the drill while holding a half full water bottle upside-down at arm's length like you would hold your pistol can show you a lot about how your movement affects your sights. Notice how the water in the bottle moves as you experiment. Try setting your feet down more gently as you move and try taking shorter steps. Your sights are moving in the same way the water does.

Drill Progress Tracker			
Date	Drill Time	Hit Factor	Notes

Notes:

Track the A Zone

Purpose/Goal:

This drill was developed by Hwansik Kim in order to learn to "track" the A zone around and through vision barriers while you move and to ensure efficient movement.

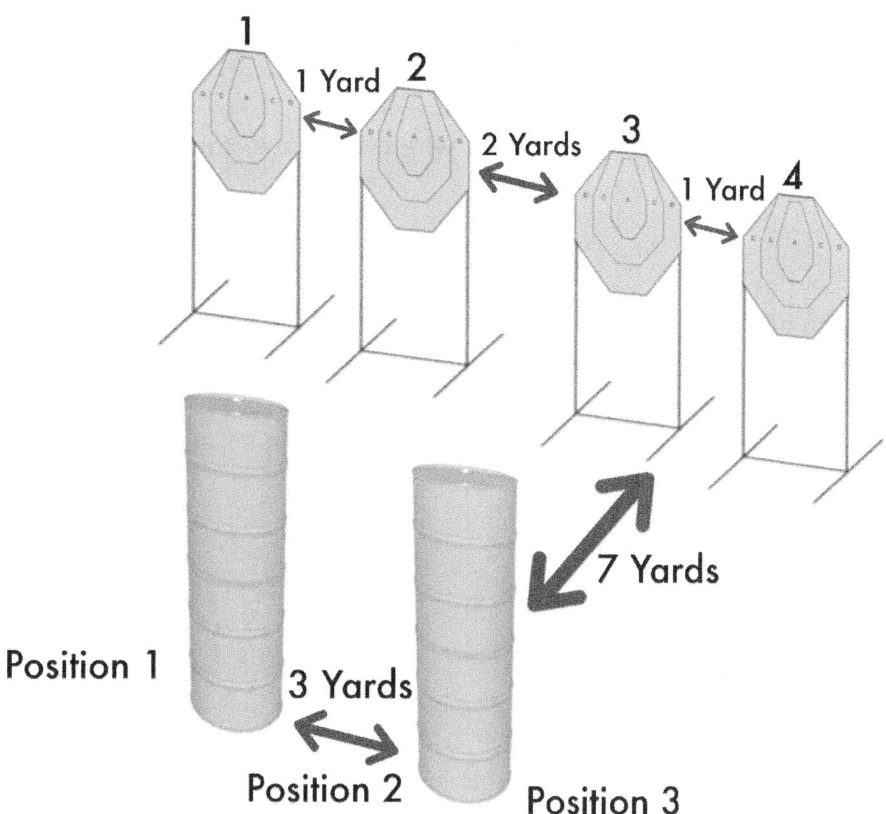

2 vision barriers and 4 targets

Setup notes:

Ensure you use an opaque vision barrier. Middle targets are 2 yards apart. Each outside target is 1 yard from the nearest middle target. Line of targets are 7 yards from the vision barrier.

Vision barriers should be 3 yards apart.

Instructions:

Engage all the targets in the sequence of your choosing. It could be any order. 1 2 3 4, 4 3 2 1, 2,1,3,4, etc. The only consideration is about where the targets are shot from. You always shoot target 1 from the left side of the vision barrier (position 1). You always shoot target 4 from the right side of the right vision barrier (position 3). Targets 2 and 3 are shot from the zone in between the vision barriers (position 2).

It is NOT a requirement of this drill that you be forced into any leaning. Do not place down fault lines.

Cues:

Be aware of the physical position of the vision barrier while you are shooting. It is common that bullets skim the vision barriers on this drill. You need to be comfortable quickly moving around and through stages and shooting scenarios similar to this exercise without shooting walls. Learning to cut it as close as you can on this drill will help.

Do a walkthrough of the drill with your arms at full extension. Use your gun for dry runs if the range permits it.

Make sure you go all the way past any vision barriers when you move. You should be able to stand comfortably when you stop.

Corrections:

Look "through" the vision barrier if possible. The key part of this drill has you moving around as you are looking for A zones, while vision barriers get in the way. If you are noticing that your hits are sporadic, this is usually the problem.

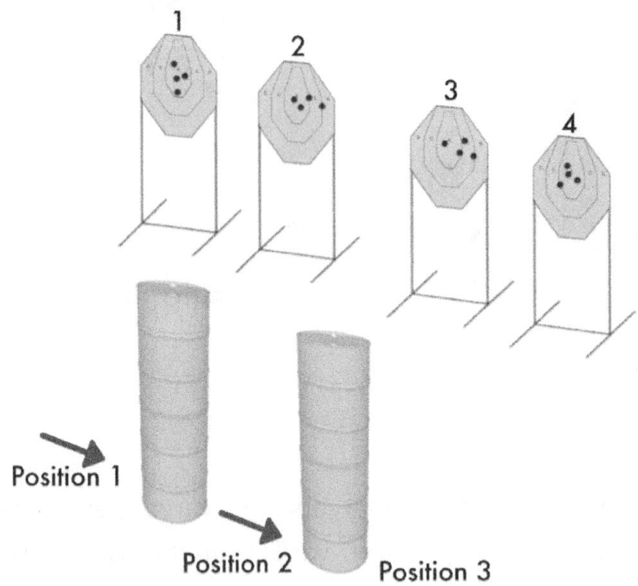

If you focus on your front sight or dot, instead of the target, expect to see hits dispersing in the same direction you are moving. Return to target focused shooting to correct this issue.

Evolutions:

A good test for this drill is to stand stationary in position 2 and engage each target. Do this until you get a good baseline for your performance. You can then take that baseline score and attempt to beat it shooting the drill in normal way, forcing yourself to use all 3 shooting positions.

Tips:

Walkthrough the exercise very carefully. Do it just like you would in a match. Make sure that you hold out your arms and practice tracking the A zone in 3-dimensional space.

Drill Progress Tracker			
Date	Drill Time	Hit Factor	Notes

Notes:

Soft Stops

Purpose/Goal: Learn to come into a shooting position, engage targets, and then leave without fully stopping.

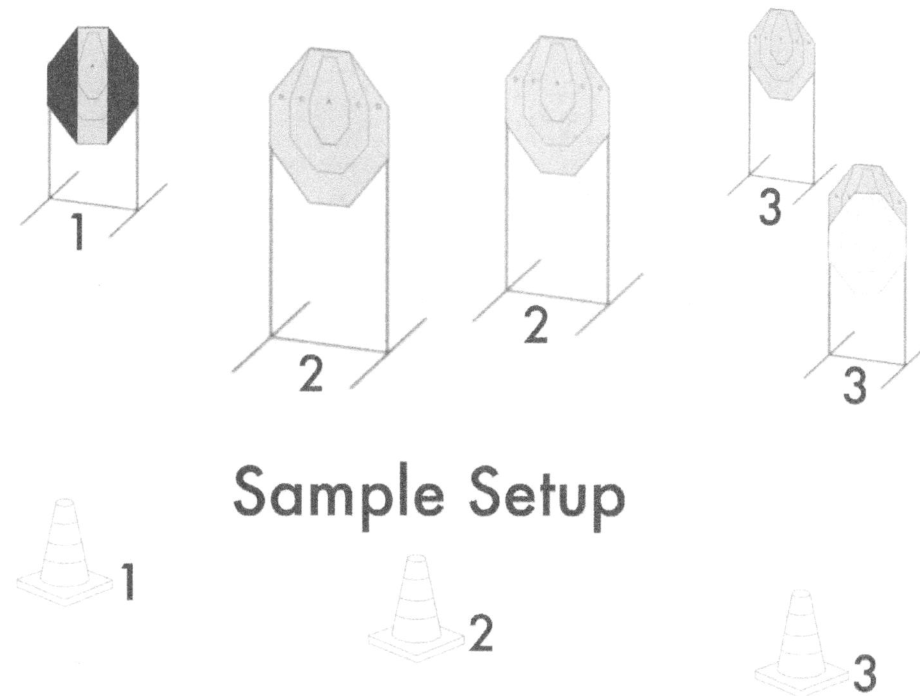

Setup notes:

This is a three-position drill. Position one and three should have at least one target set so that you must be stopped and stable to successfully engage it. Position two should be set up such that you are able to engage the targets without completely stopping.

Instructions:

Starting at position one, engage the targets from the stipulated positions in order. Attempt to slow your movement down in position two so you can get good hits on the target, but your center of gravity never quite stops moving.

Cues:

When it comes to accuracy, there are two key cues that are going to help you.

Firstly, as always when shooting on the move, make sure you are shooting target focused in position two. Getting tunnel vision and focusing on your sights instead of the target will tend to induce dragging the hits off the target in the same direction that you are travelling. If you are having this issue, remember the solution is to switch to target focus.

The second and more important cue is to have your feet stop momentarily but have your body continue moving. This might sound a bit strange, but it is a good technique for a soft stop. If your center of gravity (indicated by your shoulders if you video yourself) keeps moving, you will be saving time. Simply stopping your feet in place for a moment and allowing yourself to continue moving will feel strange at first. It will feel like you are falling through the position. However, it will allow you to shoot very accurately and save time while you do it.

Corrections:

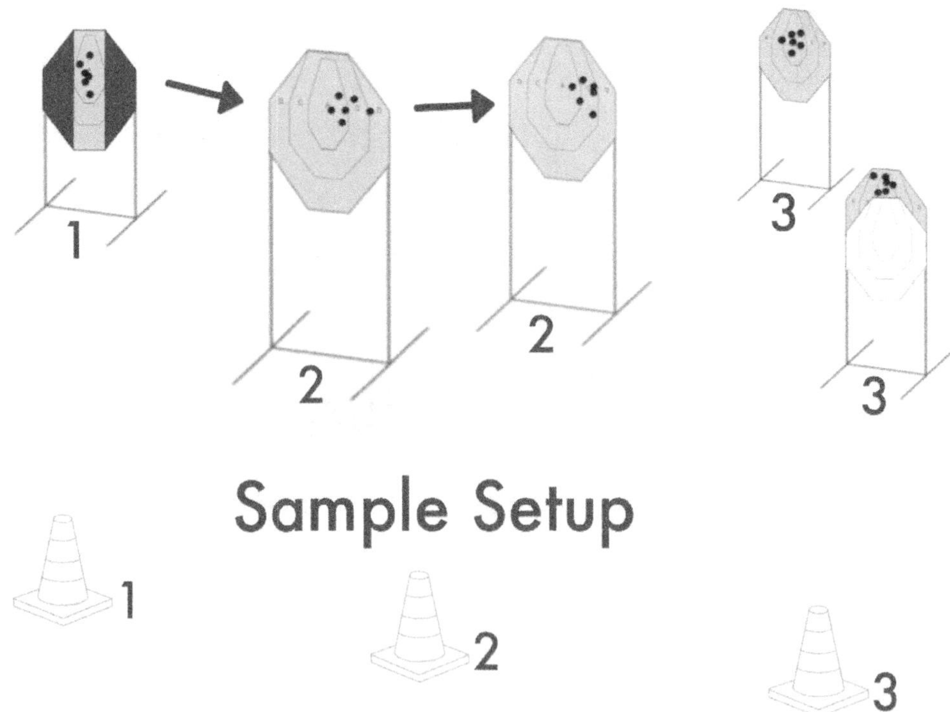

If you shoot sight focused, you will have hits trending in the direction you are travelling. It is imperative you shoot target focused.

Shoot reacting to your sights for each shot. Try to stay away from predictive shooting. If you are feeling rushed and shooting wildly you will struggle. React to what you are seeing for each shot and the results will be excellent.

Evolution:

The main variable you should play around with on this exercise is the target difficulty/distance in position two. Understanding what your abilities and limitations are is going to help you get an accurate "gut feeling" for what precisely you can get away with as it relates to shooting while you move. Do not be shy about putting no-shoots up to test yourself. Try setting the targets at very close range and see how aggressively you can move and still get acceptable hits. Experimentation is important.

Tips:

When learning proper movement technique, it is extremely helpful to have a competent training partner that can help spot problems. When it comes to movement training in particular. most people simply do not have awareness of what each part of their body is doing. The shooting mechanics layered on top of the movement and the time pressure is just too much to keep track of. Your training partner can help cut through that and inform you about what your body is actually doing.

In the absence of a training partner, use your phone to video your runs. This can help eliminate any doubt in your mind as to what is actually happening.

Drill Progress Tracker			
Date	Drill Time	Hit Factor	Notes

Notes:

Go/Stop

Purpose/Goal:

This drill was developed by Hwansik Kim in order to develop the ability to stay low and ready to move and eliminate to the greatest extent possible "false" or extra steps.

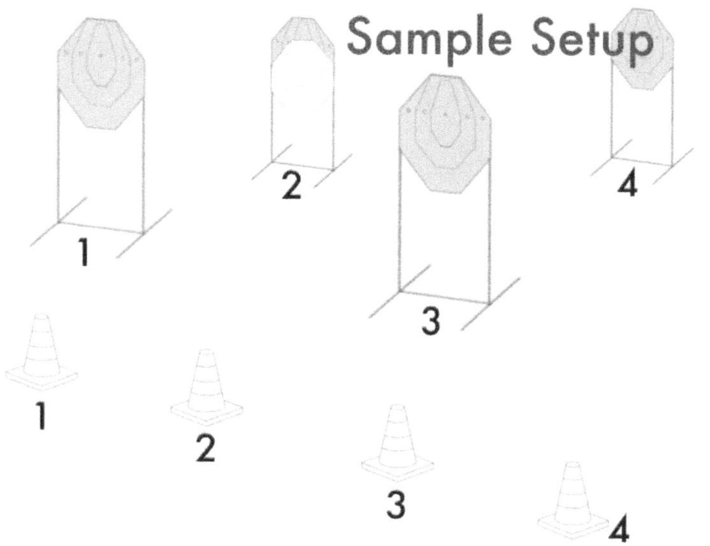

Setup notes:

Set up four shooting positions marked by cones. Each position needs to have a target associated with it.

Instructions:

Start at cone one. Engage the target associated with cone one, then move to cone two and engage the appropriate target. After cone two, move back to cone one and engage the associated target. Continue systematically working through the cones in this order, finishing after returning to cone 1. 1 2 1 3 1 4 1

Cues:

Move aggressively. This drill is physically demanding. We call it a "smoker." It is important that you leverage all your athletic ability to the greatest extent possible. This drill will not be an effective training tool without going at it aggressively to produce the errors you are attempting to fix.

Do your best to get your stance set up nice and wide. You want to have the ability to efficiently move to the next shooting position when you get done shooting.

Make sure you do not have extraneous steps or movement when you exit a shooting position. This means taking small steps to change your stance, coiling your body up like a spring, or drop stepping should not occur when you are trying to move. You should stop and stabilize in a position already "pre-loaded" and ready to move.

Corrections:

If you feel like you are stopping rough into a shooting position, you want to take short steps as you approach the next position to help you decelerate. If you attempt to stop in the space of a single step, you will likely be unable to control your body and get it stopped properly.

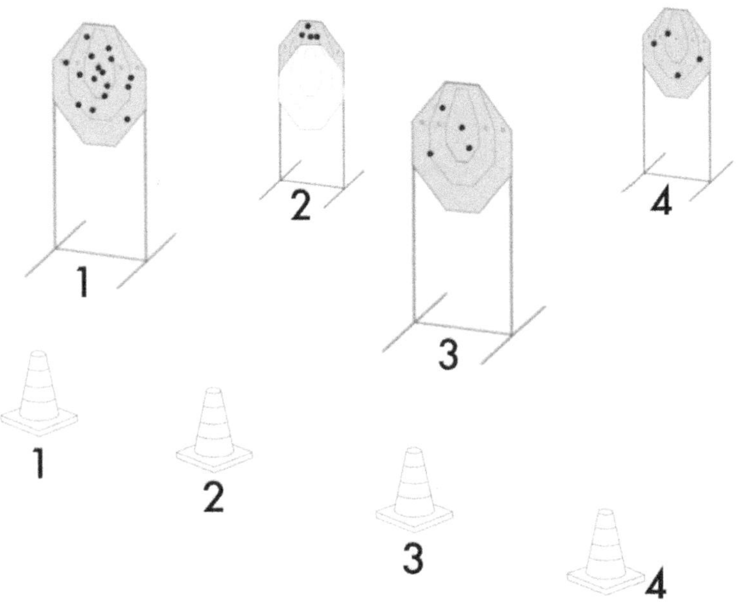

If you have widely scattered hits on the target you are engaging, make sure that you are waiting to get an appropriate sight picture on the targets.

Evolution:

Try this drill with targets of different difficulty and risk levels. Close ranged targets will place the emphasis for this drill on fast changes of direction. More difficult targets will punish you for not stopping correctly and getting to stability to shoot accurately. Work on the whole spectrum of possibilities.

Vary the direction of your movement. This drill can be run laterally, up range/downrange, or diagonally. As you improve, test out the less common movement directions to learn more. On the more difficult movement directions, make sure that you do not have "false" steps in to, or out of position. These are steps that do not move you in the direction you are trying to go, but just reorient your body.

Tips:

This drill is very physically demanding. If you are doing it properly, it will take substantial amounts of time to shoot the drill, physically recover and shoot the drill again. It is wise to set up a second drill alongside this one to avoid extended downtime and prolong the training session.

This drill is a good one to use video on. The assessment of your movement style is virtually impossible to do without seeing it from a third person point of view. If you do not have a training partner watching you, be sure to check what is going on by using video.

Drill Progress Tracker			
Date	Drill Time	Hit Factor	Notes

Notes:

Mock Stage Training

Purpose/Goal:

Learn to smoothly execute a stage

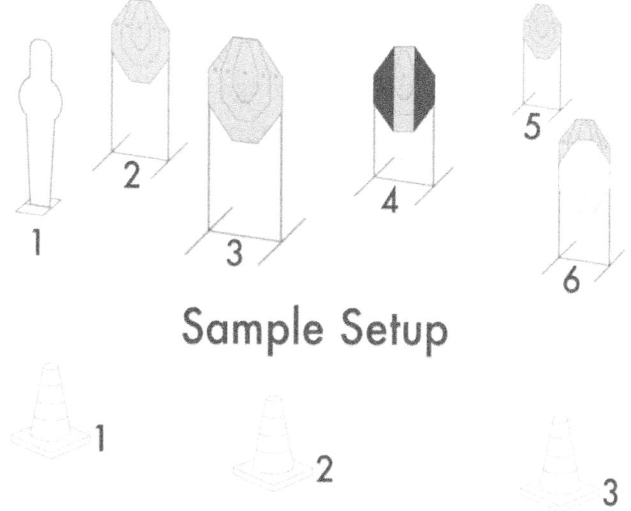

Setup notes:

Construct a multi position "stage." Using markers such as cones on the ground to denote shooting positions. Setting up non-falling steel and multiple paper targets is ideal to give target variety. Stipulate an order to engage the targets and what position to engage them from. Feel free to use the same target from more than one position.

Example: Engage Target 1-4 from position one. Engage Targets 3-6 from position two. Engage targets 2-3 from position three.

Instructions:

Shoot the stage to the best of your ability. Make sure that the stage is executed without needing to consciously think about what the next step is. Ensure that your shooting is accurate and disciplined.

After shooting your stage, change the position/target order for the next run.

Cues:

You should shoot your mock stage just like a match stage. Do not focus on training cues during your stage run.

Corrections:

Be on guard for undisciplined shooting. Apply the correct aiming scheme for each target. Do not over confirm or under confirm.

Evolution:

As your execution improves, start changing the stage. Eventually, you should be able to change the order of targets/positions every single run and be able to hold a good performance. Once you can pick an order, visualize it, and then execute it without hesitation, you are in excellent shape.

You should alternate start positions and shooting style (one handed, kneeling, prone, etc.).

Alternate between pushing for an aggressive time, shooting your "match" mode and shooting a safer style. This should expand your knowledge base and help you learn.

Tips:

The main reason to do full stage training is to observe your abilities. You should take this as an opportunity to test your shooting under a variety of circumstances. You want to make sure that you spot weak points in technique or mindset so you can do additional training on those areas.

Consider the "training philosophy" section at the front of this book. The way you shoot, your style, your inclinations, and your habits are what you are assessing when doing this exercise. You are not trying to accomplish anything specific by doing this training. The larger goal here is to see what happens and spot the 'big picture" trends.

Ask yourself the following:

- What mistakes am I making repeatedly?
- What specific exercises should I do to mitigate these mistakes?
- Am I confident that I can perform to an acceptable level on a random set of competition stages?

The above questions are just examples of the sorts of questions you should be interested in. The best way to summarize the best mindset for this type of training is, you spot the patterns in your shooting that are holding you back as a shooter. Look at the big picture.

Drill Progress Tracker			
Date	Drill Time	Hit Factor	Notes

Notes:

SPECIAL DRILLS

Confirmation Drill

Purpose/Goal:

Build an understanding of how different methods of confirmation/aiming scheme affect the outcome on the target.

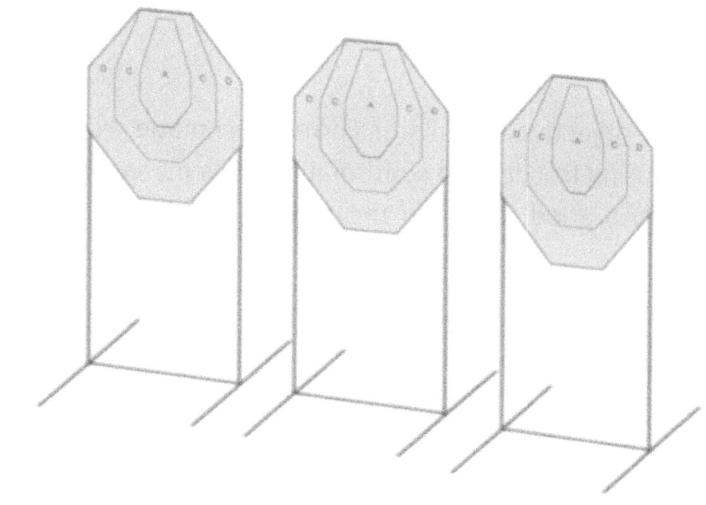

Setup notes:

Set up targets for comparison at 5 yards distance.

Instructions:

This drill will consist of many repetitions for each aiming scheme you are testing.

The start position for the drill is a two-handed grip on the gun, aimed at the bottom of the target stand of the target you are shooting.

At the tone, engage the very center of the A zone using the aiming scheme you are testing on that target. Fire one round only. Note the time.

Do the correct number of repetitions on each target. For example: Engage target 1 using confirmation 1 for 10 repetitions. Engage target two with confirmation 2 for 10 reps. Engage target 3 with confirmation 3 for 10 reps.

At the end of this test you should have a good sample of data that gives you an idea of the time and accuracy difference between different levels of confirmation. Check out the "tips" section of this drill if this is unclear to you.

Cues:

Make sure you use the confirmation you intend to.

Corrections:

This drill does not have any objective to build or correct technique. Your only job is to ensure that you actually execute each shot using the desired confirmation. This means that you need to create good data for yourself, not necessarily a good result on the target. Make sure you rigidly enforce your desired confirmation level.

Make sure you use the confirmation you intend to.

Evolution:

Feel free to attempt any confirmation/aiming scheme on any target type. This will give you more data and a good sense for what outcome you can expect given the particular aiming strategy.

This drill was developed using the following scheme:

Confirmation 1:

Kinesthetic alignment only. You "feel" your arms are pointed in the correct place and then you shoot. NO VISUAL CONFIRMATION

Confirmation 2:

You react to the color of your sight crossing your intended aiming area. With an optic you shoot as soon as you see the optical color. With a fiber optic iron sight setup, you shoot when you see the color of your front sight.

Confirmation 3:

Your dot is stopped and stable in your intended aiming area. Your dot should appear as a dot and not as a streak. With iron sights you see the front sight stopped through the rear notch.

This is a near perfect sight picture sort of setup.

As you move up in confirmation it will take more time, but the result on the targets will be much cleaner.

Shooting iron sights you might find it useful to distinguish between a perfectly aligned sight picture and seeing the front sight through the rear notch, but perhaps a bit misaligned. You might think of the sights slightly misaligned as confirmation 2.5.

There is no limit to what you can experiment with on this drill. Just remember, your goal with the drill is to put in a specific aiming scheme and then assess your outcome. You are not trying to get a "good" or "bad" outcome. You just want to see how it all works. Once you get a sense of this, it should be easy to apply these concepts to your other training.

Tips:

This drill was developed by Hwansik Kim in order to isolate the effect of the aiming strategy, confirmation level and aiming scheme on the target.

The component of target acquisition and engagement where you have a lot of control over speed is how you aim the gun at the target. More specifically, it is the reference you are using to confirm the gun is aimed. Traditionally, the expectation is that every sight picture looks the same on every target. People are generally trained in non-practical shooting context to get a "perfect" sight picture for each and every shot. As soon as you move beyond level 1 in this text that is no longer the advice or expectation.

Learning how much "perfect" sight picture you can trade away in order to go faster is one of the most important things that a practical shooter can do. As soon as you understand what sort of sight picture will produce what sort of outcome all you need to do is train yourself to address each target with the optimal strategy and your results will be excellent.

This exercise exists to strip away every other layer and show you the effect of the aiming strategy on the target outcome.

Drill Progress Tracker			
Date	Drill Time	Hit Factor	Notes

Notes:

Measurement Drill

Purpose/Goal:

Build an understanding of how much energy it requires to return your pistol to point of aim after firing a shot.

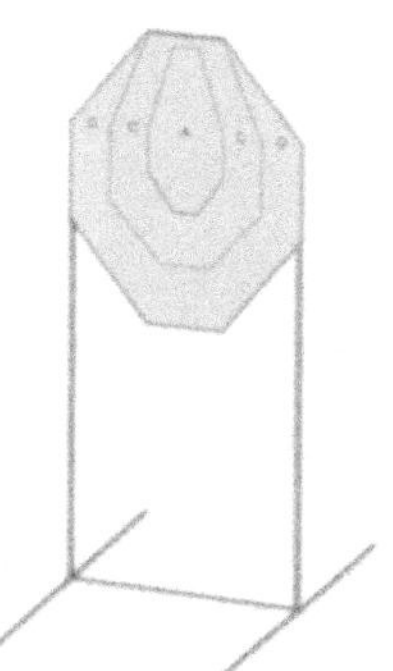

Setup notes:

This drill requires only one target. 5 yards is a good distance to use.

Instructions:

Grip your pistol properly. Engage the very center of the A zone of your target with one carefully fired shot. DO NOT PUSH THE GUN BACK DOWN AFTER FIRING THE SHOT. Fire a second shot at the point the gun recoiled to without re-aiming to your aimpoint. The distance between the two shots is the information you are looking for. This will measure how much the muzzle rises, and thus how much it should be returned. Repeat this until you have a good sense of the amount the muzzle rises.

After you understand the amount of muzzle rise, start returning the muzzle back down to the original point of aim between the first and second shots. Start going slowly (1 or 2 seconds between shots). As you continue to train and understand, increase your speed until you are shooting as fast as you can pull the trigger.

Cues:

This drill does not have any objective to build or correct technique. Your only job is to learn how much energy it requires to return your pistol to point of aim after firing a shot.

Corrections:

This drill does not have any objective to build or correct technique. Your only job is to learn how much energy it requires to return your pistol to point of aim after firing a shot.

Evolution:

Feel free to attempt this drill in unusual circumstances. Consider trying leans, awkward positions, or one-handed shooting in order to build more understanding.

Tips:

The point of this drill is to measure how much the muzzle rises when you fire a shot. This might seem like a strange thing to do, but with a little more context it will make sense.

This drill was developed by Hwansik Kim to work on the concept of recoil control. Most people have an incorrect concept of recoil control. They believe that it will take a lot of muscle mass, force, and effort to control the recoil of their pistol. The point of this drill is to facilitate you demonstrating to yourself that none of this is true. You do not need to work all that hard in order to bring your pistol down out of recoil. The muzzle of your pistol should only marginally rise when you fire a shot. The main issue you will have as you learn to shoot faster and faster is battling your tendency to overcorrect or overcontrol that recoil. Once you internalize how little force is required to return the gun it should improve your concept of recoil control.

Drill Progress Tracker			
Date	Drill Time	Hit Factor	Notes

Notes:

Sight Tracking

Purpose/Goal:

Learn to watch your sights. Test the cause/effect relationships related to your grip.

No targets needed

Setup notes:

Do not use a target. Fire the rounds in a safe direction into the backstop. Do not even aim at a particular spot on the backdrop.

Instructions:

Aim your gun in a safe direction. Watch the sights closely as you fire your gun in a safe direction. Assess how the sights move.

Cues:

Pay attention to your hands. Notice how the sights track differently as you adjust your hand pressure.

Corrections:

Keep your eyes open! If you are not sure what you just saw, you did not see enough. The gun is telling you a story as it moves in recoil, you need to keep your eyes open to be aware of the story.

Drill Progress Tracker			
Date	Drill Time	Hit Factor	Notes

Notes:

Classifier Training

Purpose/Goal:

Train on and experiment with USPSA classifier stages in order to expand your knowledge and skillset.

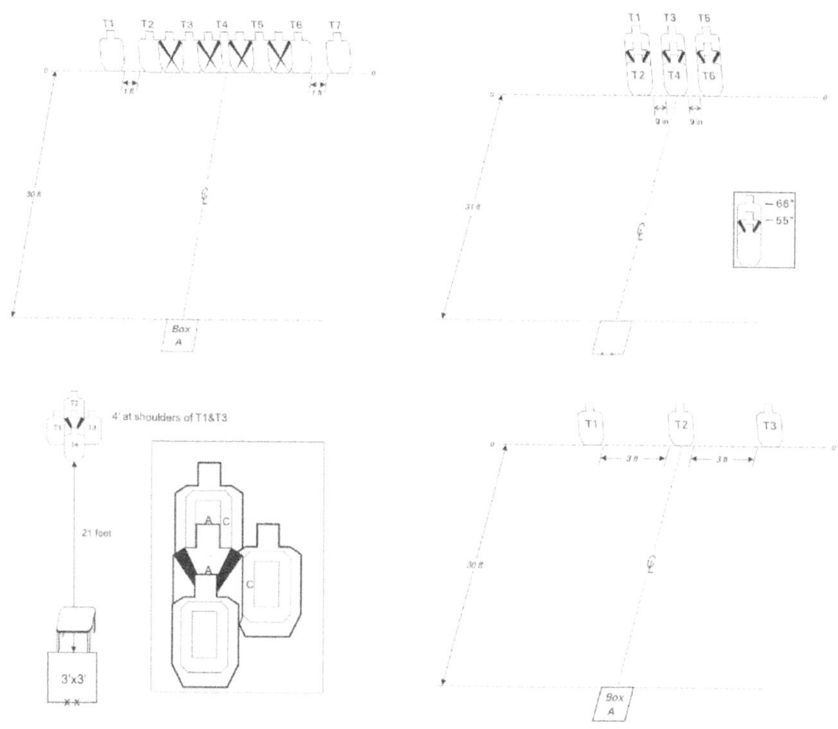

ANY DESIRED CLASSIFIER

Setup notes:

Setup any desired USPSA classifier.

Instructions:

Set up any desired USPSA classifier.

Shoot the classifier stage the desired number of times. Note time, points, and hit factor. Your goal is to competently execute the skills required. You should be able to consistently execute the classifier without incurring penalties. Your goal is to consistently shoot over 95% of the national high hit factor.

For those seeking a real challenge, your goal is to shoot 100% on your "cold" run.

Drill Progress Tracker			
Date	Drill Time	Hit Factor	Notes

Notes:

Rhythm Drill

Purpose/Goal:

"Flip the script" on target transition technique to better understand the technique.

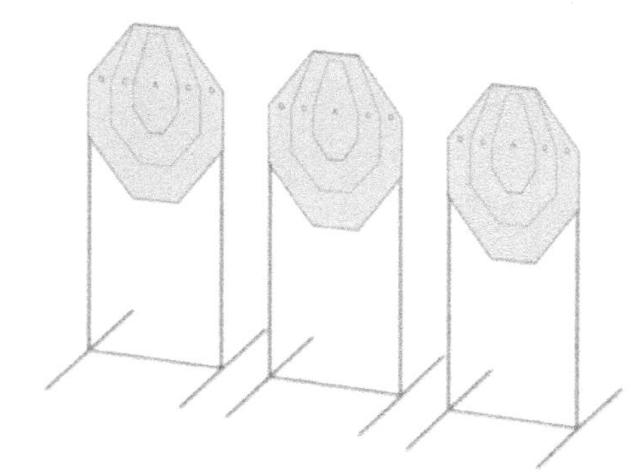

Setup notes:

Set up an "El Prez" array. Make sure the spacing is close (1 yard apart) and the distance is near (7 yards maximum).

Instructions:

WARNING: DO NOT DO THIS IN A MATCH. THIS IS A TRAINING EXERCISE ONLY.

Establish a "rhythm" in your mind you are going to shoot. Each shot must be evenly spaced. This means you will shoot every split and transition in the same time. For example: You will shoot all .50 splits/transitions. You can pick any pace you desire, but I recommend you start slowly to understand the drill. As you go along, start speeding up the rhythm.

You are REQUIRED to shoot the selected rhythm irrespective of anything else. As you speed up, you will eventually be pulling the trigger without any visual confirmation. This is a normal part of the drill.

The idea is by keeping to a rhythm, your job will become getting your eyes exactly where they need to be and bringing the gun to the next target precisely.

Keep speeding up the rhythm until you find your breaking point. Eventually, you will be unable to hold things together at the rhythm you are shooting. Back off just a little bit from that point and you will have found a good 'training zone" to stick in.

Cues:

Relax! As you speed up, there will be excess tension coming into your firing hand, your shoulders, and your arms. If you can let go of that tension, you might be shocked how quickly and effectively you can transition the gun.

Look exactly where you want to hit. The gun will go to where you are looking as if on autopilot as long as you stay loose and relaxed in your upper body.

Corrections:

Drag on/drag off transitions are the most common issue on this drill. Especially as you speed up to a .18 to .20 pace of splits (or beyond) it is very difficult to keep your vision under control. It is a very natural mistake to mentally leave a target before you are done shooting it, or to be too slow getting the gun to the next target. Remember, on this drill you are FORCED to shoot your predetermined cadence. Waiting for visual confirmation on a target is not allowed because it would undermine the rhythm aspect of the drill.

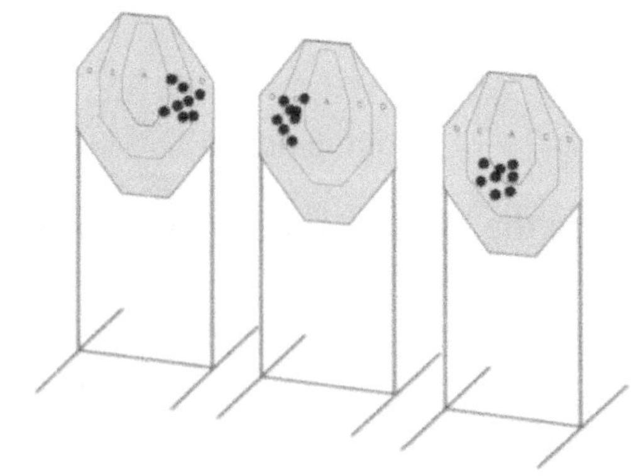

Hits clustered outside of the A-zone is indicative of looking at the wrong spot on the target. You need to get your vision to the center of the target to drive the gun there. If you aren't funding the center of the with your eyes, oftentimes hits will cluster in strange places.

Evolution:

If you are shooting at your maximum pace and still unable to break your technique, you can simply widen out the setup of the targets. This will push you to the edge.

Feel fry to apply the "rhythm" concept to any other drill or scenario. Establish a rhythm that makes sense for the situation and work within it.

Tips:

Assessing your draw speed is not a part of this drill. As you speed up your shooting, you will be tempted to speed up the draw along with it. This is unnecessary and counterproductive. The only piece you should be worried about is the actual shooting. Let your draw be what it naturally is so you are doing the exercise with a good grip.

Drill Progress Tracker			
Date	Drill Time	Hit Factor	Notes

Notes:

Special Challenges

Purpose/Goal:

Become comfortable with non-standard scenarios that may present themselves in matches. Things such as off body start positions, shooting in awkward positions and shooting one handed.

Make sure that you can aggressively execute shooting accurately in a variety of positions and circumstances.

Optimize your predictive shooting for each scenario.

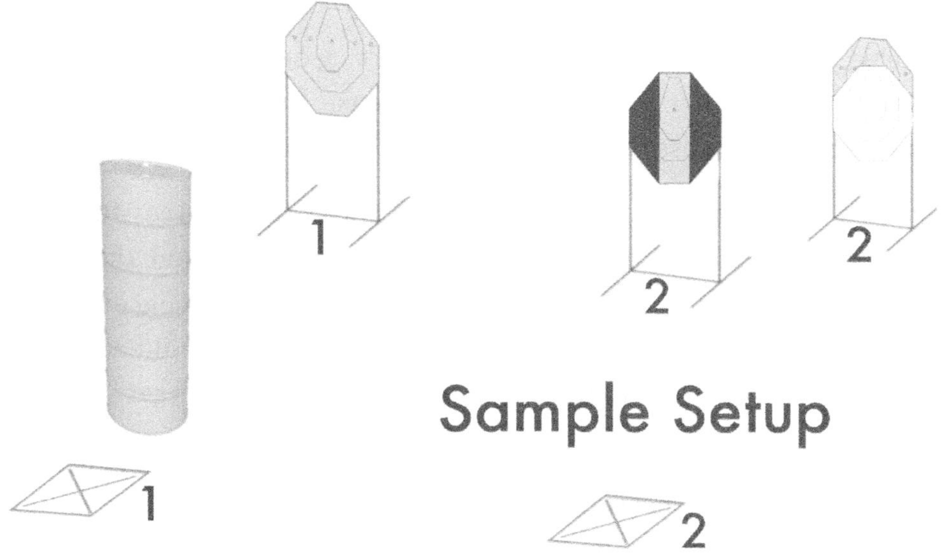

Setup notes:

Construct challenges that you expect to see in future matches. Keep the scenarios small, simple and focused.

Things like leans, crouches, one handed, prone, and other types of shooting positions and circumstances should be trained to the point that you can aggressively negotiate them at speed in a match.

Instructions:

At the tone, engage the targets in your setup while observing the special conditions you have set for yourself. Example: engaging the targets while kneeling would be the procedure if you are working on kneeling shooting.

Cues:

When the shooting is awkward or difficult, remember shooting fundamentals. Confirm sight alignment and carefully stack pressure onto the trigger for each demanding shot and you will get the best chance at your best score you could possibly have that day.

Corrections:

Pay close attention to the sight pictures you are seeing. As the shooting gets more awkward or difficult your gun will not behave the same as when you are standing comfortably in your preferred stance. If you sense the gun is not properly aimed where it needs to be then have the discipline to hold off on shooting until it is.

If the gun is not returning to your point of aim as quickly as it normally does then you will need to resist the temptation to force that to happen. It is quite common for shooters to aggressively over return the gun back to the target and induce even more errors.

Evolution:

As you get comfortable with whatever challenge you are working on, simply increase the difficulty of the challenge. Move the targets further away, add partials, make the position more demanding, or do whatever else makes sense to increase the difficulty for the given challenge.

If you are working on shooting from an awkward position and you are successful, you can modify the exercise. An example is to require you to start outside your shooting position, then shoot, and then get back out of that position. This will make the training similar to what you should expect to see in a match setting. Example: Start at position A and engage a target. Move to position B and negotiate the targets from your special challenge. Move back to position A and re-engage that target. This will require you to get in and out of your position at speed.

It is common for people to use wildly incorrect aiming schemes when negotiating special challenges. Some aggressive shooters barely look at their sights, and some people go entirely the other direction and over confirm. Be sure you are carefully assessing yourself as you go along.

Do not be afraid to try predictive shooting. There is no real downside to trying a more aggressive aiming scheme and, in many cases, you will be surprised what you can get away with.

Tips:

The best piece of advice to remember for special challenges is that you do not need to be the best at everything. You need to be able to hit the targets under pressure. Shooting from an awkward position is a challenge for everyone, and no one is going to be comfortable doing it. Suppress the feelings you likely have about being too slow and simply execute the shots.

Drill Progress Tracker			
Date	Drill Time	Hit Factor	Notes

Notes:

If you enjoyed this book, please check out these other projects:

	Practical Shooting Training Group (PSTG) is an entirely online coaching platform. The site contains drills with video explanations and written diagrams, training video, and a venue to get feedback on student submitted videos. *Available on-line at:* ***www.pstg.us***

BOOKS:

	This book answers the "how to" questions about shooting technique. How do you hold the gun? How do you shoot fast? These questions and many more are answered inside. *Available in print and Kindle on Amazon.*
	"Dry-Fire Reloaded" is an at home training manual for Practical Shooting competitors. This manual gives you a comprehensive set of drills to take your skills to the next level. *Available in print and Kindle on Amazon.*
	This book contains the live fire training exercises. The drills are put together with material to help you craft your own training routine and take your shooting to the next level. *Available in print and Kindle on Amazon.*

	Over time, I modified drills and created new ones, to highlight the patterns I was seeing so that students would understand what they were doing wrong and comprehend how to fix it. This book is the product of that refinement. *Available in print and Kindle on Amazon.*
	This book isn't about shooting as much as it is about the preparation, complicated feelings, emotions, and physiological changes that will occur when you are in a competition. *Available in print and Kindle on Amazon.*

Made in the USA
Middletown, DE
13 September 2024